Praise for William Hi _____ ....
Wonder Valley

"William Hillyard is an insightful writer who wields all the best writer's weapons—close observation, a natural fearlessness, and endless curiosity—to evoke with brilliance and beauty this strange yet telling spot on the Western map."

—Amy Wilentz, author of Farewell, Fred Voodoo: A Letter From Haiti

"[California writing] is at its best, for me, when the authors treat California as a character rather than set dressing. William Hillyard does just that in "Wonder Valley" when he recounts the tale of Ned Bray and the end of Ricka McGuire 'in this nowhere corner of the Mojave.' Part anecdote, part history lesson, Hillyard transports you so thoroughly in his descriptions that you'll need to drink a glass of water when you finish."

—Justice Fisher, Hippocampus Magazine

"Reading Hillyard's story, it's not hard to see why the work of literary nonfiction got the [Best American Nonrequired Reading] nod. "Wonder Valley" depicts a forlorn corner of the Mojave Desert in California populated by outcasts and drifters and opens with a bang—a cinematic panorama of this desolate wasteland that ends on the nude, dead body of a woman lying in the dilapidated school bus that was her home."

—Joel Warner, Westword Magazine

Welcome to Wonder Valley

Ruin and Redemption in an American Galapagos

§ § §

William Hillyard

Library of Congress Control Number: 2019915117

ISBN: 978-1-7333999-2-0

For my parents
...and, of course, Ann

Wonder Valley

You might have passed through here, maybe. Out for a drive with time on your hands, you might have taken the long-cut to the casinos of Vegas from the soulless sprawl of LA. You'd have driven way beyond the outer reaches of suburbia, beyond its neglected fringe of citrus groves, past the outlet malls and the desert resorts, past that remote high desert national park and the Marine base, past the Next Services 100 Miles sign and any reason anybody really drives out this way anyway. You'd have blown through here at 60 miles an hour, probably, along a potholed and corrugated tarmac, the only asphalt for miles. If you were messing with your radio or fiddling with your phone, you might not have even noticed the grid of washboard tracks scraped from the sparse hardscrabble of greasewood scrub in this nowhere corner of the Mojave.

You can turn off the pavement, of course, turn onto any one of the bumpy dirt roads. These are public rights-of-way, county-maintained easements between dry homestead parcels. You probably didn't, though. Few people do. And that's the way the people who live out here like it.

— Denver Voice, July 2009

Chapter 1

Jack McConaha answered my knock in an undershirt. "Come on in, have a seat," he said. "Say hello to the kids." His "kids," two toy poodles, yipped at me from the king size bed that practically filled the landlocked living room of his sprawling homestead cabin. Their bed and food and water bowls sat in the rumpled covers. The whoosh of the swamp cooler covered the room with a blanket of white noise reducing the TV at the foot of the bed to a murmur.

He disappeared to finish dressing. "Must have picked up a nail," he shouted from within the warren of the cabin. "I checked the air in my tires this morning and one was a little low." It seemed he was continuing a conversation he'd begun before I arrived. "Don't matter," he shouted, "it's just down a couple of pounds." He didn't like the Firestone tires that came on his new patrol jeep. "I'm going to replace them, get BF Goodriches. They self-seal if you get a puncture."

Jack reentered the room dressed for his desert patrol. Summer-weight camouflaged fatigues—Marine Corps issue—draped from his stout frame, a 40-caliber Smith and Wesson on his hip. The tin star on his breast designated him "Captain of Security."

I had met Jack a few weeks prior when I went to the Wonder Valley firehouse to inquire into the death of a woman named Ricka McGuire. She had died of the heat in the cream-colored school bus that was her home.

A late bloomer, I had just graduated college with a degree in Literary Journalism—essentially nonfiction creative writing—and had been fortunate enough to get a couple of my school assignments

1

published. I wanted to continue writing, maybe try to make a career out of it, something I'd always wanted to do. I had the idea to write something about Wonder Valley, about Ricka and rural poverty—that's how I shaped it. The story was to be my first since graduating college, my first without the mentorship of a professor, the first story idea I'd pitched for publication before I'd actually written it. I was nervous, out of my element. It would run in the *Denver Voice*, a magazine sold on the streets of Denver by the homeless, a magazine that had run one of my homework assignments before.

Wonder Valley had fascinated me for years. I'd been curious about the cookie-cutter cabins that fill this broad Mojave Desert basin. The cabins, skeletal and crumbling, sit equidistant on a grid of dirt tracks like hellish pieces on a giant gameboard. My parents had recently moved to Twentynine Palms, the nearest town, and, visiting them, I often heard town people nattering about those few who lived out here. They were squatters and drug addicts, criminals, the rumors went, clinically insane, pathologically dangerous. Many of them lived out there in the desert dirt and dust without water or electricity.

"They stink up the bathroom when they come in," the manager at the video store in town complained to me. "They bathe in the sink making a mess and then want to fill jugs of water to take home with them." That's why he kept the bathroom door locked. He'd hung an out-of-order sign on it. "Can you believe the way these people live?" Hearing about Ricka McGuire's death during a heat wave soon after spurred me to want to find out more. Writing her story, I found Wonder Valley to be even more haunting and otherworldly than I'd imagined, almost unbelievable in its strangeness. It was like a lost island, a bizarro Galapagos where in isolation a people had evolved, a breed apart from mainstream society, walking a razor's edge between life and death. I simply couldn't believe the way they lived. Nor could my editor.

"Can you get more of this stuff?" he asked. That's when I called Jack McConaha. The Wonder Valley firehouse supervisor had introduced us weeks before while I was researching Ricka's death. Jack was a short man in his seventies, with a penguin walk and a hairless head mottled and pocked as a Galilean moon. He peered up at me through wire-rimmed tri-focals pitched atop gristly flaps of ears. He shook my hand like we had been old friends.

"He's been in Wonder Valley a long time," she said after he'd gone. "He does security and patrols the valley. He knows it better than anybody." She gave me his card.

"Maybe I can go on a ride-along with you when you go out on patrol," I suggested when I called him, "like reporters do with the police."

"I do it all the time," he said. We agreed to meet.

Out at his cabin, he led me through the bedroom, past a pool table stacked with junk mail and old newspapers, his wife's sewing, photos and keepsakes and doodads. Jack first came to Wonder Valley as a Marine in the fifties, had been stationed at the base nearby and on his days off crawled over the washboard roads and up into the mountains in a war-surplus jeep. The Wonder Valley Jack found was then peopled by the original homesteaders. They were busy "proving-up" their parcels, building cabins and outhouses, cutting the roads. They were people like-minded to himself, simpaticos. He instantly felt at home here. When his tour in the Marines ended, he started a steel fabrication business down at the coast but continued coming back to the valley. An accident cut his welding venture short, but the severe burns he received earned him a lifetime of disability checks, the money he lived on during his forty years in Wonder Valley. After that accident, he returned to Wonder Valley for good.

"Back then Wonder Valley was like the Wild Wild West," he laughed, "You could do anything you wanted to do here, be anyone you wanted to be. I had always wanted to be a policeman, but I was too short to qualify. Out here, though, I just got a police scanner and started responding to calls." He said he beat the fire department to

3

fires as often as not. "Once there, I'd make sure everyone was safe then wait for the firefighters to arrive." Eventually, he joined Wonder Valley's small all-volunteer fire brigade and later even did a stint as its chief before the county took it over and forced him out of a job.

Jack led me on a tour of his home. It was like a Wonder Valley museum. We paused in front of framed newspaper clippings of drug busts and manhunts, of the traffic accidents he had attended to and the fires he'd fought. The Navy bombed Wonder Valley, attack planes missing the Marine Corps range in bombing run after bombing run, dropping 500-pound bombs each time, thirty-two in all. The paper interviewed Jack for the story. The dateline on the article showed it happened in the early seventies, but Jack talked about it like it was just last week. He pointed out the photos of himself with sheriff's captains and fire commanders, the luminaries he met in the line of duty. He told me about the all-night stakeouts, the search and rescues. "The abandoned cabins out here attract a bad element," he said.

"People come from LA and that mess down there by the coast and come up here to cook up drugs or dump a dead body or just wander out into the scrub and blow their own brains out." He told me about a man he'd come upon, standing in the sandy lane, bashing his wife's head in with a rock. He pointed out the commendations he'd been awarded, the citations. He told me about the people he'd helped, how they told him how much they appreciated what he did, how important his job was as the self-appointed guardian of Wonder Valley.

We stepped around a corner to where Jack kept a cabinet full of rifles, shotguns, and assault weapons. Semi-automatic pistols and revolvers hung from hooks; an antique repeater hung above a door. He opened the case and pulled a 9mm pistol from a peg.

"I prefer this one," he said, testing the pistol's weight. "The 9mm has a larger magazine. It can hold more ammunition." This was important, he said, because there was a kook out here hell-bent on

4

killing him. Years before, the man had emptied a .45 at him as he drove past. The man, Jack said, was after him still. But the 9mm's barrel was too long. "It hits the Jeep's seat and jacks my belt up all cock-eyed!" The .40-cal he usually carried was shorter and therefore more comfortable.

He holstered the pistol and I followed him outside to where his Jeep waited, a clean, new, forest green four-by-four with big gold star decals on its doors and flashing lights on its hood. Inside the Jeep was a nest with barely room for the two of us. I climbed in shotgun and propped my feet on a metal first aid kit, my head nestled in the mass pushing against me from behind the seat: blankets and jackets, shovels and jacks, jugs of water and gas, anything he might need while on patrol in the desert. The police scanner crackled to life as we threaded through the clutter of mining equipment on his five-acre parcel, the rusting metal, old car parts, wooden contraptions collected from the desert and arranged into a life-size diorama of a turn-of-the-century gold mine. We passed through the locked gate, through the wall of wind-ravished saltcedar trees, past the Marine Corps flag flapping wildly in the furnace-hot breeze and turned out on to the lattice of dusty dirt roads that divide Wonder Valley into empty rectangles of creosote and burroweed.

The original homesteaders cut these roads out here—more than 400 miles of them. Most were easements along property lines, though some zigged and zagged as they negotiated the various hills and washes of the valley. In the fifties, Federal grant money paid the power company to add these isolated residents as utility customers. The power company straightened and widened the roads, too, each one giving access to a string of power poles. They also named the roads, Jack said, taking the names from those of residents and prominent features and the like.

It was the county, however, that maintained these roads today, plowed them periodically with a grader paid for by a special assessment on meager property taxes. In fact, the roads had been plowed the morning I headed out with Jack, the washboards smoothed, the golden sand silky as softened butter under the hot sun.

"I've got to talk to that tractor driver," Jack grumbled in jest, "He's erased all my tracks!"

The trackless roads took us past the abandoned remains of old homestead cabins, stripped and bare, their windows gouged out, doors agape, each yawning a lifeless grimace over the bleak desert landscape. As we drove, Jack channeled the ghosts of Wonder Valley's past. He rattled off genealogies, reciting names as though I should have known them. Each parcel held a story, the story of a mid-century homesteader who came and cleared the land, built a cabin, an outhouse. Most of these cabins, however, now endured the whipping wind, the crackling heat, the desiccating dryness as lifeless shells.

Wonder Valley got its incongruous name from a joke, it turns out, from a sign along the paved road that once marked a homestead. It just as easily could have been called "Calloused Palms" or "Withering Heights," names of other homestead parcels in the area. Back in those days anyone could have gotten a parcel out here, got a homestead spread for the cost of the filing fee, made a claim under the Small Tract Homestead Act of 1938. Congress passed the Small Tract Act to give land to veterans of the Great War, land in this dry desert climate, a climate thought recuperative to mustard gas-scorched lungs. But the Small-Tract Act opened the land to anyone, not just veterans, made land available for health, convalescent and recreational use. Mostly, though, the government just wanted rid of it. This was throw-away land deemed otherwise useless. Now it was mostly abandoned again.

"This place here belonged to Vera Ciborowski's daughter, Anita," Jack said as we looped around a crumbling shack. "Vera owned that house back there where that pile of furniture was." The skeleton of a dog lay against the house still chained where the departed family had left it.

We drove around another cabin, circling it before driving to the next. At a small house with pasty, peeling purple paint Jack said, "This place belonged to Margaret Malone." He circled it, leaving his tire tracks on the wind-scoured sand. "Margaret Malone, her place used to be known as the purple palace because it had all kinds of purple rocks. See all them purple rocks?" He pointed to a line of cobbles painted a faded lilac, mostly buried by the wind-blown sand. "All them purple rocks—she had rocks everywhere—they made the place look like shit!"

We drove on, cutting road to road before looping around to examine another cabin.

"This one over here," Jack said, "Steve Staid—his dad and ma had the place—they gave it to Steve, they let him come out here, but he got so juiced up and screwed up. We had to call an ambulance. He died from booze and dehydration. We lost him." He paused a moment, lost in a thought. "I feel real bad about that. I'll put some tracks on it." Circling through the property, he laid a trail in the dirt and dust, marking the parcel, giving it a pulse, a sign of life.

Jack recognized his own tire tracks as we drove around the lonely cabins; he looked for others crossing over his. Cabin after cabin, his were the only ones.

Further on, we crept through another cluster of cabins. "And these two over here," he said, "there's some kind of battle in court over them." He looked around apprehensively. "Matter of fact, technically, I got no right to be on this property." He drove between the houses, laying tracks through what in suburban America would be the front yard. I sensed we were someplace we shouldn't be. "All I do is put some tracks on a property and somebody'll go and call the sheriff and—but the sheriff pretty well knows my tire tracks." He paused, pensive. "Well, they don't know these tires, these are the Firestones, they're different than my usual ones."

We drove off the property and out into the desert.

Jack talked a lot about tires and tracks. He talked about tracking criminals back to the scenes of crimes, about photographing tracks to deliver to the sheriff as evidence only to have it ignored or lost or forgotten. Until recently, Wonder Valley had been ground zero for methamphetamine manufacture, the isolated old cabins ideal for clandestine labs. A crackdown on the drug's chemical components along with stiff new bureaucratic barriers to getting electricity to the cabins had curtailed local meth making, however, forcing that industry south of the border and out of the desert. Nowadays, Jack didn't encounter much while on patrol.

We circled another abandoned shack, "Oh, and this one here," he said. "A lady had it. I came by here one day and a guy was coming out with stuff, so I held him at gunpoint for about five minutes," he chuckled. "Turns out he'd bought the place for back taxes."

Drawing a bead like that on a couple of area kids a few years ago had gotten him two years' probation for brandishing a weapon.

"I didn't recognize the kids! They'd practically grown up since I'd seen them last!" He had stopped them coming from the direction of a burglarized cabin. Their parents called the police. Jack was arrested, his guns confiscated. Anymore, the sheriff preferred Jack keep his pistol holstered and its magazine unloaded.

Jack turned his jeep from one dirt track to another, traversing the valley on forgotten rights-of-way until suddenly we were on the paved road. Heading east, we rounded the sweeping deadman's bend and up the steep grade to Sheephole Pass. "The Sheephole," as people out here call it, is the narrow gap separating the amber crags of the Sheephole Mountains from the chocolate-colored ones of the Bullions, the ranges that form Wonder Valley's northern perimeter. We stopped at the top to take in the view.

I had seen this view many times before. In fact, it was from up there that I'd first glimpsed Wonder Valley nearly thirty years ago. My girlfriend and I had taken a detour to avoid holiday traffic, following a route that would eventually, in 100 miles or so, drop us onto I-10 at Palm Springs. As we crossed this pass a thousand feet above the valley floor, the view opened up before us. The cubes of little shacks sat each isolated and alone on the grid of dirt roads. A contrail of dust marked the position of a car otherwise unseen in the heat-shimmering distance. On the way downhill, we passed a homemade sign, *Welcome to Wonder Valley* it said. We laughed. It was a joke ready-made, that name. Wonder Valley? Makes you wonder all right. Makes you wonder why the hell anyone would want to live out here.

Looking across the valley from where I sat with Jack, it was seven or so beeline miles to the Pinto Mountains, the range that forms the southern rim of the valley. In the Pintos are the adits and scrapings of the Dale Mining District, Southern California's largest gold mining region, which brought the first people to the valley, aside from the original Indian inhabitants, of course.

Wonder Valley broadens as you look west toward the snow-capped peaks of the San Bernardino Mountains, but pinches closed to the east. In fact, from our vantage, the eastern exit of the valley seemed buried under a 1,500-foot pile of rubble and stone. That's because while the Pintos run due east-west, the Sheepholes squeeze the valley closed at a 45-degree angle, leaving a blind outlet—Clark's Pass—only a few hundred yards wide at its eastern end. Joshua Tree National Park sits on the shoulder of that pass and covers the 1,200 square miles to the south.

If you follow the paved road north, up and through the Sheephole, you'll eventually hit old Route 66, then Interstate 40. From there, you'll get an idea of what Wonder Valley looked like before the cabins and the grid of roads. North from here, the Mojave opens up in a vast panorama of mountain range and empty desert basin practically to the Rockies. But even that hasn't looked that way for very long, geologically speaking.

The rocks of Wonder Valley's Bullion Mountains date just to the Jurassic period, the granites of the Sheephole Mountains only to the late Cretaceous, but a moment ago on the geologic time scale. Tectonic plate convergence along North America's continental margin caused magma to bubble up way back when in a series of events that ended about 65 million years ago. The magma that pushed up under here congealed hundreds of feet below the surface into giant granite bubbles, called plutons. Far more recently, a rift-style fault system tore the Mojave Desert asunder, spreading and rippling a vast area of the Western US, and in the process pushed those deep granite plutons up to form the Bullion and Sheephole Mountains beginning 10 or so million years ago. And the process continues today.

The thing is, I knew a lot about the Mojave Desert. I'd spent a lot of time out here. My wife—girlfriend at the time—with whom I'd first passed through here, was then a young geologist just out of school and eager to show me the desert she loved. In the desert, she said, no forest obscured the rocks. The geology, the history of the Earth, was right before your eyes. The desert was where we courted, she and I. We married a year to the day after we met. We bought a four-wheel drive truck and crawled over the desert, through the arroyos, up the alluvial fans and down countless dirt roads exploring the southwest. We passed through Wonder Valley time and again on our journeys. With her I'd seen this view from the Sheephole a dozen times before.

From there Jack and I coasted down toward Wonder Valley's basin sink, the dry desert playa that spreads like a white mirage at the valley's eastern foot. From the paved road, Jack turned down a potholed road as wide as a four-lane highway, then rounded a bend past a couple of concrete silos and stopped in a winter white wonderland under triple-digit heat. This was Dale Dry Lake on any map, but Jack simply called it the salt mine. It gathered the valley's scant rain run-off and concentrated it in a hyper-salty subsurface soup that was pumped to the surface, evaporated in ponds, kiln dried and pelletized into a dietary supplement suitable for livestock. Conveyors moved salt, white and pink and black from algae and bacteria, from snow cone pile to snow cone pile. Dolly Parton made a music video here, Jack said—he couldn't remember the song, something about salt, pointing out where she stood and sang. He had provided the security. Pitbull and Marc Anthony had made one here since.

In the distance, a dust devil kicked a mushroom into the sky, distracting Jack. "Is that smoke?" he said, shielding his eyes against the sun. Starting his Jeep, he turned it in that direction, then corrected. "I thought that was smoke," he laughed. "Oh, but there ain't nothing over that way." He waved his hand at the dust dismissively, but then fell silent. Jack had seen some fires, had lost friends in them because they couldn't escape the flames, trapped by a lifetime's accumulation of junk in their homes. His friend Dutch, for example, an old man active in the community and who had lived in the block-built homestead cabin that gave Wonder Valley its name, perished in it because he couldn't get out. He died in piles of rat-packed papers and junk-become-tinder in his home. Jack had warned the man, "One of these days you're going to be trapped." He heard the fire call on his scanner; he was the first on the scene. He found his friend Dutch inside, dead from the smoke.

We drove for a while in silence. Cabins passed without Jack's comment. He roused himself, however, as we approached the ruins of a homestead cabin virtually buried in scavenged refuse.

"Here's what you get faced with out here," he said, thumbing at the shanty. Remnants of plywood and scrap cobbled together into make-shift lean-tos and corrals of pallets littered with rubble covered the bare dirt lot. No water, no electricity, it looked more like a stockyard than a home. A silhouette stared back at us through a glassless window.

"They ain't got nothing," Jack muttered, his tinge of sympathy quickly replaced by disgust. "We gave them water and helped them, gave them food and helped them, but that's when they first moved in, but now they've got all that shit there. We've just sort of ignored it so far," he said. "We've left them alone."

I wondered who he meant by "we." It seemed anyone with anywhere to go was gone as the summer heat escalated, escaping to cooler climes, visiting the grandkids, spending time on the coast, or holed-up behind tinted windows under the blast of air conditioners. That shape in the window was the only other person I saw in four hours of laying tracks with Jack. The jeep's thermometer read 115 outside. I was sweating, the jeep's air conditioning overpowered by the roasting heat. I couldn't imagine living like that shape in the window. I later learned he had cancer. Destitute, he had come to Wonder Valley to die. This seemed like an easy place to do it. A man living in the cabin right next door to where Ricka McGuire died had, like her, died of the heat. His truck had broken down between his house and town. He tried to walk home. He didn't make it. And then there was Shawn Pritchard. Shawn grew up in Wonder Valley and lived in the cabin just next door to the east. He was with his girlfriend scrapping metal on the Marine base, out collecting bombs and bullets to recycle when his car got stuck. She stayed with it, he walked for help. The Marines found their raven-picked, coyote-eaten remains weeks later.

A guy called Nutty Ned had found Ricka McGuire's body. He lived nearby and had been worried about her. The heat had peaked at 118 degrees that day and Ricka, a woman in her sixties, wasn't tolerating it so well. Ned brought her a couple of jugs of water, but by then it was too late. I asked Jack about her. "We knew she wasn't going to make it," he replied.

As the sun drifted west, we treaded along a road that traversed a long bajada, the erosional skirt at the waist of the Pinto Mountains. Jack stopped his jeep on a hill overlooking the highway. We were close to town here, near the municipal dump, the gravel quarry, the airport. General Patton had built the airport out here, a secret base for the training of glider pilots for the World War II invasion of North Africa. As we sat there in Jack's Jeep, trash caught in a creosote shrub snapped in the wind around us. The sky was white with dust. The distant mountains floated in a silver mirage that shuddered with a shower-glass shimmer in the stifling heat. The sporadic cubes of cabins faded into the distance.

I'll tell you, for me, it takes a lot to look past these crumbling shacks and single-family slums, the trash and the junk and the beaten and abused land to see anything to redeem this corner of the desert.

But I wasn't here for desert beauty, I reminded myself.

I hadn't come here to write about the place, either, truth be told. Not really. I was here because my parents were here, had retired here, traded a house in Hawaii with an ocean view for one on acres of sand hundreds of miles from any sea. If you asked my mother, she'd tell you she was tired of the Hawaiian weather. The heat and humidity. No kidding, that was what she'd tell you. She'd tell you she moved to the Mojave Desert to get away from paradise. It snowed ten inches the day they bought their house. It was 115 degrees there now.

As much as I would rather my parents had stayed in Hawaii, however, their home here in the desert proved convenient for me. I needed a place to escape, a place to hole-up, to hide out. I'd made a mess of my life. I had lost my job and subsequently squandered our nest egg in a bad real estate deal, ruining my wife's credit and running up a tremendous debt. I'd started drinking. Our marriage was failing. I fell into a deep depression and couldn't face friends or family, so I volunteered to dog sit for my parents while they spent the summer away. I moved into their guest room. Writing was to occupy my time and maybe become a new start for me.

It had been my parents as much as anybody who had warned me away from Wonder Valley. They'd heard the stories, the rumors, had friends who had friends who had tales to tell. But it wasn't like they would know. My parents' house was in town; they had piped-in city water, trash pick-up, mail delivery, a paved access road, a supermarket and gas stations. They were, however, in the eastern-most neighborhood to have such services. Beyond them the houses thinned out quickly. From their house on, abandoned cabins outnumbered those occupied.

Their house was just over the rise from where I sat with Jack, idling. You could see the changing colors of Wonder Valley's sunset from their backyard. The sunsets out here really are beautiful. The Sheephole Mountains become enflamed, glow white-hot, which fades to a fiery red, then magenta, then purple, then, just as the sun sets, indigo black as a bruise. Then out come the stars. The heavens out here are vast, limitless in the darkness of night. I'd lie out on the concrete of my parents' driveway and count the shooting stars, making a wish on each, always the same wish. Then I'd bed down in their guest room. I was going to be here for a while. Shit happens. You zig when you should have zagged. You head down the wrong road. Things fall apart. Seems to be the story of this part of the desert.

Idling with Jack on that hill above the highway, we looked north over the valley. Jack pulled a juice bottle filled with ice water from behind his seat and poured himself a glass. He fell silent, contemplative.

"All the old-timers are gone," he said with a sigh. "None of the original homesteaders remain."

"Things change, I guess." Shit happens.

The sun colored the clouds to the west. I sunk into my seat. Inside the Jeep grew quiet, Jack and I each lost in our own thoughts, while down below us in the floor of the valley the furnace-hot wind worked to erase our tracks.

Chapter 2

A few days after my ride-along with Jack, I set out to explore Wonder Valley on my own. I spent the morning crawling over Wonder Valley's corrugated roads, turning right, left, up and down, but not knowing what I was looking for, I found nothing of interest. But then, just as I was about to give up and make my way home, I rounded a bend and came upon a woman sitting alone in a well-kempt car blocking the way. I could see her in the driver's seat, her head down as if in prayer. She didn't look up. Not another soul stirred. I hesitated in my own car, watching her, so out of place did she seem. Shaking that off, though, I got out of my car to help, convincing myself that she must be lost or broken down or run out of gas. As I approached her car, I saw she was pouring over a computer-plotted map, books and papers spread out around her. Seeing me, she jolted alert.

"I'm looking for a road," she said after catching her breath. "Mesa. It's supposed to run right by here." I didn't have a clue. I offered to look at her map with her, figuring it might guide us both out of there, but she quickly covered it. "No one's supposed to see this," she said. She was an enumerator for the Census Bureau, she explained, and the documents and materials she used in that process were confidential. She was only stopped there to get her bearings. "I've got a lot of territory to cover." As a Census enumerator, she was required to visit every cabin in her assignment area and there were many she couldn't find. None of the roads or addresses seemed to match her materials. She was frustrated and confused.

Seeing her struggle, it occurred to me, What a great story! I could write about taking the census out here! I immediately understood the challenges Census workers like her must be facing. This was such a vast and sparsely populated place with roads running willy-nilly, many unmarked. I imagined myself accompanying Census workers as they searched up and down these isolated tracks, trudged cautiously up to broken-down shacks, knocked on doors that hadn't been knocked on in years. I'd follow them door to distant door as they attempted this physical head count by hand. I almost laughed out loud picturing them getting the misfits and miscreants out here to cooperate, certain none of them would have any interest in participating in any census—or, for that matter, even being approached at all.

The Census worker gave me her supervisor's number. When I called him, he forwarded me on to a higher-up.

Meanwhile, I bypassed the homeless magazine and pitched my story idea to a *real* magazine, a big, glossy, lifestyle mag with blondes with buxom cleavage on the cover and ads for Swiss watches inside. I would be the Census Bureau's first-ever embedded journalist, I told them. Already, I explained, the material was proving to be ripe and colorful. Just a short while before, for example, a crotchety old desert rat had frog-marched a Census enumerator off his property at the muzzle of a rifle. The old man had booby-trapped his road too, a news report said, scattering nails in the soft sand and barricading parts to discourage others from approaching. The Census worker called the sheriff who confiscated the man's weapons and charged him with threatening a federal agent with a firearm. I'd heard the old man passed away before he could stand trial. Court records, though, listed his status as fugitive.

The magazine editors loved the idea. I was excited, too. It would be my first writing assignment for a major magazine, the kind of thing that could launch my career. What's more, the assignment came with the promise of a hefty check.

Even the Census Bureau gave me the go-ahead. "This story could be really good for us," the regional director said. Public concerns for privacy had given the Census a dubious cast, an image he wanted to improve. Hearing what I wanted to do, he himself pulled the strings to make it happen.

He arranged a ride-along with a Census supervisor and for two days we peered into dilapidated shacks, knocked on doors, tramped over miles of open desert. I was just settling into my new role when the director called. "Washington higher-ups want reassurance you are respecting Census confidentiality," he said.

"I'm keeping my distance," I replied. "I usually stay in the car when the guys go up to the occupied cabins..."

"You're seeing respondents' houses?" he asked, stopping me mid-sentence, a panic in his voice. "People's houses are PII! We said no PII!" PII—that's Personally Identifiable Information in the parlance of the Census. It was any information through which someone might be able to identify a Census respondent.

"How can I possibly accompany enumerators and not see the houses they're visiting?" I asked. Before I began, he'd reiterated the need to maintain the confidentiality of PII and laid down ground rules: I was not to see Census Bureau documents or maps, or approach or speak with respondents. He'd said nothing about seeing peoples' houses.

"Most of the places out here are vacant," I explained. "And I'm not going to the door with enumerators, anyway, I'm not listening to the interviews—I can't even see the respondents in most cases. They don't even know I'm there. I'm keeping my distance just like we discussed!"

"Clearly," he said, "more safeguards need to be in place. The whole thing needs to be better thought-out. As we are going about it now, the risk of PII disclosure is just too great." Citing the concerns of his higher-ups, concerns, he felt, he could not assuage, he pulled the plug on the project.

17

"Look, Bill," he said, "It's a free country. I can't tell you where you can and can't go, but I can tell you, you can no longer go around with Census employees." And that was that. My time as the first-ever journalist embedded with the forces of the US Census Bureau was over, before it really began.

But I knew I was onto a great story, a career-launching story. And then there was the promise of that big fat check, a check I desperately needed because I was otherwise unemployed.

I needed a plan B—and, just then, like an act of divine intervention, I heard an ad on the radio: The Census Bureau was hiring. Enumerators were needed for all areas of the desert. I called the advertised number immediately. I filled out the application knowing exactly what to say. I knew what they were looking for. They wanted someone who lived in the area—so I gave them my parents' address. Check. They wanted enumerators with a four-wheel drive vehicle—so I borrowed one. Check. They gave preference to those who spoke Spanish, and while maybe I wasn't fluent, I'd taken classes in college, so, check. I impressed myself with my own cleverness.

They called me within days. Then, less than a week after they'd fired me as their first-ever embedded journalist in the history of the Census, they hired me. I was now a Census Bureau Enumerator. My assignment area: Wonder Valley.

I completed training the next week. I now had a job to do, a job in addition to collecting material for a story. I was excited about it and took it all seriously. I spread my newly issued Census maps out on the floor to familiarize myself with my assignment area, its sixty square-miles rendered as thin computer-plotted lines, sparsely seasoned with the black pepper flecks of structures. I devised a strategy to proceed, deciding to move east to west, starting at the farthest corner of my AA, then work my way back.

I loaded my borrowed truck with water and lunch, and feeling fully prepared, headed out into the desert. Reaching my AA, I turned onto its most distant road and followed it toward its remotest end. The road traversed a rocky patch of desert, dropped into a deep wash, then rose again up onto a low mesa, a mesa guarded by a skull-and-crossbones sign, its crossbones disfigured into machine guns. *No Trespassing, Armed Neighborhood*, it said. I stopped there to ponder that sign. The armed part I got—armed like a Taliban stronghold or an outlaw hideout. The claim of neighborhood, however, was gross exaggeration. Neighborhood implies neighbors, people, but his was better described as habitat, home to jackrabbits and coyotes, scorpions and snakes. Creosote scrub crouched in low clumps; early summer wildflowers tinted the arid wastes yellow. Before me, a covey of quail undulated single file across the road like a deconstructed snake. Around me, dozens of skeletal cabins leaned against the whipping wind, each a pepper-black dot on my map. According to the last Census, about 1,200 of these old homestead cabins still stood in Wonder Valley, but more than half of them were vacant and most of those—like these around me—unlivable.

At one time, there'd been some 4,000 cabins out here, back when land was free for the taking, back when anyone could stake a Wonder Valley claim. You simply chose a five-acre rectangle from the Federal General Land Office map and paid your five-dollar filing fee. The Land Office had divided Wonder Valley on paper into 336-by-660-foot parcels— roughly two city blocks each—overlaying the land with a vast grid without regard to topography. There were no roads back then, of course, and few markers in the flat valley—it was up to you to find the property you chose.

Despite all this free and available land, interest in homesteading in the area started off slowly. In 1941, for example, the first-year land became available, only one hundred and forty-two families filed small-tract homestead applications. That's because by that year's end, World War II preoccupied America. Gasoline and tires for travel quickly grew scarce. The strong legs and backs needed to improve this land were sent off to fight tyranny abroad.

After the war, however, things changed. The fifties saw the advent of California car culture, the Atomic Age, the Cold War, nuclear families, bomb shelters. Hollywood Westerns fed a nostalgia for simpler times. Out here in the desert, the Old West lived. In Wonder Valley you could get your very own home on the range, claim your own personal piece of the Wild Wild West. Magazines published articles: it's easy to make a small tract claim, anybody can get land, inciting what the *LA Times* called "one of the strangest land rushes in Southern California history." By 1952 the Land Office had processed more than 12,000 homestead applications in the area, and by the mid-fifties they had a backlog of some 60,000. Lines trailed out of the government land office. Even movie cowboy Ronald Reagan staked a Wonder Valley claim.

The rules stated that once you chose your plot and located it, you had three years to "prove up" the land, to clear it, build a cabin. Ronald Reagan didn't prove-up his parcel. Few people did. Few could stand the scorching months of triple-digit heat or the icy winter chill, the snow and the flash floods, or this constant wind that blasts like a furnace in the summer and bites to the bone in the winter. Most drove the three hours out here, took one look at this dry, scruffy land blistering in the summer heat—no roads, no water—and they got right back into their cars and drove right back home. Those folks lost their homesteads, gave up their claim. Their parcel went back on the block, became available for some other soul to select.

Obviously, though, many did tough it out, the valley eventually filling with these cookie-cutter cabins. Scanning around me, I pictured people out here building them, imagined them spending their weekends banging nails into lumber and mortaring desert rocks into walls. Other homesteaders erected prefab structures or hired one of the construction companies that had sprung up across the desert offering units designed specifically to satisfy Land Office requirements. Over the years, some cabins grew into houses: rooms were added, water wells drilled, flush toilets and indoor plumbing installed, creating sprawling "builtmores" as people out here call them, warrens, like Jack McConaha's, with rooms within rooms within rooms.

After that homestead blip of the fifties, however, Wonder Valley became a blank space on the map once again. The Interstate Highways had bypassed the area, leaving the potholed road through here a superfluous byway. Homesteaders aged and died, passing properties to heirs with no interest in grandpa's wasteland clapboard shack. Forgotten, the cabins sagged into disrepair. Over time, Wonder Valley crumbled into the sort of post-modern ghost town it is today, this eerie ghost suburbia in the dry desert wastes.

Congress officially ended homesteading out here with the repeal of the Small Tract Homestead Act in 1976. By that time, about thirty-six percent of the land the Act had opened to homesteading was privately owned. The rest, the government reckoned, merited federal protection, leaving Wonder Valley a pixelated patchwork of private and protected public land.

In the armed ghost neighborhood of my AA, I pulled up to a cabin and got out of my truck. Wind rattled its corrugated metal roof, howled through the bare studs, banged its flapping door. Inside, rats' nests and regurgitated owl pellets littered the bare concrete floor. The litter covered an inscription scratched into the foundation, a date, 1952, and the initials of someone long departed. A shiver shuddered through me. I looked out again at all the skeletal cabins around me, each an anonymous mausoleum in this valley of the dead, rats and owls and animals left to haunt them.

Suddenly, as if materializing out of a cloud of pure nowhere, a man in a dust-stirring truck skidded up, out almost before it stopped. His cold black eyes drilled into me. "Can I help you?" he said in the parlance of the desert: *What the hell do you want?* His tone was gravel and dust. A silver stubble grew stunted on his cheeks, an American flag cap slouched on his head. He grinned a toothless grin, but he wasn't smiling. "Son," he said, "you're liable to get shot out here!"

A jolt of dread spiked through me. I held my Census badge out like a crucifix. At that moment, I understood why the Census Bureau had so hastily hired me. Few others were willing to work this area.

The dust-stirring man disappeared in a cloud, as quickly as he came, leaving me alone to catch my breath. This encounter had unnerved me.

I had prepared myself for crotchety desert denizens but hadn't included malevolent specters amongst the dangers I'd foreseen. To be frank, I'd been more concerned with the heat and the sun and the isolation and poor road conditions. I knew a breakdown out here could be disastrous. In fact, not long before I started with the Census, an enumerator trying to negotiate these rutted tracks in a Japanese car hit a rock and cracked his oil pan. His oil ran out and his engine seized before he could make civilization. His long walk and hundreds of dollars in tow fees weren't covered by his fifty cents-per-mile Census Bureau reimbursement.

Over the ensuing days, I soon discovered other unforeseen dangers, as well, like people's dogs—pit bulls predominantly—chained to the front stoop if you were lucky, or let to run wild if you weren't. Soon after I started with the Census, a pack of feral dogs chased me to my truck, encircling it and growling threateningly at me until I sped away. In training, we were admonished not to leave our car doors open when approaching a house—an open car door risked the exposure of PII to wandering eyes. But after that encounter, I always kept my door open in case I again needed to flee vicious dogs. I got good at the routine and consequently was only bitten the once.

I'd gone up to a scroungy place where an old dog with a gray muzzle bared its teeth and growled at me from inside, smashing against a duct-taped window as I approached. Other dogs joined in as well, howling and barking, banging against the door. No one answered.

When I returned later that day, a truck was there. The dogs piled out the door when the cheerless owner opened it. "Can I help you?" the owner said, staring at me defiantly. The dogs yelped and jumped around me, jockeying for attention. The old dog with the gray muzzle trickled out last. "They won't bother you," the owner said as the old dog with the gray muzzle clamped its jaws down on my arm just below the elbow. I sprang back, prepared to run, but the old dog just stood there looking up at me, silent.

"Did you get bit?" the owner asked, a cold smirk drifting across his face.

"YES!" I cried, my elbow quickly turning blue. I examined the bite for punctures.

"Which one did it?"

"The black one!" I pointed an accusatory finger at the old gray-muzzled dog while cradling my throbbing arm.

"Oh, it couldn't have been that one," the man said dismissively.

As I rubbed it, my arm turned a deep, ghastly purple. I held it as I proceeded with the interview.

"Is this your usual home?" I asked the man. He nodded, staring at my black and blue swelling arm. This dog bite was a boon, I realized. Now a little concerned that his dog had just bitten a Census worker, the man was giving me the interview without the fuss I'd come to expect. I continued rubbing my aching arm as I wrote down the man's responses to keep the bite fresh in his mind.

You learn to work with what you're given, I guess. I was nothing if not adaptable. Over the days and weeks, I fell into a routine, most of my time spent looking for occupied homes. As an enumerator, of course, I had to visually inspect all the tumbledown cabins in my assignment area, but Census Bureau protocol forbade me from simply marking them down as vacant and moving on. Instead, I had to find "proxies"— neighbors or knowledgeable persons—to attest to the "occupancy status" of each one. According to Census procedures, I could consider none of these broken-down, dilapidated, windowless, bare stud-walled, gaping-roofed and clearly uninhabitable piles of rubble out here unoccupied until a proxy told me so.

To find proxies, I looked for signs of life: dogs, laundry on a line, green trees, junk and trash. I headed for any place with a car with all four tires parked out front. I pulled up at one such place, for example, a place surrounded by a clutch of broken-down shacks. As I approached, I saw a woman through a window washing dishes, her gray hair pulled tightly into a bun. Reaching her door, I didn't knock. Seeing me, I overheard her talking over her shoulder, something about the goddamn something or other. A man soon answered, a man with a deeply grooved face and no front teeth. His eyes fixed on me through the door's tattered screen. "Can I help you?" he said in the parlance.

"Does anybody live in those places?" I asked, pointing to the broken-down shacks, aware, I'll admit, how ridiculous the question sounded. The man just looked at me silently through his tattered screen like I was some kind of dumbshit. "I have to get confirmation," I explained.

He just rolled his eyes. "Well, that one there was old man so-and-so's place 'til he died," he offered finally, pointing at a tumble-down pile of two-by-fours. "That one was never nothing, just a shed." A smile crept to his face, "And see that place over there? Stay away from it. One night a SWAT team came rappelling out of helicopters raiding it. It was a meth lab."

Once he got started I had trouble keeping up. He pointed at places and rattled off road names, none of which matched what was on my Census-issued map.

"My map shows a road," I said, "it runs right by your cabin..."

"Sweeney?" the man said.

"No, it's..."

"Halston?"

"No..."

"Coyote Trail?"

"No...umm..."

"End Run?"

"No..."

"Prickly Pear?"

"No...on this map...it says this should be Piedmont?"

"Never heard of it. This road here is really Sweeney but them people over there changed the name to Halston. And that jerk on the end, he wants it to be End Run. Prickly Pear is that up there, but it's just that old lady's driveway. Everybody wants to call these roads something different and the county just lets them. They don't give a shit. It gets so confusing. I once had a tractor-trailer pull in here looking for an address. Turned out he was twenty miles off. I never could figure how he got that rig across the wash." I snickered and suggested maybe that truck was still stuck out here, its driver struggling to turn the thing around to get out.

"Oh, it'd be completely cut apart for parts by now." the man chuckled. "You don't know the people out here!" I laughed, picturing that semi being carved into pieces like a whale being butchered by Inuit.

§ § §

After the homestead blip, the population of Wonder Valley spiraled downward leaving the vacant, forgotten cabins to the elements and any drifters to alight in. Eventually, others arrived, most just sort of finding themselves here. Over the years, mental institutions resettled patients out here, too, and prisons dumped inmates out on early release. Many of the remaining cabins had their windows scrapped, their metal scavenged, stripped to bare shells, their doors and chairs and siding and walls hauled away to be sold or repurposed or burned to heat newcomers' homes in the freezing high-desert winter. Open squatters' fires on bare concrete floors sometimes spread to walls, the roof. "Improvement fires" the fire department called them. They let them burn, let them prove-up Wonder Valley by removing another run-down shanty. Remaining homesteaders burned down eyesores, too, tore down drug dens, dismantled desert blight. A federally funded program, "Shack Attack," actually paid contractors to demolish the development it once encouraged.

After Congress established the nearby Joshua Tree National Park in the nineties, however, campers and hikers began to venture out this way again. Desert off-roaders pushed out of the new park probed into the valley, too. The motorhomes of migrating snowbirds traced Wonder Valley's forgotten byways in search of isolated nests in which to overwinter. Their fixed incomes found affordability here. Writers and artists found they could survive here on the proceeds of their art. The population swelled. By the turn of the new century, about a thousand artists and retirees and drifters and squatters peopled the three hundred square miles of the valley.

While working on the Census, I got so I could tell what kind of person lived in any particular place before I even pulled up. A fenced parcel, chain-link and no-trespassing signs, for example, protected a retiree. Inside the gate, they'd beaten back the forces of nature, scraped clear the unruly scrub, leaving a bald pate of dust as a protective moat. Those who answered my knock were wary, wanted to see my badge, prove who I was, avow that their information was not going to be sold to telemarketers. They complained my visits were annoying interruptions, keeping them from TV, I could only imagine, Fox News piped in through satellite dishes. Despite their rush, though, they'd often drag the interview out, hold back details, obfuscate. Not a few of them told me that their race, when I asked, was Martian.

The rare raked-sand, Zen-garden parcel, on the other hand, held an artist, gathered desert detritus meticulously integrated into their landscape. They'd offer me herbal tea or a complaint about the bother or a lament that their pristine desert vistas were lost to the single-family favelas of their neighbors. "Can you believe the way some people live out here?" they'd say.

The single-family slums the artists lamented often flooded over acres of desert, the sagging shacks at their cores surrounded by dissected heaps of splintering lumber and bent-metal scrap, beached cars and weathered furniture, drifts of trash and debris. A stockade thicket of scraggly trees often walled them from the world.

The ghosts I'd see drifting around these places from a distance often went phantom as I arrived, leaving a place seemingly haunted by just the murmur of a radio or TV. Only with persistence could I conjure them forth.

At one isolated cabin, for example, I could get no one to respond to my knock. The cabin had all the signs of occupation: laundry on the line, a dog tied outside, the usual accumulation of junk and rubbish around, but would fall eerily silent when I pulled up. I went out to the place every day and at varying times over the course of a week. Each time, I'd find the "Notice of Visit" I'd left during the previous trip gone, yet no one ever appeared. I was desperate to find someone, not simply because I had to get the enumeration, but also as a proxy for the broken-down shacks all around it.

One time, as I walked around the cabin, knocking on doors and windows, a truck appeared from the barren nowhere and a kid got out. "Can I help you?" he asked, before banging on the cabin door calling out a woman's name.

"Who lives here?" I asked. "Can you tell me about these vacant cabins?"

"I don't know," he said, seeing my badge. "I'm not from around here." He then jumped back into his truck and as fast was gone.

On another visit, a taxicab with a turban-wearing driver came down the rutted road and across the wash, then out of the cab almost before it stopped jumped a man in a fedora. "Can I help you?" he asked.

He carried a bottle of Black Velvet and told me about the steaks he'd brought to grill, but he had no steaks, just that bottle of whisky. I asked him who lived there, about the cabins around. "I don't know, man," he said, throwing his hands up in surrender. "I'm not from around here." He stood there looking at me with a big grin, leaving me completely bewildered.

Then, a week later, my phone rang. It was the woman from that isolated cabin.

"I found your notes," she said. "Sorry, I've been sick, I really think the Census is important, I want to participate." Someone, it seems, had told her she'd lose her benefits if she didn't answer the Census questions. I was pretty sure that wasn't true but decided it best not to contradict her.

Out at her cabin, she answered the door in a nightie. "Come in," she said. "Sorry about the mess, I've been sick. I had the flu for three days. The medication makes me sick, it messes with my immune system, let's go back here. Don't mind the mess." She was pinging, redlining, 10,000 rpm, flying through words. She wore her auburn hair piled on her head, scooped and stacked there, stray tendrils sprouting from the nape of her neck, looping to her shoulders. She'd been pretty once, I thought to myself.

She led me into her bedroom, a cave with windows blackened, clothes scattered. She sat on the bed, a mattress on the floor, and patted a spot for me next to her. She bounced her leg up and down as she jammered, going on about her life, her health, the hem of her negligee creeping up her thighs, her breasts swimming freely in her top. We Census workers were admonished in training not to go into anyone's house, to do all interviews at the front door, yet here I was practically in bed with a woman wearing nothing more than a nightie in an isolated cabin in the middle of flippin' nowhere. I could barely write her responses the bed was shaking so. I took my job as an enumerator seriously and prided myself on being professional, but, here, sitting on the bed with this woman, I found my palms were sweating. I felt the heat of a blush flush my face. I stammered through the interview. "Did you live here on April first?" "Is this your usual home?" "How many people live here?" "Your name?" "Sex? —sorry, I have to ask…" "Age?" "Date of birth?" She answered everything in a breath, going on about the neighbors, the crumbling, tumbledown cabins all around her, shaking her leg, jiggling all over, until I quickly stood up to leave, my face flush, my hands shaking, certain I was going to be fired, and she was talking, talking, as I backpedaled to the door, goodbye, goodbye, thanks for coming, and out the door and into my truck, I fled across the wash and as fast was gone.

Phew. I stopped a safe distance away to catch my breath. I felt I'd escaped an enchantress or something. The dangers of Census work out here were indeed many and varied, I laughed to myself.

§ § §

Unlike that strange woman's place, the occupied places in my AA tended to be clustered together, around powerlines and away from the washes and flash flood zones, making typical enumerations bee-to-blossom hops from door to door. One big section of my assignment area, however, turned out to be completely depopulated, devoid of residents entirely. In the middle of it, a string of cabins stretched across a low hill, the road out to them a single, seldom-used track. The cabins all appeared well-maintained and livable, their windows covered and locked, the isolation protecting them from scavenging. The lack of trash and tire tracks, though, made it clear no one had been to them in a long time. Vacation cabins, I concluded, and now that it was summer, there was little chance anyone would come out. Shit.

I hiked cabin to cabin, sticking a Notice of Visit to each, leaving with a futile bang on the door for good measure. At the last one of the string, a cacophonous din of buzzing responded to my knock, followed by a black rain of insects. Tiny bees by the hundreds tumbled out of the eaves and onto my head, into my eyes, down my shirt, tangling in my chest hair, climbing over my sweaty body. They followed me like a cloud as I ran to my truck. They crawled around on my face, into my ears and nostrils until I wrenched the truck to a halt and flung the door open and dashed into the scrub ripping clothes off as I ran. A hundred yards out, sweating and out of breath, I stopped to survey myself for damage. I hadn't been stung. In fact, I wondered if I hadn't just imagined it all, the heat and isolation taking its toll. I stood nearly naked in the middle of the desert, thanking god there were no witnesses. I returned to my truck certain I'd never find a proxy for those cabins.

Later that day, though, out of the blue, a woman called. She owned the last one of the string. "It's my family's cabin. We don't come much—in fact, I haven't been here for years—but I came out today and found your notice." The cabin had been in her family for a generation, she said, her family had homesteaded it, and so-and-so had the one beyond and such-and-such the other and they had all been friends and used to all come out together, but now everyone had scattered to the wind and none of them ever came out anymore. She gave me all the information I needed. I crossed the cabins off my list. Check, check, check.

A miracle, I thought, the timing unimaginable. The Census Bureau owed me a medal for this one, some kind of Employee of the Year award. Enumerating above and beyond the call of duty. One thing still nagged me about that, though: How was it possible that that woman wasn't chased away by the bees?

I shrugged it all off and congratulated myself again for a job well done. I was getting really good at this Census stuff. I was having fun, too. I loved being out here having a reason to investigate the skeletal cabins and ghost-town shacks while tracking down the spirits that haunted them. This was all going to be stuff for my Census story, of course. I was writing it in my head as I drove around—Wonder Valley, this otherworldly place through the eyes of a Census Enumerator.

I breezed through my assignment books, every shack, hovel and house in my assignment area counted and crossed off. *I am an enumerating god!* I told myself as I strode up to the final cabin in my AA with a swagger. I'd earned this cockiness, I figured. Not that this was a competition or anything, but if it were, I'd be winning. Within the next five minutes time, I'd be the first enumerator in the area to have completed his Census assignment.

This last place was no different from so many others I'd enumerated: a small boarded-up shack facing the wide-open mountains. It sat alone, all by itself except for a clean little Korean car parked out front. I couldn't imagine how that car got down that rutted, sandy road. As I approached the place, a man walked out from around back. "Can I help you?" he said.

He was young for these parts, I noticed—late 20s or early 30s tops, with hipster's tussled bed head and groomed three-day beard. The gods were indeed smiling upon me I thought, figuring with a young person I'd avoid all the rank bullshit I'd come to expect from the older residents. I mentally shortened my estimated time to completion to three minutes.

"Hi," I said, giving the guy a little wave. "I'm with the Census."

"I do not live here," the hipster replied. "I am here only for the day." He was European, his accent French, I thought.

"No worries," I said, remaining casual. "Is there someone else I can talk to?"

"The owner, he is not here," he replied in his halting French way.

"When is he going to be back?"

"I do not know."

"Well, when did he leave?"

"I do not know."

I wasn't sure he understood me, that I was with the Census and it was my job to ask these questions. Surely, they must have the Census in his country. "I'm with the federal government," I said, holding up my badge. I was employing a technique I'd adapted from TV cop shows and honed sparring with the reticent old hermits I'd been dealing with. "I'm here to take the Census. I need you to answer a few questions for me." I flipped open my notebook and clicked my pen, prepared to write—part of the method I'd sharpened.

"I know who you are," the hipster spat back at me. "You are on private property! You must leave!"

His hostility caught me off guard. I quickly regrouped, however, looking up at him and pulling my shades off with a practiced TV detective's flourish. "But it's the law," I said, commencing a spiel I developed to strike fear and garner respect. "The Constitution of the United States mandates all residents submit to..."

31

"Bah!" the hipster growled. "You do not frighten me, Mr. Federal Agent! You must leave!" It was like I was suddenly in a scene from a Monty Python movie. *Your mother is a hamster and your father smells of elderberries!* I filled in the dialogue by rote. *Now go away or I will taunt you a second time!*

"You are on private property!" he spat at me again.

"But..." I mumbled. Flustered, I held my badge aloft again, my amulet of divine government authority. The hipster just crossed his arms defiantly and stared at me through black, soulless eyes.

Collecting myself, I whipped my phone from my pocket and held it out, preparing to dial. This was my ultimate mind trick, *I'm calling back-up!* its clear, unmistakable message. If this guy'd watched any TV at all he'd know shit was definitely about to hit the fan. But he just stared at me, leered at me. It was like he was trying to get into my head, infect me with the evil eye or some kind of wicked gypsy juju. I shifted foot to foot. I tried to maintain eye contact, but I couldn't. I broke. I shoved my phone back into my pocket and I flipped pages on my clipboard, scanning for I don't know what. After a moment, I stuffed the clipboard under my arm with an aggressive finality. "I'm going to have to come back," I threatened, as dire as I could make it, *this isn't over!* I backed to my truck and got in. I pretended to write while I watched him through the windshield, wondering in that instant if he was even real, if he wasn't maybe some kind of apparition, a figment conjured by my vanity, my hubris, a spectral smack-down by the gods of enumeration. I started my truck and quickly got the hell out of there.

When I rallied my nerve to return a few hours later, the little Korean car was gone. Already the wind had erased any sign of it. I left a Notice of Visit on the chain link fence and returned to check on it every day for a week afterward. No one ever returned. There were no proxies, I never checked the place off. I finally handed my maps and books over to my boss at the fast food joint he'd taken as an office, that one cabin un-enumerated.

My boss scanned my entries landing on that one unfinished line. I began to fidget. My mind fumbled for an excuse—it wasn't like I could tell him I'd been foiled by a spectral French hipster with a manicured three-day beard and tussled bed head. "There was someone there," I stammered in explanation. "The place was boarded up, but some foreign guy was there though I don't think he understood me or at least didn't seem to know anything..."

"Boarded up?" he asked. "So the guy didn't live there?" After I shook my head, he checked Uninhabited in my book, then closed it. Then he stood up and stuck out a hand. "Good job," he said, "pleasure working with you." I thanked him and turned to leave feeling foolish I'd let myself get so worked up about that cabin at all.

§ § §

I went home to my parents' house and plopped myself down on the couch. It was all so anticlimactic. I don't know what I expected, a gold watch? Enumerator of the Year? I was now unemployed again, and that fact left me with an emptiness I hadn't expected, a feeling of loss. Working for the Census had given me reason to get out of the house, to drive around Wonder Valley and explore, to meet people. I'd only been hours without it, but I already missed it.

I still had that Census story to write, I reminded myself. Get that done and there'd be so much more I could do out here. I started to gather my thoughts. I replayed the experience over again in my head, blushing openly when my thoughts fell on that French hipster guy. I'd made a fool of myself out there. I shuddered, too, thinking what I might have said to my boss had he pressed me about it, what kind of ridiculous, laughable excuse I'd have come up with in that moment. I didn't believe in apparitions or any of that nonsense, but I'd gotten myself kind of freaked out. I chalked it up to fatigue, the heat. I'd been really hustling out there, like I had something to prove.

But what was that hipster guy doing at that place anyway? I couldn't stop dwelling on it. He didn't live there—it was boarded-up. It made no sense. Same with the woman at the bee cabin. She'd said nothing about the bees, but surely they'd have chased her off like they had me. Then there was that guy in the fedora? And the taxicab? A taxicab with a New York, turban-wearing cabbie? Way out there? And what about that jiggling enchantress? And that dust-stirring truck man, appearing out of nowhere, warning, "You could get shot out here!" It was all just so weird. I remembered the guy who'd frog-marched the enumerator off his property at the barrel of a rifle. I'd heard he died. I decided to go check his place out.

Driving there, I came to a barricade of barbed wire blocking the way, scattered nails and glass in the sand beneath it. I paused, looking around, and, seeing no one, swung my 4X4 wide past the barrier, fishtailing up over the berm and through the soft sand to rejoin the road on the other side. Weeds grew in the road's ruts, no tracks marred it. Easing forward warily, I came to the man's house.

It looked normal, like a regular house, with cedar fence and a few young trees rustling in the soft breeze—the trees still a vibrant green, clearly watered and well cared for. I didn't find the hermit's thicket wall of saltcedars I had expected, nor the cars on blocks or drifts of scavenged cast-offs littering the yard. It was just a normal house, something you'd expect in a normal neighborhood, not out here amongst these ramshackle shacks, not housing a crotchety old desert rat brandishing firearms. I debated whether to knock on the door.

As I stepped out of my truck, though, another truck turned toward me. Shiny and new, it barreled at me. It careened around the buried barbed wire barricade and out of the truck almost before it stopped, the driver with a chrome garden spade sending a flurry of sand into the air while prairie-dogging up and glaring at me between shovelfuls. I moved to get back in my truck, but then it dawned on me.

The driver, a woman, stood upright as I approached her.

"Can I help you?" I said, you know, like you do out here. One of her wheels was buried to the hub in the sand.

"Oh, hi," she said, jabbing the spade into the ground. "Thanks for coming over. I think I might be lost." She raised her Census badge. "I'm looking for a road, my map shows it runs right by here..." I laughed. After weeks with the Census, I knew this place. I pointed the way.

Chapter 3

"I want to see everything," the editor at the big glossy magazine said. "Send me all of it, everything you got, and we'll figure out how to cut and shape it from there." I typed my Census story out as he instructed me, stream of consciousness, chronologically, starting with the forays I'd made as an embedded journalist and continuing to my last days as an enumerator. In detail, I described tramping to the skeletal cabins and rattling around the open desert. I wrote about finding proxies and fleeing pit bulls and that strange black rain of bees. For days on end I steadfastly worked on it, honing and polishing, taking breaks only periodically for excursions out to Wonder Valley to jog memory or clarify my confusion. Finally satisfied with my work, I emailed it off. The editor called a couple days later.

"There's some great stuff here, really great stuff," he said. "If you can write like this, you'll do fine in this business." I beamed at that. He was a renowned editor with two Pulitzer Prize-winning stories under his belt and many more nominations. It was an honor to be able to work with him. His praise of my writing meant more to me than anything, more even than the big fat check he'd promised. I knew before we got too far into the editing process, however, I'd need to tell him about the letter I'd received from the Census Bureau. I figured it was probably nothing—I didn't even work for them anymore—but I thought I should at least run it by him.

The letter reiterated the restrictions I was subject to as a Census Bureau employee. It reminded me I'd sworn a lifetime oath to uphold the confidentiality of PII, and that any violation of that oath carried a fine of up to $250,000 and up to five years in prison. More concerning to me, though, it said I was also prohibited from disclosing any of the details of the programs I'd worked on as a Census Bureau employee, particularly, but not limited to, the operations and the assignments I'd been given. To cap that all off, the letter said that the terms of my employment specifically forbade me from writing or publishing anything at all about the Census, under penalty of fines and jail time.

I read the letter to my editor. "Send it to me," he said.

He forwarded it to the lawyers at the big glossy magazine. Within hours he called me back.

"On the advice of our attorneys," he said, "We can no longer pursue this project." All contracts expressed or implied, he said, were hereby void. He then advised me, in the strongest possible terms, to find a good lawyer, tersely informing me that in case of prosecution he and the magazine would be obliged to testify against me.

"You swore an oath," he said, "It's the same oath members of the CIA and FBI sign." Just writing the story, I'd broken the law, he said. I'd crossed the line, overstepped the big fat black line between embedded reporter and sworn federal employee.

I deleted the story from my hard drive and purged my email, suddenly very aware of what I'd done. How did I not realize this at the time? In enumerator training they'd reiterated these restrictions over and over to us—not mentioning writing specifically, but hammering the prohibitions on information disclosure. I had known from the beginning that the Census Bureau considered everything confidential, the maps, the documents, everything, and while I always thought that overkill, nonetheless I knew the rules.

But I'd invested so much in this story, more than just time, but hope, too. I'd been counting on it, needed it more than I cared to admit. It was going to be something I could show, something to account for the time I'd spent out here: a byline in a big, glossy magazine. Instead, I was humiliated, ashamed. I didn't know how I was going to tell my wife, Ann.

I'd been cavalier, reckless. I'd charged headlong into this without considering what I was doing. This was how I lost my last job and how I squandered a nest egg in that bad real estate deal, how I ruined my wife's credit and ran up a tremendous debt. Those times, as now, I hadn't thought my actions through before I charged into them, and each time, it had cost me dearly.

The thing is, at one time, that kind of boldness had served me well. I had climbed the corporate ladder quickly through my twenties, had earned a director's title and a six-figure salary by my mid-thirties—all without a college degree. With dual incomes, Ann and I had built a great life together, had a nice home, nice cars, even a yacht. With our disposable income we bought a string of rental properties, too, amassing that nest egg.

But then, just before my fortieth birthday, I lost my job. Fired.

I don't know what happened.

Or I do, I guess. As I said, I had always been a bit cavalier. Cocky, arrogant. Believed the adage that it is easier to ask forgiveness than permission. But now, supposedly old enough to know better, the traits that had gotten me up the corporate ladder so quickly, got me unceremoniously knocked off of it.

The company that fired me was a gift-basket company, a seasonal mail order and internet concern with a mom and pop façade concealing a corporate-industrial machine within. I was director in charge of the company's several call centers. My job was to train and manage the dozens of new employees we hired weekly as basket sales ramped exponentially toward year end, culminating with more than a million baskets sold and shipped in just the two weeks before Christmas. My role was dynamic as I scrambled to head-off problems, avert mishaps and forestall the unplanned. My management methods, in the face of this, were largely seat-of-the-pants, responsive, not prescriptive. I was a firefighter, and I was good at it.

This all baffled the boss hired over me, however. An accountant by trade, he valued rubrics, standard procedures. He was a show-your-math kind of guy who came in insisting on structure, detailed processes, reports and spreadsheets, accountability. While I saw myself as a captain at the helm of a weather-battered ship, he felt my job should be as simple as connecting dots, dots pre-ordered and laid out for me through strict prior planning. This rigidity infuriated me. My boss prided himself on an almost religious adherence to his textbook MBA dogma and had a self-righteous way of speaking down to me that reminded me of my father. He shared my father's unbending sense of right and wrong, too, and his same refusal to even try to see if there was value in my way of doing things. Immediately, he triggered something in me, and my reaction to him was visceral.

My father wasn't an accountant but a military man, a high-ranking officer. Deployed abroad, he was gone frequently when I was young, but had been a loving, even doting father when around. As his eldest son, he saw budding genius in me, deemed I had a gift worth developing. He set out to shape me, challenge me, continually piquing my intellectual curiosity, stressing the importance of thinking critically, of weighing options, of avoiding seeing things as binary, right, wrong, black and white. "Use your head, son," he'd say. "Don't believe everything you read." I lapped up his attention. I craved his praises, swooned at his endorsements. Everything I did, I did for him, for his approval.

I think it was his deployments, though, that most shaped our relationship. Returning from sea, he could plainly see the acute influence school and TV and the greater world was having on me while he was gone, and this fretted him. I had developed a temper I couldn't control and a headstrong manner of challenging authority and questioning dogma.

My father had grown up poor, the only child of a domineering mother and a drunken, jailbird father, but he had bootstrapped himself out of that hole by parlaying an Academy appointment into a successful Naval career. His dysfunctional childhood had taught him to compartmentalize, a skill that served him well in the military, but also freed him from reconciling factual and ideological conflicts. The military further conditioned him not to question, to follow orders and obey the chain of command. Challenging authority, then, was more than simply disrespectful, it bordered on treason.

By contrast to his upbringing, however, I had a solidly middle-class childhood, one with freedom to think and dream. The frequent moves we made to accommodate his duty station transfers forced immersions into new environments on us kids, too. My siblings and I were perpetually the new students in school, the outsiders in the community, and often markedly different. We were the only white family in an all-black Washington DC neighborhood, for example, and the Yankees when we arrived in Mississippi. To adapt, we became chameleons. Forced by circumstance to time and again put ourselves in other's shoes, we quickly learned to pick up on cues, adopting the accents, the mannerisms, and appropriating the culture of the neighbors we found ourselves among, the styles, the music, Earth, Wind, and Fire and Parliament in Washington DC, Lynyrd Skynyrd in Mississippi. This all seemed to baffle my father.

"Why can't you just be yourself?" he'd say. But I was being myself. I was being the chameleon I'd learned to be. The strategies he saw in us weren't simple affectations as he alleged. They were more than simple artifices to cover insecurities. This was willed assimilation. My southern drawl was not a put-on as he accused, it was the way I came to speak.

As my life and experiences diverged from his, I began to feel his disappointments and disapprovals ever more deeply. "Where do you come up with these things, Billy?" he'd say in response to a thought or opinion I was testing that ran contrary to his own. "Why don't you use your head?" These criticisms pierced me. They also confused me, too. I was using my head, just as he'd taught me, weighing all sides. The problem, I came to realize, was that I was drawing conclusions that conflicted with his, that challenged his, a luxury as a Naval officer he himself didn't have.

Moving to California as a teen was the most difficult move for me, a junior in high school. The moved ripped me from a network of friends. What's more, I felt I'd moved five years into the future, such was the cultural shock. Eventually, I adapted, though, swapping my drawl for surfer's slang and immersing myself in punk rock and new wave music. My father, on the other hand, saw the stubby corduroy shorts and hot pink shirts, the music and androgynous mannerisms as a personal affront, things I willfully did to spite him. By this time, his disapprovals no longer cut me, though. They infuriated me. "Fuck you" became my attitude.

§ § §

As I turned eighteen, the Navy transferred my family to Hawaii, but having graduated from high school, I jumped ship. For a while I wandered nomadic, spent a year sailing the South Pacific on a 35-foot sailboat before returning to California. There I worked manual labor and moved couch to friend's couch. Eventually I started taking classes at night, interested in a degree in anthropology, prompted by my experiences growing up as well as my more recent travels. My new adult lifestyle exhausted me, however. The physical demands of menial jobs, the fast food, the drinking and partying, late nights after classes followed by early morning clock-ins. Run down and on a poor diet, chronic symptoms manifested: diarrhea, excessive weight loss. I began missing work, skipping classes, eventually losing my job, then failing to make rent. School I abandoned as I sunk into a deep depression that I treated with ever more alcohol. Anxiety to the point of panic kept me from sleep. I burned tanks of gas at night just driving around, going nowhere, listening to the radio and trying to quiet my own thoughts. I estranged myself from friends. I needed help. I called my mom. She sent me a ticket to fly home.

In Hawaii, nothing changed. I got a job as a waiter and partied until daybreak. I slept the day away on the couch in my parents' living room, right next to my dad's recliner and the TV. He and I rarely spoke. Finally fed up, though, he'd had enough. He sat me down in the formal living room of his home.

"Since you've been back here," he said," I've taken a long, hard look at you." He pointed to the way I was dressed: short turquoise shorts and a polo with the collar popped up. "What are you doing out all night like *that*? I don't even know what to think about you. What's your mother to think about you?" It suddenly occurred to me he had concluded I was gay. He grew silent, looking me up and down with disgust, disgraced. He took a deep breath, then, bracing himself up like the military officer he was, assumed full responsibility for the situation. He looked me squarely in the eyes. "I am a failure as a father," he declared.

I knew immediately what he meant. He thought himself a failure because he thought me a failure. He'd failed to shape me to his design. I'd gone bad, spoiled, and was now beyond saving. He had written me off. In his eyes, I was beyond redemption and he felt at fault for that.

But I wasn't a failure! I was simply young, making the mistakes of youth. I knew that even then. I was trying to find my way by trial and error. I wasn't unredeemable. I craved redemption, in fact, I craved it from him. In the face of his mounting disappointment and disgust, I longed for his approval.

But seeing him there as he stood before me, seeing him so self-assured in his judgment of me, so righteously self-effacing in his censure of himself, I knew he was right. He had failed me. He had failed me and was continuing to fail me when I'd needed him most. In that moment, I divorced myself of him. I left Hawaii vowing to prove him wrong, vowing to succeed to spite him.

I found my redemption within a month of returning to California. Ann and I married a year to the day later.

This was the long-suppressed baggage my boss at the gift basket company had inadvertently unpacked. Triggered by his judgmental stubbornness, his deprecating way of speaking to me, I felt sixteen-years-old around him, and that angered me all the more. I came to hate him. His very manner was an affront to me. I avoided him, defied him, side-stepped him, subverted him. He didn't tolerate that for very long.

Firing me, he spoke about the growing he thought I needed, how I should use this experience to become a better employee at my next job. Fuck you, I thought. I'd show him. I'd call some contacts, land another job, a better one, leapfrogging up the corporate ladder as I always had. But I couldn't. With no college degree and a bad-conduct sacking, I couldn't even get an interview. There'd be no next job.

As it happened, however, we were in the middle of a real estate boom. I bought a house, no money down, and flipped it before the first mortgage payment came due, netting myself a $250,000 profit. Fuck you, I thought of my boss. Fuck you, I thought of my father. I bought another place and flipped it again. I paid off our home. I bought my father-in-law a house and an exotic European convertible for myself. And when my parents moved from Hawaii to the desert, I never told them I'd been fired. I told them I was rich. I'd made it big in real estate.

As my parents looked for a house here, I laughed at area real estate circulars advertising Wonder Valley shithole shacks for prices approaching $100,000. Who would buy such things? I thought. I was smart, a thinker. I knew the game. I was in it to win.

I knew the real estate bubble wouldn't last; I saw what was going on. I had planned my way out, one last big deal, a deal that would leave Ann and me financially secure. I'd acquired a house on a large lot, a house I could have flipped with minimal effort for tidy profit, but I wanted to do something big. To take advantage of the property's multi-family zoning, I'd build condominiums. To do it, though, I'd need to move quickly. Against Ann's wishes, I tore down the house to expedite construction and mortgaged our home for the cash to finance the project. But then there were the city's statutory whims I hadn't fully considered, and the red tape, the design standards and review committees, the fire codes and the handicap requirements, the parking and turnarounds, drought-tolerant xeriscape and aesthetic façade articulations, the clock ticking and expenses mounting. Architects and engineers, redesigns, resubmittals, insurance and fees and mortgage payments on high-interest loans, the months and money draining away from me. I knew real estate values couldn't hold—my father didn't raise no dummy. Getting final city approval, I rushed the project to market, putting it up just as it was: a bare patch of land and green-lighted plans. And the offers came. I wouldn't make money, but I felt I'd dodged a bullet. I patted myself on the back for my quick thinking.

The buyers, a group of attorneys, left $80,000 on the table when they backed out of the deal and walked away from their deposit. They couldn't secure the financing. Nor could the next buyers. Nor the next. No one could. This was something I hadn't foreseen: The balloon didn't pop; all the air had quietly seeped out of it. Banks stopped writing these risky types of loans, curtailing new construction long before real estate prices actually tumbled. By the time the economy finally dropped in a tailspin, I was already stuck with a very costly piece of dirt.

But, to finance it, I had mortgaged our house with a revolving account, a credit card, more or less, a temporary thing, I'd thought. After the crash, though, I could barely afford the minimum payments, and couldn't refinance it into a more stable loan. I had to carry the mortgages for the other real estate I had, too—or rather Ann did, I didn't have a job. The house of cards fell. Ultimately, I lost more than a million dollars, two lifes' savings. And I had squandered all the equity in our home—we were on the verge of losing it, our home of twenty years.

As a concession to Ann after losing my job, I had returned to college, taking a couple days a week to attend classes. I was retooling, I told her, thinking ahead. I'd get a degree in something practical, something that would lead to a decent job when the real estate thing played out. But making all that money in the real estate boom, I figured I'd never need to work again. So, when a professor praised my writing, stroked my ego, suggested I had talent, I switched my major to Literary Journalism. Literary Journalism isn't journalism, per se, but writing about real people and events—which sounded great to me. There were no jobs in this field, of course, but I didn't care, I was never going to need one.

I was a junior in college when the attorneys backed out of the deal for lack of financing. The economy and my financial world all came crashing down just before I graduated. While my classmates, kids in their early twenties, advanced to internships in corporate communications and the like, I slipped into idleness. Retreated into my shell. Ann slaved to keep our financial lives afloat while struggling to keep me buoyed as well. But I was scuttled. I couldn't bear to even look at her, couldn't bear to see friends or family. I needed out. That's when I called my parents and offered to dog sit. They thought I was retired. I never told them I was destitute.

§ § §

When I was little, I wanted to be Jacques Cousteau—the French oceanographer-explorer-cum-TV star. I wanted to study marine biology, travel all over the world, visit exotic locales, swim with dolphins and sharks and tell the world about them, how precious they are, how all these living things and places and people have value in our over-populated, globally-warming world and should be protected, saved.

My dad dissuaded me. "There is only one Jacques Cousteau," he said, "Be realistic, son, that job's been taken. No one will ever pay you to do that." And no one yet has. But that hadn't stopped me from wanting it. Before I met Ann, I'd wandered the world as an amateur explorer. I've crossed the Equator by plane, by boat, by bus, on foot. I've battled 40-foot seas on that 35-foot sailboat, been chased by a wild orangutan in a Sumatran jungle, stared into the black pupil of a communist Kalashnikov in the rainforest of Guatemala. I once saw a moonbow in the middle of the Pacific, a rare rainbow cast by the moonlight, arcs of purple and indigo and violet. I was in the doldrums just south of the Equator, three weeks' sail from Hawaii. The sea there was black and calm, crude oil. Lightening-lit squalls passed around me under the fullest moon imaginable. I was alone except for the dolphins. For three or so nights prior, dolphins came up to the boat deep in the night, so close I could reach overboard and touch them. That night, their oily backs rising from the water reflected the moonlight and the moonbow. I knew I was seeing something few people would ever see.

I was alone on deck that night, but not on the boat. I was there with a man, a man in his forties, the man who owned the boat. He had invited me to sail with him to Tahiti and then we were going to continue around the world. I was twenty at the time, looked younger, just the kind of boy that man liked. I hadn't realized that until we were far out to sea. I probably should have. If I hadn't been just twenty, I certainly would have. I spent weeks alone terrified of that man. He never touched me—he wasn't that kind of guy, he said—though he assured me he could have, any time he wanted, and there'd be nothing I could do about it. Nobody would know. I'd just fall overboard, he said, be lost at sea, never to be seen again. I never told anyone about this.

In Tahiti I awoke on the boat one morning with one of that man's new-found friends masturbating, his hand down my pants. I fled the boat to a park on shore where I met a local high school teacher who saw my trauma. He took me back to his place where, after feeding me, he pressed me for a blow job. Alone, terrified, and suddenly homeless on an isolated island, I called my mother in Hawaii. As she would again a few short years later, she sent me money and an airline ticket home.

§§§

The catalytic converter on my exotic European convertible failed as I was bringing it up to my parents' house. The back pressure blew out a cylinder wall, the car careened to the side of the road like a downed Japanese Zeke. We had no money to fix it. I drove the four-wheel-drive truck I'd borrowed from my father-in-law for the Census after that.

"Just come home and get a job," Ann said to me when I finally told her the Census story had been killed.

"I can't," I said. "I'm dog sitting," That was no excuse and she knew it. She knew my parents had a regular dog sitter who could take over at any time. She worried for me, though, worried about my mental state. And I missed her, missed our life together, but I knew there was no going back to that. I had fucked it up. I'd pissed away all our years of hard work and planning in one cavalier transaction. I wanted to stay in the desert because out here I didn't have to see the toll my repeated fuck-ups were taking on Ann, the physical symptoms she suffered, the rashes on her body, the hair loss, as she struggled to pay bills, her earnings going straight to creditors to pay off my repeated messes. Out here, no one knew me as Ann's deadbeat husband, the unshaven slob who drove his wife into debt, who sat unemployed in front of the tube all day, not even trying to find a job.

But I had tried to find a job. I'd been away from the workforce for too long, though, certainly too long to be considered for a job at the level I'd had—even with a college degree. Too much had changed. I read want ads now and found I didn't know the jargon, couldn't understand the requirements—I didn't even understand the specifications for the job I'd been fired from, though I'd literally created that position for myself years before. Everything now was so specialized, requiring specific knowledge and skills, the ads in language designed to exclude outsiders. I simply couldn't talk the talk. I'd tried to break the code in the ads and concluded they were channeling for youth, women, anyone but a middle-age white man like me. No one wanted someone of my age and demographics anymore.

Besides, I didn't want a job. I wanted to be Jacques Cousteau. I wanted to swim with the dolphins, travel the world, live without the banality of regular, mundane life. I just wanted to stay in Wonder Valley, to explore this bizarro desert Galapagos further. I wanted to make it my Galapagos, to be its Charles Darwin. I felt I'd spent all my life preparing for something; all my years of travel, that degree in Literary Journalism, were all for something, but I never knew what it was. Maybe this was it. Maybe this was what I'd shifted gears for, what I'd retooled for, gone to college and studied Anthropology for. Maybe I'd just had a false start with the Census story, maybe that was all. I could still call Tim, the editor for the homeless magazine. He wanted more Wonder Valley stories. I could find more. I could stay out here, and I could write.

Chapter 4

It was three o'clock in the afternoon when I joined others sitting in cars or milling about in the cracked, sand-covered asphalt parking lot of The Palms bar waiting for it to open.

"She's late," a man said to me from the cockpit of an old van. He blew out a lungful of smoke, then dropped a smoldering butt to the ground. I gave him a puzzled look. "Tonya," he said. "She's late."

The man, George, drew a fresh cigarette from a pack on his dash. His van reeked of gasoline, which he sold, he said, from jerry cans in the back. That those jerry cans leaked was made obvious by the fumes as well as the steady drip coming from within the vehicle.

"Should you be smoking in there?" I asked him.

"Oh, I sell cigarettes, too," he said, holding up a carton of Marlboro, oblivious to the obvious danger. "I buy them on the Marine base." He laughed a nasally laugh, then sparked his lighter and lit the cigarette. I backed slowly away.

At that moment, a truck towing a beat-up brown Isuzu glided into the parking lot behind me. The towed Isuzu coasted around its tow truck on momentum as the two vehicles glided side-by-side into parallel spots in front of the bar. It appeared practiced. The driver of the Isuzu checked her make-up in the rear-view then threw open her door and stepped a high heel onto the cracked pavement. She traded a couple of quips with some guys out front, then walked around back and unlocked the bar's heavy wooden front door from the inside.

If I'd come to Wonder Valley to study the wildlife, The Palms was its Serengeti plains. It was the community's watering hole, its sole

49

business outside of the salt mine, and was the reputed gathering spot for the artists and retirees, the misfits and miscreants. I was here to go to work. When the door opened, I filed in behind everyone else.

It was bright inside the bar at that hour. Daylight through dingy windows illuminated an old booth in the corner, slapdash paintings on the walls, an antique rifle hanging in the hall. Sand crunched under foot against the bare concrete floor. Those quicker than me grabbed the free-moving barstools at the bar. I landed in one that was bolted to the ground

Behind the bar, shelves—waterbed headboards, actually, propped one against another and shimmed more or less level—held a clutter of half-filled liquor bottles, Slim Jims and lighters. Used t-shirts and caps filled a rack against the wall. A bookcase sold paperbacks for a dollar. DVDs and video cassettes. Motor oil. The balls got stuck in the pool table. The jukebox didn't work. The CD in the CD player skipped. Above me, the blind eye of a dusty Super 8 film camera stared down at the till, an old-fashioned cash register left in the open position.

"What can I get you?" Tonya, the bartender, asked, wiping the bar down in front of me, the bar still sticky from the night before. "A beer?" she asked, "Or I can make you a cocktail, as long as it ain't anything fancy. I can make you something, you know, like Jack and Coke, except, right now we're out of Jack."

I pointed to the draft beer. Tonya shook her head. The keg beer, she said, was for the weekenders and passers-through who stopped by in the cooler weather. By summer, it seemed, the keg was flat and the beer warm. I squished my face in a puzzled look. "You want a Natural Ice?"

I had already heard other customers calling for it, asking for Nattie Ice or Naughty Ice or just plain Ice, or more likely, Tonya just knew to put one in front of them. "Nattie Ice has a full percent more alcohol than the draft beer," a guy sitting down the bar offered.

"I'll have one of them, then, I guess." It cost me a buck.

Behind me, a guy with slicked-back hair and a white Fu Manchu entered the bar and slipped into the booth in the corner. His name was Bill. Bill was followed in by a thick-built man with red hair and a perpetual sunburn. The name patch of his mechanic's shirt labeled him 'Bill,' too, though that wasn't his name. Everyone called him Red.

I met Mark Bennett and Denise and a guy called Desert Dave. Clyde Eddie came in and ordered a vodka cranberry, though the drink he received appeared to lack any measurable amount of cranberry juice. Clyde Eddie was called Clyde Eddie to differentiate him from Scruffy Eddie who sat a couple stools down from him next to a lanky cowboy called Slim. Dingy and Fluffy were a couple who grabbed beers from the bar and disappeared with them out back following a guy named Roofer Richard. Biker Richard, on the other hand, brooded over a beer not far from Pizza Richard, so called, I deduced, because he worked in a pizza parlor.

George, the old man from the van outside, shambled in from the parking lot after everyone had settled, and eased himself onto a barstool. He humphed and grunted, his tired, wet gray eyes peering down at the loose change he dumped on the bar and began to slowly stack, a hat slouched on his head, his gray brillo of beard resting on his chest. Tonya set an Old Milwaukee in front of him and slid one of his piles of coins into an open palm. She dumped the change into the drawer of the cash register before turning back to the others at the bar. She talked inhumanly fast, teasing and taunting and joking with everyone. Invariably, however, someone had challenged her to a game of pool or she was outside smoking a cigarette when anyone wanted another beer. They had to wave at her or get someone to elbow her until she noticed them, then she'd race over, snatch up their empty after bringing the refill, crushing the can flat as a hockey puck with her hands.

As I sat there watching her, a man with a strawberry beard wandered over to me.

"Hi, I'm Curtis," he announced. "I'm the Wonder Valley drunk!" He flung his arms wide open as he said this, inviting me to give him a once over, a quick up and down, and see for myself that what he said was true. He fixed me squarely with one blue eye; the other wandered skew-whiff off into space. He then bent forward to let me feel the soft spot in his skull and trace the scar ear-to-ear across his head while he told me how a boat on a lake sent his nose through his brain and crushed his forehead flat. "I'm a dead man walking!" he proclaimed, once again throwing his arms wide for me to take him all in.

Tonya came over and Curtis called for a Nattie Ice.

"How you going to pay for that, Curtis," she asked him, hands on hips.

"I'll pay you back when I get my money," he said, throwing his arms wide for her. "On the first of the month." Tonya shook her head, rolling her eyes at me. Curtis stood motionless and for a moment I thought he was going to cry, but then he looked over at me then leaned in and said, "Hey boss, can I borrow a twenty?"

I slid Tonya a dollar for his beer. Satisfied, he moseyed away.

Not long after that, George ambled over.

"Do I know you?" he asked.

I reminded him we'd only just met in the parking lot.

"Oh," he said, "I thought maybe I knew you." He lifted himself up onto a stool. "I was a substitute teacher in town, a lot of people know me," he said. He leaned over to me. "My ex-wife was married nine times," he said. "I was her third. Her first B." He laughed a nasally laugh as though he'd made a joke. "We had lunch together one time on base. She ate a tuna fish sandwich and got pregnant!" He laughed again. "I told Mary that in front of Laura and Laura stopped eating tuna fish!" More nasally laughter. "Mary was so mad at me!" I didn't know who or what the hell he was talking about. It was like he was delivering a comedy routine pared down to the punchlines, a routine he recited by rote, going on about how his grandfather had built a clipper ship in Nova Scotia that sank on its maiden voyage, about his MBA in finance, his master's in taxation, his law degree from a university in Ohio. "But I could never pass a bar. Get it?" he said. Again, he erupted in nasally laughter. Tonya came over and offered to shoo George away, but he paid her no mind.

"I asked Tonya to marry me once," he said. "But only for a year, just long enough for her to fix up my place." He laughed again. Tonya rolled her eyes.

"It'd take more than a year to clean *that* sumbitch up," she said.

George told me he lived on Virginia, a road he made a joke about, referring to a Virginia I didn't know, a woman I suspected was long dead. He told me about the bitch he lived with—that's how he said it—and he laughed his laugh again. The "bitch" was a female dog that adopted him soon after he moved to Wonder Valley and had a litter of puppies under a decrepit travel trailer in his yard. Those pups grew and bred into a pack of some thirty feral pitbulls that George fed, he said, but couldn't get close to.

He continued like this for twenty breathless minutes, delivering his abridged shtick between nasally guffaws until he slipped off his stool and went out front to smoke. I grabbed my beer and escaped out back before he returned for an encore.

A big patio with a fire pit spread out from The Palms' back door. Next to the patio, a hose dribbled well water into an old iron ore cart that dripped a beard of green slime into a rusty bathtub made into a pond. Desert Dave and Slim sat on rusty bar stools under a big mesquite tree smoking cigarettes. Others occupied benches up against the bar's back wall. Dingy and Fluffy sat together in what looked like old church pews out in the dirt. The pews faced the stage, a platform of battered, splintering plywood topped by the inverted steel skeleton of a skateboard halfpipe. Behind the stage was an old silver-sided motor coach, the aluminum bus, I was soon told, that Mary, the bar's owner, and her kids lived in when they first bought the place.

A hard-looking man in a cowboy hat sat at a rickety picnic table under camouflage netting draped from a date palm tree. He gave me the once over.

"Pull up a seat," he said after a moment. "I'm Roger." He jutted a hand at me. Like George and Jack McConaha, Roger first came to the area as a Marine. After a tour in Vietnam, he spent his career as part of an anti-terrorism team, a quick response unit sent to protect American diplomatic installations around the world. He returned to Wonder Valley to retire. Still, nearing seventy, he was top-to-bottom a grunt, from the tattoos on his tightly wound biceps to his ruddy, deeply lined face and his dark eyes that drilled into you as he spoke. Despite his intimidating appearance, though, he was quick with a story or a joke.

"Just passing through?" he asked me.

"I'm a writer," I told him. It was the first time I'd ever told anyone that. "I'm thinking of writing about Wonder Valley."

"Well, there's plenty to write about around here." He told me his wife Darlene had been a Palms bartender until she died. After that he married Darlene's sister, Diana. Diana often bartended at The Palms on Sundays and for events.

"The bar opens at nine on Sunday mornings," he said, "and with everyone drinking all day, the place is a shit show by the evening. That's why I like to be here when she's working. I've broken up a lot of fights." He smiled. It occurred to me that breaking up fights was probably something he enjoyed.

"One time," he said, "this Mexican sonofabitch was smacking his girlfriend around in front of everyone and I couldn't stand for that. So I hit him. Hit him so hard it sent his glass eye skidding across the floor!" The guy left, Roger said, but returned with family and guns. They pistol whipped Roger, then shot up the bar. Roger laughed a rasping smoker's laugh as he crushed out his cigarette. "The sonofabitch went to jail for that and from there he got deported."

We talked more about Wonder Valley and his time in the

Marines, taking turns returning to the bar for beers. As we spoke, the bands of clouds grew magenta across the sky, the Sheephole mountains glowed golden. The sun set and we were now on the patio alone.

"Whelp," Roger said, standing up and dusting off his Wranglers. "I'd better get home, too." We shook hands and he left me there by myself. I sat for a minute watching the colors change in the sunset, then went back inside the bar.

Most of the others had drifted away by then, too. Pizza Richard was long gone, as was Biker Richard and Roofer Richard. Both Eddies were gone too, as well as Red and Desert Dave and Slim. Only George remained, humphing and grunting to himself from behind a pyramid wall of empty beer cans. He was waiting for his dinner. Taking a seat near him I asked him about the food.

"You like diarrhea?" he replied, laughing his nasally laugh. Still, he said, he ate at The Palms every night—every night but Tuesdays, the bar was closed on Tuesdays.

"You have to tell Tonya what you want so she can call Laura next door to come and cook." Laura was Mary's daughter. A short while later, she shuffled around the corner from the kitchen with George's food A woman in her thirties, she had the self-conscious posture of a child, with greenish eyes and tow-colored hair and thick, full lips that hung open seemingly of their own weight, giving her a slightly bewildered appearance. She slid George's food in front of him without looking at him, then turned to leave. She headed straight out the back door and into her car, driving away. I never got the food I ordered. I contented myself with beer.

After the sun set, it was dark inside The Palms, but it was a warm, cozy kind of dark. Strings of Christmas lights lit the bar itself, and there was a light over the pool table and a lamp swagged over the corner booth and the regular with the white Fu Manchu. Tonya walked over and clicked it on for him.

"George makes him sit in the dark," she quipped. George, it

turned out, was the bartender on Sunday and Monday nights, Tonya's nights off. I thought about the stories Roger had told me about the bar fights and stuff on Sundays and I couldn't imagine George in that kind of situation.

Behind us, the door creaked open and Jill Davis slipped in, landing in a stool a few down from me. Seeing her, George struggled up and started her way, but Jill stuck her hand out to halt him. He turned around and returned to his seat humphing and grunting, not saying a word.

"I have all his stories memorized," she said. "The ex-wife, the tuna fish sandwich, all of them."

I'd met Jill when I was writing about Ricka McGuire. She had the place next door to where Ricka died and had shown me a human femur she had found in the wash at the end of the valley. When the cops refused to come, she took the bone to the sheriff's station in town and left it on the counter after failing to convince them of what it was she held. A search and rescue ensued a day later, the cops interrogating Jill, threatening her with arrest.

Like me, Jill was new to Wonder Valley. She had bought that cabin over by where Ricka died as a getaway for herself and her husband. After an unexpected divorce, though, she found herself living in her second home primarily. She and Tonya had become friends.

"I prefer to come to the bar after everyone's gone," she said, speaking loud enough for George to hear her. "If only I could get George to leave me alone." She took a sip of tequila from a shot glass, pushing her short-cropped hair out of her dark brown eyes. She was about my age, I figured: late forties. I liked her.

Another woman, Kassandra, arrived a few minutes later and sat next to Jill. She held herself upright on her stool with her legs crossed, her arms folded in support of her buxom chest. Tonya poured her a glass of white wine.

"I worked here for a while when Mary first bought the place," she said after introducing herself. "I tried to teach her what I knew about running the bar." Kassandra said her mother had owned The Palms thirty years ago. She had worked in the bar even before she was of legal age.

"It was just a little shack when my mother bought it," she said, "She added the back room and built the kitchen while she owned it." The Palms had been one of four bars in Wonder Valley back then. There was Barnett's out by the dead man's bend. The regular with the white Fu Manchu had owned that bar, ran it for nearly twenty years. He sold it to some guys who were having trouble keeping up on the payments when it suddenly, inexplicably burned down. Then there was The Mouse Trap over by the airport. A man called Mouse owned that one, though Diana, Roger's current wife, ran it when Roger was married to her sister Darlene. It was now just used for storage. And finally, there was The Way Out. It was still there, in fact, I'd seen it, way out on the highway. It still had the beer signs in the windows, the booths inside, the pool table. The gas station pump islands still sat in the parking lot. But The Way Out went out when the valley did, it seems, when the homesteaders died off and the gold miners gave up and the artists and retirees had not yet returned.

"The Palms went out, too," Kassandra said, "My mother got tired of it and lost interest in running it. She kept shortening the hours until no one came anymore. Then she sold it." The men she sold the bar to subsequently ran the business out of business, and for a time Wonder Valley had no bar, no businesses at all, in fact—even the salt mine had bankrupted—until Mary bought The Palms and reopened it.

Kassandra turned back to Tonya and Jill. George drank beers by himself, humphing and grunting and stacking his empties onto the pyramid. I sat with my own beer, now a little unsteady on my stool. I'd been drinking since three. It was ten when Tonya came around from the back of the bar and clicked off the beer signs and the light over the pool table. The regular with the white Fu Manchu drained his beer and quietly left. I finished my own as Tonya poured herself a drink and counted out the till—twenty percent of the take was hers, plus tips—then she stashed the rest in the secret spot for Mary to collect in the morning. I dropped a few dollars on the bar, setting my empty on top of it. I nodded my goodbyes and headed out. Tonya locked the heavy wooden door behind me and George as we left, slipping the wooden bar through the metal rings barring it closed. George climbed into his van and it gasped to life. I got into my truck and started it, too. It was dark, not another car for the twenty or so miles I could see. I slid the shifter into reverse and cranked the wheel, my headlights opening a path through the desert darkness which I followed to my parents' house in town.

Chapter 5

It was Nutty Ned who first told me about Tom Whitefeather. I'd been visiting Ned frequently since writing the Ricka McGuire story, once a week or so, checking in, hoping for gossip. He knew I wanted to write more about Wonder Valley, and on one visit, he offered Whitefeather up as a suggestion.

"I told him about you, man." he said. "He wants to meet you. He used to live at the Cat Ranch, but then he went to jail. You should go talk to him. If you want a story, you should go talk to Whitefeather."

Whitefeather was a desert rat, a fit man in his fifties with thick black hair, close-cropped under a battered Marine Corps boonie hat. He scraped his living from the desert, collecting cans and working odd jobs to get by. When I met him, he was squatting in a rock-walled cabin encrusted to a flank of Valley Mountain, the rocky crag that scars deeply into Wonder Valley. He had been friends with the owner of the place, had been there drinking with him when the man shot himself. Whitefeather simply moved in. The half-drunk jug of wine the two men had been sharing at the time of the suicide still collected dust on the floor beneath the rocking chairs where Whitefeather and I sat in as we talked.

"Ned says you're a reporter," he said, focusing in on why he wanted to meet me. "Maybe you can help me." He opened a battered briefcase and withdrew a sheaf of soiled papers. "I've been charged with a felony. I could go to prison, but my public defender won't listen to me about my case. He's not putting any time into it. He doesn't care." He held up the tattered pages in his lap. "This is all evidence that proves my innocence," he said, "There's receipts and affidavits and all kinds of stuff, but he doesn't even want to see it."

"I'm confused," I said. "I don't know how I can help with that."

"Well, maybe if a reporter was hanging around and all, my attorney would think the case was a big deal and spend more time on it." He pulled his boonie hat from his head. "Those cops that arrested me didn't know what they were doing," he said, arguing his case before me. "They were at the Cat Ranch when I got there, but they were lost. They had a warrant for someone I'd never heard of at a cabin nowhere near there! They were way off!"

"And they arrested you by mistake?"

"Not exactly." He drew some crumpled pages from the sheaf of paperwork and handed them to me. His arrest report. He'd been charged in violation of Section 597, paragraph B of the penal code of the State of California.

"What is that?"

"Too much pussy!" he quipped and winked. Then he pointed to the text of the charge: Felony cruelty to animals. The arrest documents alleged he failed to provide his dozens upon dozens of cats with proper food and drink and shelter from the weather. "Too much pussy, get it? But what they're saying isn't true! I was good to my kitties, ask anybody!"

On the morning of his arrest, he explained, he had gone to the Cat Ranch, as he called it, to bring his cats food and water. He was already living at the rock cabin by then but his cats remained at the Cat Ranch, the homestead parcel he lived at before his friend died. When he arrived there that morning, he found two patrol cars out front and two deputies inside. Immediately, the deputies confronted him.

"Are these your cats?" a deputy with a raptor head and deep-set hawk eyes demanded. "How many?"

Whitefeather told them eighty, though he admitted to me he wasn't quite sure of the actual number. To the deputies he stammered excuses about how he had tried to keep the place up.

"This place looks like the county dump!" the deputy railed in response. "You can't tell me this place is maintained!"

"Sure," Whitefeather said, recanting the story to me, "the place had gotten away from me a little, what with having to cook for the kitties every day and haul the food and water all the way from here. But I did my best. I cooked for them every day, ten pounds of chicken with two pounds of dried beans. I'd add potatoes and rice and sometimes canned vegetables to that and boiled it all together for eight hours. Every day!" He then pedaled over Valley Mountain's jagged crags to the Cat Ranch dragging a red wagon filled with food behind him. "And I'd return again with ten gallons of water! Every day! I did this every day!"

According to the arrest report, the deputies had been at the Cat Ranch for forty-five minutes before Whitefeather arrived. They documented the conditions: an overwhelming stench of cat urine and feces. The smell of decomposition. No food, no water for the cats. They photographed them amid filthy squalor and even video-recorded a dead kitten lying on the kitchen floor, another cat eating it. They noted the bones of dead cats strewn about the place, gnawed-on and half-eaten, paws and fur still attached. And then there was the whole cat, rotten to a pool of putrescence curled up in the fridge—you could still see its little ears and eyes and nose, the report said. I read it with disgust.

"It's all lies!" Whitefeather cried. He sprang up, spilling papers to the floor. "But my kitties were healthy—not like they say! All the work I did around here was just for them! When I worked I asked people to pay me in cat food rather than cash! It was not at all like they said!"

After his arrest, the report continued, a county animal control officer trapped fifty-three cats at the Cat Ranch. They took the cats to county shelters and they destroyed them.

"Because of this, I spent five days in jail," Whitefeather said, "and the charges are still hanging over me. I have to be in court, constantly, but I have no car!" To get to court, he said, he had to wake up at two in the morning and head out from the rock cabin on his bike. He followed a path of his own tracks over hardpan scrub and sand patches, across abandoned homestead parcels and in and out of washes until he finally reached the paved road. Then, turning his back to the rising sun, he'd pedal the last dozen miles to the bus stop in town. Already, he'd made the trek a dozen times, he said, first for the arraignment, then each of the fact-finding hearings, then the readiness hearings and postponement after postponement after postponement.

"On court days, it's imperative I get to the bus stop early," he said. "So, I get there early and wait, maybe scrounge some butts and roll a smoke. If I miss the bus, I'll miss my court appearance, and if I do that, I could get another felony and more time in jail."

§ § §

The following day, I went with Whitefeather to the Cat Ranch. Driving up, the place looked like a fortress that had succumbed to siege. Bunkers of cat shit and sand, three feet high and ten feet in diameter, rose up next to the bomb crater pits the sand had originally been quarried from. A palisade of up-ended plywood, sun-burnt and sand-blasted, reared up beyond them, the fortifications Whitefeather had created to keep marauding coyotes at bay.

Inside a worn gate, the acrid reek of cat piss hit me like a cold-cock. Nothing I read in the police report could have prepared me for it. It invaded my nose, soiled my tongue, pricked at my eyes. Its stench washed through my hair. For the rest of the day I wore it in my clothes. I fought not to wretch. As we entered the cabin, the remaining cats scurried into hiding. Litter and trash and gnawed-on bones covered the floor. Dry, dust-colored twists of cat shit hung weightless from the edge of plant pots, filled the basin of the sink, the rumpled covers of the bed. A litterbox overflowed, more shit than sand. Dusty bags bulged with garbage. I couldn't believe the condition of the place.

"I lived here for three and a half years, and the place wasn't like this then, ask anybody." Whitefeather pulled his hat from his head and wrung it in his hands. "I love my kitties. All of them had names—well, except for the last few litters, but there were just too many, it had all just gotten away from me." He showed me the raked-up heaps of shit ready to be hauled out and dumped outside, except his wheelbarrow had a flat. "I've patched it over and over," he said. He showed me the bones the cops saw strewn about the property. "See? Goat bones. Bones from the goat I slaughtered to feed the kitties. Not cat bones!" He told me about the little kitten the cops found dead. "I'd seen that kitten the night before when I came to bring them their water. It ate well, but later it seemed sick, like it was on its way out. I picked it up, and it felt limp. I put it with its mama and was going to come back the next day with a box to carry it home to nurse back to health. And that was what I was doing when I showed up and the deputies were here. I was taking care of it. Everybody knows that."

§ § §

Later, at The Palms, Whitefeather took a sip from his beer. "Wonder Valley is a good place to hide out," he mused. "It's a good place to fly under the radar. I'm not here because I want to be." He lowered his head, then raised it and looked over at me. "If you had the kind of past I've had, you'd understand." He took another sip of beer and fell silent again. I leaned in close to him, waiting. "Marine Corps," he whispered, staring off into space. "Sniper, black ops." He turned to me again. "In 'Nam—De Nang, originally, doing wet jobs deep up-country, then elsewhere around the world. I can't tell you everywhere they sent me in those eight years but suffice it to say that the jungles of South America are as dank and nasty as anything in South East Asia." He stared down at his beer. "You can't just leave that life behind, you know, you can't just walk away—they won't let you. That's why I'm here."

It seemed everybody in Wonder Valley knew not to talk to Whitefeather about his time in the Corps. They just quietly nodded a knowing nod for his sacrifices, bought him beer at The Palms, gave him cigarettes. They slipped him a couple of bucks for his kitties to make sure he got by.

I too began helping him out. I started taking him to his court appearances, and on the way home, through a drive-through for a burger. I began taking him to the grocery store in town, too. There, he never asked for anything for himself, just gallons and gallons of milk for his cats, though I often bought him ground beef or a steak or eggs so he'd have something other than the Top Ramen he typically lived on. I usually left a few beers with him as well.

For his part, he introduced me around Wonder Valley. He seemed to know everybody. "He's a reporter, he's helping me with my case," he'd say as he related his legal woes to listeners, asking for moral support and accepting condolences over his lost kitties in the form of beer and cigarettes. He accepted these offers gratefully and sincerely and promised work in return, but his pledges were always waved off. As I got to know him, we became friends.

Whitefeather's real name was Thomas Ritchie. Whitefeather was his Indian name, he told me, the one his mother gave him as a child. He didn't remember much about her, though. In fact, he said he didn't remember much about his childhood at all. It was just a flash of images, a slideshow with no chronology, no narration, out-of-order snapshots of a little boy in San Diego. He remembered getting hauled into the police station with his brothers, his earliest childhood memory. Police picked them up while eating out of trash cans in a back alley. His two older brothers, aged four and five, fended off the stray dogs with sticks so their little brother could eat. Tom was two. I confirmed all this with his brothers, who I located through the internet. Tom hadn't seen or spoken to them in thirty years. They figured he was dead.

They told me they were all taken from their drunken, drug-addled mother after that, and again at various other times and returned to her again and again until ultimately authorities removed them to an orphanage. Tom got a toy tool set for Christmas that year, wooden hammer and screwdrivers, the first thing he'd ever had that was truly his own.

Time and again, Tom's brothers escaped the orphanage, leaving little Tom alone until they were apprehended and returned to the home. Finally, authorities shipped the boys off to live with relatives in corn-country Iowa.

Tom had a fondness for cats even back then. In fact, his brothers told me he seemed closer to animals than he ever was to people. While his brothers teased, tormented, and tortured the farm cats, Tom fought to protect them.

In Iowa, the boys grew up and attended high school, hot-rodded the corn tunnel roads, pilfered liquor to swill under the cover of darkness. In the late sixties, Tom's brothers shipped off to Vietnam: one became a sniper in the Marines, the other went into the Navy. Tom, still in high school, knocked around the Iowa town until a family with a cute daughter knocked on his door. When they knocked, the missionaries and their daughter, Tom let them in. They prayed. When they asked to come back, Tom looked at the cute daughter and said sure. Together they read the Bible, and, for Tom, the world finally began to make sense. Soon he found himself a member of the Jehovah's Witnesses, living in their dorms in Brooklyn. He evaded military service as a conscientious objector. The Vietnam sniper thing was just a cover story, it turned out, a facade he borrowed from his brother's life and used to justify his presence in Wonder Valley, an armor he used for protection as much as a ruse to earn a living. I wondered what else he was bullshitting me about. I dug up a couple of his ex-wives and called them, too.

In the years after he left Brooklyn, he had married and divorced and married and divorced. He lunked around the country, held good jobs at times through the nineties, banging nails when construction was booming, worked as an exterminator, sometimes living in a proper apartment, bringing home a proper paycheck. He was forty-two when he got the first of a string of DUIs, lost his driver's license. He was in the desert by then, Palm Springs, at the beginning of a slow spiral—a third marriage in a drugged-out and drunken fog, a second and third DUI that finally got him convicted and sentenced to a bullet: one year behind bars.

His third wife left him while he was in jail. That was his last real home. Paroled, he moved into an old broken-down camper, towed it up to Wonder Valley, dragged it around until some kids gave him a couple kittens and he ended up at that rickety shack people began to call the Cat Ranch. By then, Thomas Ritchie was Whitefeather.

§ § §

One morning, a couple weeks later, Whitefeather and I, driving by the Cat Ranch, saw a car there, a new, red rental car. Upon inspection, we found a man in the back of it, asleep, hugging himself against the morning chill. Recognizing the man, Tom knocked on the window. Inside, Jan, the owner of the Cat Ranch, woke with a start. He sat up and looked out at us in a jet-lagged daze. He had arrived after dark from Germany, where he lived. He had not yet seen the condition of his property, not seen the placard tacked to the gate warning against admittance under penalty of a misdemeanor, calling the Cat Ranch "Unsafe for Human Habitation." He had received the notices of violation from the county, though, the requirements for the abatement of the cat urine and feces and the list of infractions tacked onto it, including structural defects and building code non-conformities in the decades-old homestead cabin such as wrong-size windows and too small rooms, as well as the bills for the fines incurred for non-compliance. Waking and looking around that morning, he quickly turned testy.

"I let you stay here!" he snapped at Tom. "I gave you money!" He spun in circles, growing increasingly appalled as he struggled to avoid the waist-high mounds of cat shit, his arms held as if to avoid touching anything. He wore shorts and sandals, the sun already pinking his balding head, reddening his nose.

An artist, Jan had bought the Cat Ranch years before as a place to produce his art. To him Wonder Valley was both an up-and-coming artist Mecca and a place between worlds. "It's crazy," he said to me later. "You drive out from Los Angeles, past the last of civilization, the trappings of American excess so glaring, and into a land of tumbleweeds and people from another century living with no water or electricity. Only in America!"

Jan thought of the Cat Ranch as an *objet trouvé*, a random and uninspired work of art. In fact, he saw all of Wonder Valley as an artifact, an *assemblage* of detritus that so perfectly embodied what he saw as the waning of the Yankee empire. Whitefeather was living at the Cat Ranch when Jan bought it, and he liked the idea that what he thought of as a "feral person" would occupy the space. He allowed Whitefeather to continue to stay in his broken-down motor home parked out front, to look after the place or whatever, to be part of the art. Whitefeather had only the two kittens back then, the one male and one female. Jan went home to Germany after that, and never, until now, returned. Finding his artwork now destroyed, though, he was furious.

"You were supposed to clean this place up," he ranted. "You were supposed to get rid of this trash! I paid you!"

"You only gave me $800 dollars!" Whitefeather retorted, incredulous. His clenched jaw jutted out from the shade of his boonie hat. "Only $800 in three years!"

"I gave you $1,000 dollars!" Jan snapped, backing up, nearly tripping into a pile of dusty turds.

"It was only $800, remember? You took $200 back because you were going to LA and needed the cash..."

"Yeah, well, I gave you $800! I paid you! I paid you and you did nothing! You were supposed to take care of the place, you call this taking care of the place?"

"I...I moved that pile of trash there," Whitefeather said pointing to a heap of rubble, trying to draw me into the argument. "That stuff used to be *inside* the cabin! You should have seen this place before! What did he expect for only $800 in three years?"

"I paid you $800! *I* paid *you!* Most people have to pay rent to stay in a house! Look at this place!" Again, Jan spun in circles, his mouth agape, stammering, speechless. A dust-colored cat slunk haltingly past.

After his arrest, the court mandated that Whitefeather have no contact with animals as a condition of his release. But Animal Control had only picked up fifty-three cats from the Cat Ranch, leaving the rest.

"What was I supposed to do, let them starve?" He kept feeding the remaining cats, pedaling to the Cat Ranch from the rock cabin under cover of darkness, a bag of cat food strapped to the front basket of his bike. When Jan showed up at the property dozens of cats remained. Seeing them, he grew crimson with frustration.

"You have to get the rest of these cats out of here or I'll call animal control," he said with resolve.

"You do that and I'll sue you!" Whitefeather screamed. He clomped after Jan who had tramped away over the trash and rubbish, a matted tomcat hissing down at him from the cabin's corrugated metal roof. He wheeled around.

"You have three days to get these cats out of here."

"I need a week."

"Ok," Jan sighed, "you have a week." He then slipped into the cabin leaving me and Whitefeather where we stood.

§ § §

"Hindsight is 20/20," Tom said to me later, at the bar. "I shouldn't have taken that female kitten, for one thing, if I'd known how this would all turn out. That was my mistake—I'd never had a male and female before." Still, he wouldn't have tried to get them neutered. "I don't believe in that," he said. "It's against the will of God. These kitties are God's creatures, not mine." That's also why he never gave any away. "I just couldn't trust anyone to take care of them, not the way I can. What with the coyotes—and you know the way people are out here."

At his trial a few weeks later, however, Whitefeather told the court he simply couldn't afford the spaying and neutering costs: $125 each. He told the court how he'd tried to get county vouchers, talked to a woman who approached him while he was buying bags of cat food, offered to give him spay/neuter vouchers, but the vouchers never arrived. He told the court how he just couldn't find the kitties proper homes.

The jury sat through days of testimony, pictures of countless cats amid filthy squalor, the description of the eye-burning stench, ninety-some-odd exhibits, debates about cat bones and goat bones, and a video of an emaciated cat eating the head of a dead kitten. "Thomas Ritchie couldn't care for all the cats," they heard. "He let them breed rampantly with no thought as to the consequences." They heard how he worked not for money, but cat food, how he bought it by the 16-pound sack, a dozen at a time. What they didn't hear is what I knew about him, that the cats gave him purpose, meaning. They were his Wonder Valley identity. Along with his sniper story, he wielded the cats and this trial to an end. I watched him employ the same tactic in court. Yes, of course, he was overwhelmed, he said, but he tried the best he could. He was the victim in all this.

"I prayed to God just this morning," jurors heard him say to a deputy. It was the recording from the back of the patrol car at the time of his arrest. *"I prayed to God to help me, to lift this burden, and when I arrived, you were here."* The jury let out an audible sigh.

In the end, they deliberated for eight hours over the charges in the case of The People vs. Thomas Ritchie. Ultimately, they found Tom not guilty. When I later asked them about their decision, they said it was a matter of degrees. "Sure, he was guilty of something," the jury foreman told me, "but not a felony." Then he complained of the waste of time and money this trial had been, here when the county was going broke.

Tom welled up with tears when the jury announced their verdict. He left the courthouse that afternoon acquitted of all charges. I drove him home, passing through the dots of desert towns, past the Marine base and the national park, back to Wonder Valley, the setting sun at our backs. "Thank you," he said to me. "Thank you for all you did."

I forced a smile at him as he spoke, but I couldn't share his high spirits. I was disappointed. I'd hoped he'd be convicted. A conviction would have meant he'd have lost his remaining cats and have been prohibited accepting more—and a probation officer would verify his compliance. He could have gotten out of this desert then, gone to stay with his brothers in Iowa maybe—they had invited him.

But Whitefeather was no one without those cats. Somehow blind to their suffering, they made him feel needed, gave him a reason to live. And, as I said, they had also become such a big part of the role he played. The cats and the pending court case and the Marine Corps sniper charade were what he had to offer to the valley. He gave people the gift of their own altruism. And it worked. People with little more than he had made sure he stayed housed and fed.

Without the court case hanging over him, though, he'd now have to rework his identity, revise the hat-in-hand shtick that had kept him and his cats in food and beer. He was going to have to figure something out because he had hungry mouths to feed: his old motorhome and a broken-down travel trailer next to it, and the bedrooms of this rock cabin as well as the guesthouse next door, were rapidly refilling with cats.

Chapter 6

Through the summer, my parents came and went from their travels. When they were home, I tried to disappear to Wonder Valley early and spend the afternoons at The Palms. My relationship with my parents had reverted quickly, as if I were a child, sixteen again, my mother expecting me home for dinner by six, reminding me how upset my father got if he had to wait for his meal. I dreaded it. Dinner with my parents meant Fox News babbling in the background, amplifying my dad's Tea Party, jingoistic opinions which themselves echoed the network's dire warnings about the Muslims and the liberals in a feedback loop. My snarky comments often led to flare-ups which ended in the silence of forks clicking on plates until my father retreated to his lounger and the company of the tube. I knew from experience the situation couldn't hold. Our coexistence was becoming untenable. Then, one evening at dinner, my father addressed me calmly. He coolly detailed his suggestion. I called Ann right afterward to pitch the idea to her.

"My dad knows of a cabin in Wonder Valley I can rent," I said. "And, it's super cheap! My dad says the owner just wants somebody in it to keep an eye on things. Besides, to do the kind of research I need to do, I have to be out in Wonder Valley more, full time, not just commuting from town." I knew I'd have to get her on-board with the idea—she'd be the one paying the rent—but I had already committed to it. I had agreed to rent the cabin sight-unseen. "Things out here are really starting to pick up for me," I told her. "I need this."

§ § §

71

The next day, I drove out with Whitefeather and turned off the paved road. I had no address for my new cabin, just the street name—Naborly—and a description—white with green trim. Naborly Road was broad and well-maintained, though sparsely populated save for a few abandoned shacks and what appeared from the distance to be a child's cobbled-together play fort, although a massive one. It stood back off the road, a crenellated wall of scavenged plywood and bent, banged-up metal surrounding a decrepit cabin and a commuter-type city bus. Flags like military pennants snapped in the wind over the compound: an upside-down American flag, a Confederate flag, a German SS flag and a Nazi one with a swastika, as well as the Arizona State flag, flying with the others like some kind of new racist standard. Whitefeather and I just gawked as we rolled by.

Across from the compound, on Naborly Road, a minivan watched us. A menacing figure filled its cab; his tan arm, pudgy as a baby's leg, held a camera. He kept it trained on us as we drove.

Then, a half a mile further, Naborly Road abruptly ended at a tee. We came to a halt, dust swirling around us as I looked around. No white cabin. Somehow, we'd missed it. I eased forward and cranked the wheel around, returning back down the road. A desert iguana scurried away on two legs, a Barbie doll velociraptor.

Returning to the crenellated fortress, I saw it. Crouching as if hiding in the shadow of the flapping fascist flags, was my cabin. The malevolent minivan, gunmetal-gray, idled opposite it.

I eased into the cabin's dirt drive and killed the engine. Slowly, behind us, the van skulked across the road, crunching the hard-packed sand, halting when it reached us, the driver leering menacingly, the camera still trained in his thick-fingered hand. A gray beard like a bandana masked his face, cheap iridescent shades concealed his eyes. Cold hostility filled his voice. "You the family?" he asked.

"No," I answered with as much fuck-you as I could muster. I

didn't want any trouble, but I didn't want to appear soft either.

"You buying the place?"

"No.

We stared at each other in a standoff.

"I'm renting it," I offered finally.

"Was that you flying over here yesterday?"

"Yeah," I said. I had no idea what he was talking about, but at that moment I wanted him to think I had an air force, and maybe ground support, and if he was thinking of fucking with me, well, he'd better think again.

"Well, tell Fangmeyer you met the asshole," he sneered.

Fangmeyer was the owner of the cabin, my new landlord. Looking back at the man I found myself nodding my consent, as if to agree to not only tell Fangemeyer, but to also acknowledge the truth of his statement, that he was indeed an asshole.

§ § §

In contrast to the asshole's place behind me, the little cabin I was renting sat barely discernable from the landscape. Bleached white like the bones of the dead, it was a fossil on a barren gravel yard, empty except for an old Chevy, chalky-white and oxidized by the sun, its hood ajar. The cabin had been vacant for years, though Fangmeyer came out from town frequently to check on it.

"So, you met the asshole," Fangmeyer said when he arrived at the cabin a few days later. "Because of him, I always come out here prepared." As he took me through the place, he pantomimed how he chambered a round in his 9mm before opening the front door. He then crept through the cabin, checking each nook for intruders while sighting down the barrel of the imaginary pistol gripped tightly in his outstretched arms. This was all meant to be instructional.

"You can't be too careful," he said. "The threats and harassment from that asshole are constant." The asshole, he said, was trying to take the side road the cabin shared as his own property, preventing anyone else from driving on it. And he dragged an old piece of carpet up and down the road out of spite just to create dust.

"He has spotlights shined at the bedroom's back window all night and even bent the bottom of his own fence up so his dogs could torment the neighborhood—the dogs even mauled a kid as he walked to the school bus stop. And he accuses me of spying on him!"

Fangmeyer ran through the quirks of the cabin with me, the bad propane valve, the water storage tank and pump—there was no well, the water had to be delivered. "Oh, but don't drink it," he said, "that asshole behind might have poisoned it." Fangmeyer always brought his own from home, a five-gallon jug of water he could trust, with back-ups on the floor sealed and labeled with the date he had filled them.

He walked me through the use of the security cameras. "They're infrared. You can see the whole property from all directions on the two 32-inch monitors." The cameras were arrayed in banks of four, motion–activated. They recorded everything on internal hard drives. There were also half a dozen dummy cameras pointing this way and that to confuse interlopers. He reviewed the recordings as he spoke, jotting the comings and goings of the neighbor behind in a small notebook: *Tuesday 11:42 he left for water, 1:04 he returned; Thursday 3:43 he dragged the side road, Friday, 10:30 he left for town.*

He then pointed out the binoculars, gave me a run-through on the night vision scope. He handed me a motion detector that fit into one of the fence posts and sounded an alert should the asshole neighbor park in a camera blind spot. He showed me the lockbox behind the door—there was a pistol in it. Walled into the wall of the closet was a rifle—unregistered. "Just kick it in right here if you find yourself in a siege situation." He himself carried a 9mm in his belt, a .38 in his pocket, a two-shot derringer in his shirt. He suggested I get a gun too.

At The Palms that afternoon, I mentioned Fangmeyer's warnings and others quickly chimed in with stories of their own about the neighbor behind me. Red, for example, said the guy tried to keep him and others from driving on the public roads, not just the side road he was trying to take as his own, but Naborly Road, the main one that passed in front of my place. "He follows me, too," Red said, "and he's always taking my picture and harassing me and my wife." He caught the guy stealing his mail once, he said, but confronting him, the guy beat his ass. He said the asshole was in cahoots with Brian, the neighbor to the north of me, and together they called the police if he saw anyone driving too fast or too slow or cutting anywhere across the desert or taking too long at the mailbox getting their mail. "They called the police on me so many times and I spent so much time in jail that when I got sentenced to 90 days for my second DUI, I already had 88 days in the bank. I was out of jail within hours!"

Others had stories for me too. Gary, hearing I'd rented the place, came over the next morning. He was an elfin man in bib overalls with a thick gray beard he hadn't shaved since he was discharged from the Army after Vietnam. He had retired to Wonder Valley from a job as a heavy equipment operator and built a nice new home next to his homestead cabin on the paved road. He told me he'd had problems with the asshole neighbor from the time he moved in.

"That asshole takes pictures of me in my own home!" he said, taking a swig from a longneck he held pinched between two fingers. "He stalks me in town and even parks next to my house at night and shines his headlights through my kitchen window. He's frightened my wife to the point she won't come to Wonder Valley no more. She'd rather live with her son because she's afraid." The trouble really escalated when the neighbor kidnapped his dog, he said. The dog had wandered across the desert to his property and he snatched it.

"My dog ain't no desert dog," Gary said. "It ain't no scroungy, half-feral mutt like that asshole's are. He's a Bassett Hound, pure bred. My best friend." The first time the neighbor grabbed the dog, a sheriff's deputy negotiated to get it back, threatening him with jail time for theft if he didn't return the animal.

"The second time, he hauled my dog to the pound—but not the pound in town, one 70 miles away! He hates anyone associated with me or Red or Fangmeyer. Everybody knows that." He shook a cigarette from a pack of Camels. "That's why he tried to draw Rick Swan into the feud." He pinched the filter from the cigarette and dropped it to the ground. "Rick lived up there near Red. He's one of Red's good friends." He lit the frayed end of the cigarette and drew in a breath of smoke. "And I'll tell you this," he said, looking up at me while blowing out a cloud. "When Rick Swan's cabin mysteriously burned to the ground, we all knew who done it."

§ § §

The asshole's name is Craig, Craig Nolan. He lived in the old commuter-type city bus parked behind the fortress wall on his compound. I rallied my courage and went with a box of beer to talk to him.

"I saw Gary over there yesterday," he said. "I bet he told you all about me." We sat in the dirt outside his municipal bus. He poured vodka from a plastic jug into a tumbler of cola.

"I don't want any trouble," I said. "I'm just renting the place." I didn't want any part of the Naborly Road feud, as I'd heard people call it.

Craig took a sip from his drink. "I'm not like all the others out here," he said. "I always had a job. I worked on the Marine base before, then was the manager of the dollar store in town." He had lived out here for nearly twenty years, he said, first in the homestead cabin on his property, and then the commuter bus after he filled the cabin with stuff rendering it unlivable. Before Wonder Valley, he'd lived in LA, drifting here slowly, first by the beach, then an inland town, then further and further east, landing here because it was where he could afford. He bought the property with a girlfriend, he told me, a mean woman who took no shit from anybody. He eventually bought the cabin next door, too, bought it for his mother. He tore the walls and windows out of that cabin to remodel it, but his mother preferred living in town, so he never finished the remodel. It sat gaping, yawning, open to the desert. He'd lived there alone since the mean woman turned that meanness on him and left him.

After the dollar store closed, he couldn't find another job. He collected unemployment while it lasted, he said, then got by reselling salvaged junk and working swap meet booths selling flags. Mostly, though, he just holed-up in that fortress compound.

"I keep tabs on the riff-raff out here. I monitor their comings and goings. You know the way people are out here, running around drunk, stealing. But you don't see me running around, breaking into people's cabins, you don't see me driving where I don't belong, like Red and Gary, tearing up the desert or cutting down people's private roads as a shortcut to the bar."

That was why he closed the road in front of his property to traffic. "I got the only place on it. No one else needs to be driving on it. I'm the one who maintains it, too." He towed that homemade drag up and down it not just to create dust, he said, not just out of spite. It was to erase tire tracks so he could monitor the road's use.

"But Fangmeyer thinks he can just drive on it anytime he wants, so I can't tell if drug dealers or thieves or whoever had been driving by—and Fangmeyer never even lived here. He lives in town and only comes out to fuck with me. He's always driving his damn jeep around his property and across other people's, tearing up the land and riling up my dogs."

Craig had half a dozen dogs, Belgian Shepherds—not purebred or anything, but dogs he planned to breed and sell all the same. Craig said that when Fangmeyer came out he'd throw table scraps to the animals attracting coyotes and other vermin, letting Craig's dogs eat the bones and scraps, too. Then his dogs started dying.

"Fangmeyer was throwing out them scraps and suddenly, one a day, my litter of puppies died. And then the mother went. Fangmeyer had poisoned them. Or Red did. Or Gary. Or somebody poisoned my dogs. You just don't lose a whole litter at once like that!"

Craig said yes, one of his dogs got out and bit a kid one time. "But that kid was retarded or something. He had wandered onto my property, opened the gate and walked past the no trespassing signs. He let the dogs out. Then he ran and the dogs chased him, what else you think they would do?" Because of that, Animal Control seized his dogs, took them to the pound. They destroyed them before Craig could come up with the nearly $500 each to retrieve them. All he could save were two.

"One Fangmeyer poisoned," he said. "The other Rick Swan purposely hit and killed on Naborly Road. That is why I hate Rick Swan. And Fangmeyer."

"I've never met Rick Swan and barely know Red and Gary and Fangmeyer," I said.

"Yeah, well Fangmeyer deliberately bends the bottom of my fence out so my dogs will escape." He said that was how the dog got out, the dog Rick Swan killed, though it was clear to me that the dogs were simply digging under the fence. I had seen Craig's dogs running loose, chasing cars as they passed, and I worried they'd get hit.

"When Rick saw one of my dogs on Naborly, he purposely punched the gas and ran it over. And Gary came along behind and swerved out of his way to hit the dog again!"

To hit a dog deliberately, just out of spite, seemed almost unbelievably barbaric to me. "I can't imagine they'd do that," I said.

"No matter what Gary says, I know he ran over my dog. I heard it squeal until it finally died. He ran over my dog because he was pissed off I'd taken his dog to the pound." He took a swig of his drink. "Gary lets his basset hound run loose up the road. It shits in front of people's cabins. I raise peacocks, and when that dog came up to my fence, I thought it might kill my chicks. So I caged it. The next time I drove it to the pound, one where I thought Gary would never find it. If it happens again, I won't hurt it, not like they'd done to my dogs, but Gary won't find that dog in this county, in this state, anywhere ever again."

It was Gary who was the problem, he said, Gary and Fangmeyer. Before they showed up, he and Red had been friends.

"After Red met Gary, they started running around, driving and drinking, cutting across the desert where they shouldn't be, going where they had no business going, and probably stealing stuff from the junk cabins and abandoned cars." To combat this behavior, Craig started a neighborhood watch with Brian, the neighbor to the north. Together, they called the police whenever they saw anything suspicious.

"Red is a registered sex offender, a convicted child molester," Craig said. "But when me and Brian put out signs warning people, Red retaliated. He attacked Brian, yelling and screaming at him, zooming up and down Naborly dusting him out. He threw caltrops on his driveway"—spiked balls welded together out of nails that pierce your tire when you run them over then shake loose into the dirt for you to run over again and again. "That's why Brian has all the lights." At night, Brian's place was lit it up like a maximum-security prison, his lights with the ones Craig shined through my bedroom window made it nearly daylight bright at my cabin at night. "Brian had to get a restraining order against Red, but Red consistently violates it and challenges the violations in court using video from Fangmeyer's security cameras. He started attacking me, too. He put boards hammered through with nails across my driveway. He throws rocks at my van. We call the cops to have him arrested, but the cops don't do anything, nothing ever sticks. I don't know why. Me and Brian figure he must be some kind of police informant, or something."

When Red and Craig fought at the mailboxes, though, they both went to jail.

"I caught him messing with my mailbox. I beat Red's face black and blue, his eye was swollen shut, but through his fat lips he said to me, 'I'm going to get you. I'm going to burn you out.'"

§ § §

When I brought up Craig's side of the story at The Palms a couple days later, Gary shouted, "Bullshit!" He repeated his story about his dog, about how the asshole stalked him, taking pictures. Red told me again how Craig had beat the shit out of him. And Whitefeather, the smoke from his hand-rolled cigarette curling around his face, brought up Rick Swan's place. "It was arson, proven," he said, "someone kicked in Rick's door and doused his cabin with gasoline. That asshole Craig did it. Ask anybody." Others out on the patio that night chimed in about Craig as well, the stuff he did, the things they'd heard, someone had to do something!

"Someone should do to him what he done to Rick! Someone should burn him out, burn *his* fucking cabin down!" I don't remember who said that. It was all just empty words, I figured, the beer talking, just the guys puffing themselves up to one another. But then, a week later, in the still air of dusk, three thick, black columns of smoke, visible for forty miles around, rose from Craig's compound, so that when I returned home, drove up Naborly Road to my little cabin, I saw Craig's Nazi flags and fortress wall and his cabin and old commuter-type city bus, gone.

As it happened, Red was the first to see the smoke. He climbed to the roof of his place half a mile away. The fire department showed up on the scene within minutes, the sheriff to Red's shortly thereafter.

"The fire? Couldn't have happened to a nicer guy," Red told deputies, "but I didn't start it." He had an alibi, he said. He'd been home with his wife the whole day.

There were no witnesses. I wasn't there and Craig had taken a friend to a funeral and was gone. There were cameras on my cabin, though, cameras aimed at his place. They were motion activated, recording when they detected movement.

On the day of the fire, at 18:03—6:03 PM—narrow, shimmering shadows triggered one of them. It recorded the shadows climbing across the desert and quickly broadening to a dark cloud churning with heat. Five minutes later the west-facing camera clicked on, triggered by something, Craig's spite flags perhaps, or his cabin or the tinder-dry junk or the old city bus behind the fortress wall roiling in flames that popped with blasts as the fire's heat cooked off the rounds of stockpiled ammunition. That camera recorded the fire department arriving, it recorded them backing away and letting the fire burn. Six minutes later, flames ate through the power lines and the cameras on my cabin went dark. Holy shit, I thought. I felt complicit in a crime. When I brought up the fire at the bar, everyone grew quiet. "Couldn't have happened to a nicer guy," Red said again. But, again, he denied doing it.

§ § §

A week after the fire, I went to see Craig. He had relocated into the cabin next door, the one he had bought for his mother, the one with no walls or windows or doors. He had no electricity. The tires on his water trailer had melted in the fire. He had no water and no way to get any. It was 110 degrees out. I beeped my horn.

"*WHAT DO YOU WANT?*" he roared as he burst from the cabin, all six-foot-whatever and two hundred and fifty pounds, fists clenched.

He stared at me in cold fury, then softened. He slouched against the wall. "I got fucking nothing!" he bellowed suddenly, shaking. "They took everything from me!" That rekindled him. All emotions, sorrow, despair, turned to anger. He flared, but just as quickly burned out.

He stared in silence at the blackened waste, the charred hulk of the commuter bus, the waste land ash pit of the cabin, the single nightmare trunk of a burned and blackened tree.

"Huey Lewis," he murmured. He was making a mental inventory of his loss, remembering each of his CDs, his books and DVDs, family mementos, the photos and documentation, the evidence against Fangmeyer and Rick Swan and Gary and Red. As we stood there, a thermal rose from the ash pit. A churning column of charred papers lifted skyward, swirling like buzzards over the carcass of the cabin, reaching three hundred, four hundred feet into the air. It felt ominous, like it meant something, a warning I should heed.

A week before the fire, Craig found footprints on his road. He tracked them, he said, tracked them as they came from the east and curved north behind Brian's. It was Red, he told me, he could tell by his shoeprints.

"Why didn't Fangmeyer's cameras record him walking around? Huh? Why didn't he give that video to the fire inspector?"

The fire inspector had visited Fangmeyer at his home in town. He reviewed the footage of the fire on his big plasma screen. But the recording begins with the cabin fully engulfed in flames, there was no footage of anyone arriving before the fire or fleeing from it. Fangmeyer didn't tell the fire inspector about the person walking around Craig's cabin the week before. He saw that person, though, saw him on the recording. I saw that person too. I couldn't tell who the person was, but it did look to me like it could have been Red.

The fire inspector told me that three distinct columns of smoke indicated three distinct starting points: evidence of arson. But maybe the flames simply jumped quickly from the cabin to the bus, he said, and as the electrical line burned through, it started the third fire. His report was pending.

"I don't think it was arson," Craig told me later. "It was an electrical fire." He'd heard rumors that if the power line started the fire the power company took responsibility for the blaze. A power company-started fire could mean a payout for Craig, a new start. Arson means he can expect nothing. He was being hopeful.

Everything on Naborly Road quieted down until a few weeks later when Craig ran into Gary in town. Gary mouthed off to Craig and Craig stabbed Gary's tire with an ice pick. It was all caught on a liquor store's video cameras. Gary filed for a restraining order, but Craig ran the process server off at the barrel of a shotgun. Gary then asked me if I'd serve the papers for him. I called Craig to let him know I was coming before I drove over. I wore a collared shirt and slacks to serve the papers. I had told Craig I was a writer, but rumors were circulating that I was an undercover cop or FBI or a narc or something and I wanted to capitalize on that.

I stood with Craig as he read the documents. From his tumbledown cabin, no walls or windows, I looked out over the ash pit of his place, the charred hulk of the commuter bus, the single nightmare trunk of that burned and blackened tree. From there I could barely make out my little cabin, bleached white like bones of the dead, sitting on a low knoll on Naborly Road. It was so unremarkable over there, almost unnoticeable, and I thanked God for that.

Chapter 7

It wasn't long after I moved into my cabin that I found myself at Pizza Richard's formica table watching him hold court. He sat in a leather desk chair, leaned back almost reclined. Whenever anyone passed him a joint, he'd take it. He'd wave it around absentmindedly as he talked using it to dot the period on the point he was making, "Oh yeah, yeah, *exactly*," his perfectly white, acrylic teeth shining like piano keys from under his boot-black mustache. Eventually, though, somebody'd elbow him or he'd catch a glimpse of the smoldering baton in his hand and, clipping a pair of surgical pliers to the wet end of it, he'd jut his chin skyward and stare cross-eyed at its glowing cherry as he drew a bit of the smoke in through his pucker. Other times, though, he just passed the joint along, not hitting it at all.

"Yeah, it's my weed," he said, "but, hey, hey, I get it for my friends. *Exactly*." He traded pizza for the pot during his stops around the valley as he made his way back home from work.

I had gotten to know Pizza Richard from The Palms. There, he was always quick with a story or a self-deprecating laugh. He seemed to know everyone, too, and introduced me around while drawing me into his circle.

He spent his weekends away, which was why I didn't see him at the bar all the time, working down the hill at a pizza place. He returned to Wonder Valley on Mondays, making his stops along his 100-mile route: the Indian casino for gas, the smoke shop for tobacco, the liquor store for beer—a 30-pack, enough for the night— and then his rounds around the valley, trading pizza for pot and promises, finally ending up at the bar with any surplus pies. Tonya immediately put a Bud in front of him.

"It's frees," he said to me in that way of his, adding S's to the end of words, "That's the deals. A trade for the pizzas. *Exactly.*" He clinked me in cheers.

Pizza Richard bought beers freely for the entourage that surrounded him. When he stood to leave, the bar stood up with him. I'd watch them all go, me and George often the only ones remaining. One day, though, as he readied himself to leave, he looked around as if to see who was eavesdropping, then leaned over to me, fixed me with his eyes, one blue, one brown, and said, "Hey, hey, you, uh, want to come overs? Come back to my place, drink some beers?" I nodded, feeling finally part of the club.

In the parking lot, he grabbed beers from the cooler in the bed of his truck and offered them around. "It's OK," he said, handing one to me. "We stick to the dirt roads. *Exactly.*"

I joined the caravan that threaded behind Richard across the valley: Red on his ATV, Whitefeather with me, Slim and Desert Dave, Gary, up the rutted dirt tracks, through the wash, traversing the valley to a little one-room shack out by the Sheephole. Curtis, the Wonder Valley drunk, walked in soon after.

"I like all the company," Pizza Richard explained as we sat around the formica table at his cabin. "But I got to be careful. I don't want absolutely everyone to come over! I mean, come on! I can't supply beer and weed to the entire valley!" Still, out at his tiny little one-room cabin, he seemed to always have a full house. Almost every night a bunch of us would follow him from the bar, drink his Nattie Ice and listen to music or watch concert videos on TV. Tuesday nights at Richard's were Taco Tuesday. The bar was closed that day, so Richard's Taco Tuesday was the event of the week. For the tacos Richard pilfered frozen ground beef from the pizza parlor, as well as pizza cheese, and lettuce and tomato from the salad bar. Someone, Denise or Clyde Eddie or even Bartender Tonya, would fry up the tortillas in Richard's electric skillet while Pizza Richard sat at his formica table in his leather desk chair, a bandana around his head, rolling a joint or two from shake in the styrofoam lid of a pizza parlor to-go box. More guests would trickle in. We'd sit around the formica table or on the bed or on the couch pressed nose-close to the television eating pizza tacos and drinking beer after beer and gossiping and trading news and rumors about the valley into the wee hours of the morning.

At Pizza Richard's, I made mental notes about the things I saw and heard. Taco Tuesdays were tribal, almost ritualistic, the caravan to Richard's, his taking his seat in his leather desk chair, his throne at the head of his table. With a wave, he granted permission to drink his beer, pass his joints. Visitors filtered in and out to pay homage, to quietly borrow money—or repay it, with interest in the form of a T-bone steak bought with food stamps or handyman work on his cabin. It had all the excitement of a high school house party. His beer was a magnet to those who couldn't afford a buck for one at the bar. Side deals were made, barters arranged, favors indulged. Everyone arrived showered, their hair combed, dressed in their best, a regimen otherwise reserved for court appearances and funerals. On Taco Tuesdays, we rode Richard's ATVs around his property, shot his rifle at beer cans from the lazy boy on his front porch. Any alcohol-induced catty bickering and petty fighting was resolved quickly, at the risk of eviction—not by Pizza Richard, but by other guests who policed the party by pressing combatants to turn hostilities into hugs and I-love-you-mans or get the fuck out. And this was all to a music bed of classic rock. I was here as an anthropologist, I told myself, cracking open another Nattie Ice. I was Margaret Mead, Franz Boas, my research was immersive.

I had already concluded that Wonder Valley was the bottom of a kind of metaphorical vortex, a place where those shaken loose from society rolled, spiraling downward. And once you were here, if you'd no one to throw you a rope, you might never climb out. As I listened, I heard a commonality in everyone's stories: They'd all once lived in the real world, the world outside of Wonder Valley. They'd had jobs and families and lives out there, and it had all gone to shit for them. They'd suffered mental illness, substance abuse, cause and effect in a vicious circle, spiraling into this vortex. Of anyone, though, Pizza Richard seemed the least affected by it. He seemed happy here, and I suspected he was the one person I'd met who wouldn't get the hell out of Wonder Valley if he could. He seemed worry-free and content where life had landed him.

He had a job, for one thing, had worked at the pizza parlor for nearly twenty years. His brother had opened it in the town where they grew up and Richard started working for him when he last got out of prison. Richard had been in and out of lockup his whole life prior to that, had gone to juvenile hall for petty crimes as a child, spent his high school graduation there, in fact, for selling reds to a narc. After a first long stint in jail he moved to Oregon where he met a woman, married, and had kids before becoming the Backdoor Bandit, made famous in the Portland papers for his basement backdoor smash and grab. He burglarized from his bike, riding around the rich neighborhoods, casing a place, kicking in the door, grabbing the jewelry and valuables, stuffing it in the victim's pillow case, and toodling Santa Claus-style to the pawnshop to trade it for the cash he needed to maintain a smack habit far richer than his job as a short order cook could support. His career as the Backdoor Bandit ended when a neighbor saw him break in. Cop cars screamed up to a house and found him hidden behind a basement couch. Guns and flashlights trained on him, "Let's see just how slowly you can climb out from back there," a cop said.

For that one heist he did three years. His wife left him while he was in prison. After his parole, prosecutors charged him with another 200 burglaries. He skipped town. On the lam in Phoenix, he became Richard Smith, remarried, had more kids, worked again as a short order cook. After a drunken motorcycle wreck, he developed a taste for painkillers, pharmaceuticals washed down with liquor—bourbon his preference—a fifth a day. He started robbing pharmacies for drugs. Again, they caught him. He did more time. Then they shipped him back to Oregon for the 200 unpunished burglaries. He never saw his wives or children ever again.

He'd been clean since then, though, never touched hard liquor, lost that taste for hard drugs. He'd worked at the pizza parlor since his brother opened it and had been married to the third wife just as long. He moved to the one-room cabin in Wonder Valley with her— it came with her son living next door, as well as his kids and nieces and nephews. Rent was cheap. He figured they could save money. He'd get up early Friday mornings, drive the hundred miles to work, spending nights with his mother. After she died, he moved into the bed of his pickup parked behind the pizza parlor. Then his third wife died, so, now, on Mondays, he returned to Wonder Valley and the tiny one-room cabin alone.

Well, not exactly alone. As I said, most nights Red would show up. Me and Whitefeather. Sometimes Desert Dave and Slim. Gary. Dingy and Fluffy. Curtis would walk over. Together, we all drank a lot of beer, a thirty-pack or more a night. And even when he was away at work people came over and drank his beer and maybe grabbed a couple cans for the trip home. In fact, I'd been to Richard's cabin with Whitefeather before I'd even met him. We popped in and helped ourselves. Red was there every day, too, to check on Richard's dogs, so that by the time Richard got home, any beer he'd left was gone. And as Richard's one-room cabin was way out by the Sheephole, it cost Richard nearly $10 in gas for his beer runs to buy more. This worried him. He was turning sixty-two, retirement age, and needed a nest egg.

"I've got to start saving money, man!" he said to me one night. The expense of all the beer was putting a strain on his finances. To make matters worse, that stepson lived next door—and the stepson's kids, and grandkids, nieces and nephews.

"They play video games all night and the TV is always on, and they run the AC all summer!" Pizza Richard paid the electric bill for both places, that was the deal. "But $300 a month? I mean, come on!"

"Why don't you move?" I suggested. "Find something cheaper, closer to town?" I was thinking of Whitefeather's guesthouse; it was on the property next to the rock cabin Whitefeather had taken as his own. "The owner of the property is dead, there's no one to kick you out until the county auctions it off for the unpaid taxes, but that would be years from now." Whitefeather's guesthouse was bigger than Richard's little homestead cabin, I told him, and with a little TLC, it could be much nicer too. "It's a lot closer to town," I said. "More than ten miles closer."

"That's more than twenty miles round-trip!" Richard said, mulling it over. "Like a gallon of gas!"

I figured such an arrangement would be a win-win for both Pizza Richard and Whitefeather. Whitefeather had been kind of cast adrift since his trial ended. After evading that felony conviction, his survival lost the urgency in the eyes of others. I helped him out where I could, and others bought him the occasional beer in The Palms, but his cats were multiplying and taxing his resources, his only income now coming from aluminum cans he foraged while walking the desert. His electricity had since been cut off for lack of payment and he was losing weight. I was beginning to worry about him.

I drew Whitefeather into the conversation. He thought it a great idea. "I live right next door, on the same property," he said. "I can take care of your Chihuahuas while you're down the hill. I'll watch the place while you're gone, keep these low-lifes away from your beer."

Pizza Richard and Whitefeather settled on rent: $100 a month, plus electricity—and beer. The next week, while Richard was down the hill at work, Whitefeather moved the junk from the guesthouse to the yard, relocated the cats to a camper, and painted. Richard bought the materials and paid Whitefeather cash for doing it, plus beer and weed. Red helped, and Desert Dave and Slim and Clyde Eddie.

The next Monday, after work, Pizza Richard came home to his formica-topped table and big leather desk chair now set up in the rock guesthouse's living room. In his chair, he tied a bandana around his head and pulled off his work shirt. That evening, he held court bare-chested in the early autumn heat, his arms colored with the veiny lines of faded tattoos, Aries, the ram, his astrological sign, but others too faded to see and lost even to his own memory, or so he said when I asked about them. His arms, tan to the shoulder from the sleeveless muscle tees he preferred, seemed stitched to his stringy, patchwork corpus, itself stretched taut with the sinewy scars of the skin grafts from that drunken motorcycle accident, burns that came as he lay unconscious, shirtless, on the summer asphalt, his flesh literally cooking on the road like the proverbial egg.

Once Richard was home and in his leather desk chair, he rarely moved. You get up to get a beer, get him one too. They were in the cooler, or the freezer, or the fridge. And see who else wants one. Whitefeather would take one. He could drink beer, a lot of beer. That was OK, that was the deal, he got beer, all he could drink. But Red could put it away, too, plenty, and when he left, he'd take a beer in hand and a couple more for the road, tossing the cans out into the desert, not even bothering to recycle. Curtis might arrive already drunk, but he could always drink more, often leaving half-full cans scattered around the cabin. Add Desert Dave to that, and Slim. Dingy and Fluffy. I'd drink a few, and so would the others who dropped in unannounced now that Richard didn't live way out by the Sheephole. We'd all shoot the shit, gossiping about the valley, have a beer or two or three, maybe take a couple to go or just sit and talk into the wee hours, going through two or even three thirty-packs in a night.

"That's like $50 a day, man!" Richard said, calculating the impact in his head. "Or more! Like $500 a month!" He now had to run to town every day to buy more, $5 a day just in gas. "I don't mind buying beer for my friends, but, hey, hey, I mean, come on!"

Chapter 8

I have no idea how George Stadler got my phone number. I'd never heard of him and no one at the bar seemed to know who he was either. Somehow, though, he'd heard I was a reporter.

"I got a story you won't fucking believe," he said when he called. "We could sell it to *Life Magazine* or something, make a movie out of it, about the cocksuckers out here in Wonder Valley and the fucking Army and how all these sonsofbitches have been fucking with me my whole life!"

He wanted to meet me, but he wouldn't tell me where he lived. He was laying-low, he said, hiding out from the cocksuckers out here determined to get him. He had to check me out first, vet me through some sophisticated system he had. I wrote him off as a kook. Then, the next day, I heard on the news that he shot at a meter reader who had come onto his property to read his meter. The report said he'd been arrested. That confirmed it: he was a kook, a dangerous one.

I drove to his place the next week following the cryptic directions he sent me via email, no road names, only landmarks. I was to turn off the paved road at the abandoned jojoba farm and creep up a little-used dirt track until I reached a "No Trespas" sign.

Behind the sign a 50s-vintage singlewide slouched beside the charred remains of a burned-down cabin surrounded by a riprap of wheel-less cars and sagging travel trailers on a packed-dirt homestead parcel. I turned in and hesitated there in front of the singlewide, idling. Finally, I blew the horn. A full minute passed in a silence interrupted only by the banging clatter of an aluminum panel slowly being stripped from the side of a motor home by the wind. Suddenly the door of the trailer flew open and George Stadler filled the breach. He was buck naked.

"Hold on," he said, "let me put some clothes on."

After a moment, he reemerged, bare to the waist. He was a barrel-chested man, a formidable fighter I thought, seeing him for the first time. But old age and ill health had ridden him relentlessly. His biceps and forearms—once his guns—now sagged, spindly. Nitroglycerin patches stuck like post-its to his chest. The wind tussled his hair, still a youthful strawberry; his only gray hairs curled from his chin, framing his jaw and his sparse, blackened teeth. He lowered himself into an old kitchen chair in front of the singlewide and launched into an incomprehensible monologue.

"Nobody fucks with me!" he began. "Not these classless cocksuckers out here, not Jack McConaha and his band of criminals, not even the pigs or the US fucking Army! I'm on to all their shit! It's taken me twenty-two and a half years, but now I know the shit that goes on! They harass you to get your property, see, that's what they do; they're after your land. And there's no one who'll do a thing about it—certainly not the crooked cops, they're in cahoots with Jack McConaha's gang! They've been fucking with me from my first trip out here, slashed my tires, death threats, condemned my cabin on false information, incarcerated me on false charges. I spent thirteen hundred days in jail before a jury declared me innocent! Now I'm onto these sonsofbitches. And someone is going to get hurt, someone's going to get hurt real bad! Because nobody fucks with George Stadler!"

From his vantage from the single-wide, he had a sniper's view over the riprap cars and trailers, over the jojoba farm, all the way to the paved road. "Anyone stupid enough to drive in here will hear the boom of my .44 before they ever lay eyes on me! That's one thing for sure!"

I asked him about the meter reader.

"They said he was a meter reader, but I know he wasn't no

fucking meter reader. Everyone knows there ain't no meter readers anymore, the meters are all digital!" He leaned in close to me. "Here was the trick they pull on you out here. They pretend they're out reading your meter, see, but you won't get a bill, and you go in and say, 'I didn't get a bill,' and they say 'Oh, they just missed you last time. We'll get you next month.' The next thing you know they're out here to cut your power off for lack of payment. It's been going on for a long time—that's how they get your land. So coming onto my property to cut my power will get you shot—which was what must have happened to that so-called meter reader, I don't know, I wasn't here at the time." He laughed and lit a cigarette behind cupped hands, taking a drag and blowing out a lungful of smoke. "I was out toward Arizona—at least that's what I told the crooked cops when they showed up. You see, the cops don't come to my place by themselves or empty-handed, they come with a SWAT Team, helicopters, the whole fucking shop! Wait here." He stood and went inside, returning a moment later with a wooden box. From it he lifted two replica black powder revolvers.

"The pigs searched the place, but they didn't find any guns here, just these old Colt pistols—perfectly legal, don't need to be registered—they couldn't have been the weapons used in the shooting because they don't shoot bullets." He laughed a rheumy laugh again as he popped the revolver's cylinder open. Shiny, brass .44 Magnum cartridges filled it. "They don't shoot bullets unless you happen to have a conversion cylinder like I do, which the stupid fucking pigs probably don't even know about and at any rate didn't even find!" He snapped the gun closed and handed it to me, butt first. I took it gingerly, worried about leaving fingerprints.

"But the news said you were arrested." I was confused.

"Not for the shooting!" he said. "They got nothing on me for that! They arrested me for outstanding warrants." A Failure to Appear, it turned out. He had a standing code enforcement order to remove the junk cars stored on his property and had been arrested because he'd refused to comply. I looked around at the rip rap surrounding

93

us. "We're not talking about these cars here," he said. "This ain't my property. The code enforcement shit is about the cars on *my* property, the place the cocksuckers out here had condemned on false charges. The pigs arrested me, but there wasn't a fucking thing they could do to me because those cars are evidence, stored there as evidence of a crime from when this bunch of Guatemalan motherfuckers went over there with end loaders and semis and stole all twenty-two of them, plus six motorcycles. They broke into my cabin and wrecked my fucking campers, too. After I got them back, code enforcement tried to force me to get rid of them, but they were evidence of a crime. There's one straight cop out here and he told me so. I was only in jail a few hours before the judge sent me home!"

I was confused. It seemed he was telling me that he was living here in this singlewide—squatting, I assumed—but had another cabin somewhere else. I had no idea how Guatemalans and code enforcement related to the meter reader and his arrest, though. "Start at the beginning," I said, trying to redirect him.

He lit another cigarette and inhaled deeply. "This here property ain't my property. My property is north of here, near that goofball Nutty Ned. I bought it in 1988, before that cocksucker ever came out here. I'd come out here to die."

His heart was failing, he said. He had no medical coverage and was losing the fight to get the medication he needed, the nitroglycerin patches, the drugs to treat strange symptoms that flared periodically in him, swelling his joints and ever further damaging his heart. He told me he had contracted this strange illness in 1956 while in the Army, had his first illness-induced heart attack at twenty years-old, and developed a heart murmur while aboard a Navy transport ship on deployment to Europe. He said he spent three months in an Army hospital in Germany where doctors found unidentifiable spirochetes, a type of bacterial pathogen, in his blood. They evacuated him stateside, sent samples of the spirochetes to the Centers for Disease Control in Atlanta. They declared him unfit for further military service, to be discharged immediately with a full pension.

"All this is in my medical records," he said. "But I ain't got no medical records. A fucking Army colonel took them, left Germany with them under his arm." And since then, all record of Stadler's military service had disappeared, his discharge papers, everything, gone. He showed me a letter from the National Personnel Records Center: the US government had no record that George Oscar Stadler had ever served in any branch of the military at all.

The letter was the same boilerplate letter I'd received when I tried to get Whitefeather's Form DD-214, his Marine Corps proof-of-service document. I figured Stadler's story was just another replay of Whitefeather's sniper horseshit. Whitefeather had said his service was so secret, records of it had been scrubbed. Stadler, on the other hand, told me his records had been destroyed because he'd been a guinea pig for biological warfare tests. He said the spirochetes in his blood were weaponized bacteria, that he was an unwitting participant in the CIA's covert human research program code-named Project MK-Ultra.

"Without my medical records, the fucking Army wouldn't discharge me," he said. "They fucked with me at every stop. Just bounced me around, from Great Lakes Naval Hospital to Fort Sheridan to Fort Benning, Georgia. At Benning they stopped treating me, withheld my medications, but refused my medical discharge!" They held him in limbo, he said, stuck where he'd fallen between the cracks of Army bureaucracy. "I sat out the rest of my enlistment there, unable to work and doing nothing except passing time. Finally, I just packed my duffle and left, drove myself back home to Ashland, Wisconsin and dumped my gear at the fucking recruiting office where I'd enlisted." He brought home a new wife with him, Shirley, a Michigan Finn he met at Benning. She was expecting their son.

Stadler rolled cigarettes and smoked them one after another as he spoke, pausing only to pick the occasional bit of tobacco from his tongue. He said he brought his small family to California chasing work in the sixties, but his marriage dissolved when Shirley became mentally ill and was institutionalized. He battled flare-ups of his mysterious disease over the next thirty years, he said, working intermittently during remissions. He boasted repeatedly of being the best, brightest, most capable mechanic, machinist, carpenter, electrician, computer technician, farmer, lover, and fighter that anyone had ever seen, but the flare-ups of the disease would take it all away. Neil, his son, grew up on the road as Stadler jumped from place to place, job to job, hassle to hassle. Through all this, they had only each other. As Neil reached adulthood, Stadler said, he would disappear for weeks or months or years on walkabout only to return to find his father in much the same place he'd left him.

Stadler had been homeless, living in a motorhome at a Santa Barbara beach, when cops started hassling them, writing him tickets, threatening to tow his camper. Stadler sued them. I verified this through court records. It was around this time, too, that the State of California declared him indigent and fully disabled. He began receiving $400 a month of Supplemental Security Income. The $400 wouldn't go far in Santa Barbara, as expensive as it was, so a social worker suggested the desert to him. He took the money he won in his lawsuit, and, with son Neil on walkabout, he left Santa Barbara for that cabin in Wonder Valley. He paid cash for it, $9,500.

"I thought I'd be left alone out here," he said, "but the classless cocksuckers started fucking with me from my first day out! On my very first night they smashed all the windows of my car, slashed the tires, and left a note: *If you move out here, we're going to shoot you in the ass and burn you out.* And I said, 'We'll see who kills who.'"

Stadler droned on about Wonder Valley in what seemed to me to be an extended paranoid delusion about the classless cocksuckers, about how Jack McConaha was in cahoots with the cops and a man named Ted Meyers.

"They 'tacked' my road!" he said. They dumped roofing nails on the washboards causing him flat tire after flat tire, sometimes all four at once. He said Jack and Ted Meyers would follow him everywhere, forcing him to move his post office box to a hamlet up on the Interstate sixty miles to the north.

"The post office in town, see, they started throwing away my Social Security checks. And I didn't get utility bills for over a year!" To throw pursuers off his trail, he said he left for the hamlet at four in the morning with his lights off to get his mail, and when he went, he didn't go directly there.

"I drove east to the Colorado River, then looped north, then west. Two hundred miles one way! I could hear them talking about me as I drove away. 'He's just left,' 'He's traveling east.' I had a scanner, see, one that could pick up people's cordless phones. They say you can't hear a cordless phone from more than five hundred-feet away—well, they couldn't, but I could! I could listen to them over miles and hear everything they were saying!" Through that special device only he had, he said, he could hear them planning how they were going to get him.

§ § §

I went to see Ted Meyers. Ted lived in a spic and span, bathroom cleaner-blue cabin with toilets as yard-art not far from Stadler's old place. Stadler had told me that Ted, like Jack McConaha, had been fucking with him his whole life. As proof, he boasted of beating Ted's ass back in Detroit in 1956.

Ted was from Detroit, he told me, but would have been too young to have known George Stadler in 1956.

"I don't remember Stadler moving to Wonder Valley, either," he said, "but I remember his son Neil showing up. I remember Neil riding up and down the roads on a motorcycle, naked, yelling obscenities!" The problems with Neil came to head when Neil opened fire on Nutty Ned, which led to a stand-off with deputies. Stadler had told me about this previously, told me it was he who had tried to kill Nutty Ned before Ned could shoot Neil, but the cops hauled Neil away for the crime. He had since been committed to

Patton State Hospital, the hospital for the criminally insane.

"The nails on the roads started soon after that," Ted said. Back then he operated a water delivery business that had him driving all over the Valley. "Do you know how expensive the tires for a water truck are? I complained about Stadler to the sheriff, but of course they could do nothing. No one could prove it was him doing it."

After that, Jack McConaha began keeping tabs on Stadler, staking-out his cabin and tailing his movements. In addition, as chief of Wonder Valley's volunteer fire brigade, he had special access to sheriff's deputies. "Off the record, they suggested I fight fire with fire," he told me. "So I drove up to Stadler's place with a fifty-pound box of roofing nails. When I returned the box was empty. I got a phone call from a neighbor the next day: George Stadler was stuck in the sand up there with all four tires flat!"

Then suddenly, randomly, it seemed to those who remembered it, Stadler opened fire on Jack McConaha.

Stadler had told me the story: "I was coming back from a mail run when McConaha zoomed up and pulled across the road, blocking my way. He had his gun drawn, but I just drove around him, flipping him the bird. But when McConaha shot my rear window out, the game was on! I opened up on him with my .45, emptying the clip while he zoomed away like the chickenshit he is!"

A witness who had just then been driving east, though, told me Jack wasn't stopped or pulled across the road at all. "He was right behind me in his jeep," she said, "when I saw the driver of an on-coming truck stick a gun out of the window. I thought he was pointing it at me!" As he passed her, she heard the gunfire.

Jack didn't know anything was happening. "I saw everyone simultaneously duck as I passed The Palms, but thought it was a prank!" It was the witness's husband who called him and told him he'd been shot at. The husband had been in the front yard and had seen the whole thing, saw a man coming the other way shooting, the

.45 slugs hitting the stucco of the bar. The eyewitness evidence proved insufficient, however—neither could identify Stadler—and the charges against him were dropped.

But something had to be done. Ted Meyers contacted code enforcement. Living in a homestead cabin without electricity or indoor plumbing was illegal, he argued. Based on the complaint, the county inspected Stadler's cabin and condemned it.

Stadler grew furious relating the story to me. "The crooked cops and the cocksuckers with the county red-tagged it on false, trumped-up information!" But there was nothing he could do.

Evicted and with nowhere to go, he moved to the hamlet sixty miles to the north on the Interstate, where, a short while later, during a traffic stop, a Highway Patrol officer arrested him for making and possessing an illegal explosive device.

"I had merely *found* that stuff," he told me when I asked him about it. "I found some black powder and Pyrodex and iron pipe and caps and was taking it to give to some local miners—maybe they could use it for blasting—when that crooked cop stopped me. He said it was a routine traffic stop, but then he started rooting though my back seat, performing an illegal search, uncovering what he said was bomb-making materials." Stadler had been heading in the direction of Wonder Valley.

A court-appointed psychologist found Stadler mentally incompetent, unable to stand trial. They ordered him to Patton State Hospital for treatment, the same institution that housed his son. It would be two years before he was back in court. Then he got a venue change. He tried to have the judge removed, filed writs of habeas corpus, fired his public defender, then the next one, then the next one, then the next one, until, finally, two years, nine months and ten days after his arrest, he stood trial.

"Carrying pieces of pipe ain't illegal!" he crowed. "Nor is transporting a pound each of black powder and Pyrodex—two pounds of black powder is, but one pound of each isn't!" A jury acquitted him of all charges. "Ha ha!" Nobody fucks with George Stadler!" He moved back to Wonder Valley upon his release.

§ § §

When I next visited Stadler, he repeated what he'd told me about the classless cocksuckers in Wonder Valley, how they have been fucking with him all his life, how they followed his son on his walkabouts, chased him across the country trying to kill him. This time, though, he produced computer printouts as proof, printouts of names from internet directories, last names that matched last names of people here, McConahas and Meyerses in Ashland, Wisconsin and Detroit and Georgia and here, look, they'd been fucking with him the whole way, proving in his mind that they'd been after him for years. They were why all the bad that had happened in his life, them and the army. The Army, he reiterated, had maliciously destroyed his service and medical records to cover up a conspiracy.

The thing is, his service records *were* probably destroyed. A fire in 1973 had destroyed the National Personnel Records Center and 80 percent of Army personnel records, Stadler's likely among them. When I wrote the Army and asked for his records, that's what they told me. But after his discharge, Stadler had done one thing that was pretty smart: he recorded his discharge papers at the Ashland County courthouse. And the records were still there. I found them on file in Ashland, Wisconsin. They say Stadler had been drafted in 1955 and had served two years in the Army as a communications specialist. He received an honorable discharge.

His medical records were another matter. Stadler had been begging, pleading, harassing, cajoling veterans' groups around the country for years hoping for help finding the medical records lost in 1956. He showed me the letters he'd sent. Finally, though, he caught the attention of a veterans' advocate with AmVets, a veterans' service organization. This advocate found records, hundreds of pages, representing only a fraction of the total.

"George might be a little strange," the advocate told me over the phone, "but what he's saying is true." Stadler, however, could produce only half a dozen pages when I pressed him.

The pages did indicate Navy doctors declared him one hundred percent disabled in 1956. Based on the symptoms, they had diagnosed him with Rheumatic Fever, an illness caused by the streptococcus bacteria, a follow-on disease to strep throat. Stadler said it destroyed his heart; the records mentioned a murmur. The Navy treated the swelling in his joints with aspirin. The records make no mention of spirochetes, though it seemed too random a thing for him to just make up.

I had come to the conclusion as soon as I met Stadler that he was insane. Paranoid, delusional—I don't know what—but I was certain he was crazy and more than a little dangerous. To make him sound all the crazier, he had a verbal quirk, the royal "we," referring to himself in the plural: They've been fucking with *us*, it took *us* twenty-two and a half years, but now *we're* on to their shit. I wondered if he was schizophrenic or something. Maybe that mysterious disease was the cause. Blaming spirochetes was so specific it seems unlikely he'd have had come up with that without some basis, something he heard, something discussed by his doctors, possibly. The thing is, it's well known that spirochete-caused diseases can lead to heart problems, joint and muscle pain, and eventually can lodge themselves in the brain causing psychosis—syphilis being the most well-known example of this. As I looked into it, I found that some epidemiologists believed Lyme disease, another bacterial disease caused by spirochetes, has similar long-term effects. In fact, some researchers even theorized that the Salem Witch Trials were a response to the mental illness exhibited by Lyme disease-infected people, that the 'mark of the beast' was in fact the tell-tale bullseye rash of Lyme. The disease is thought to have once been widespread across America, but as farming cleared the land across the country, it became isolated to remnant patches of hardwood forests, particularly the patches around Lyme, Connecticut, where the disease was first identified, and, more interestingly, Ashland, Wisconsin, Stadler's home town, the place he'd visited immediately prior to his illness. And while the disease is now well-known, scientists hadn't identified the Lyme spirochete until the seventies. The disease would have been a mystery to Navy doctors in the fifties. It's entirely possible George Stadler suffered the long-term effects of Lyme gone decades untreated.

But maybe Stadler's insanity was something else, something simpler. Maybe the "we" was he and Neil, father and son, together through thick and thin, homeless together, father protecting son as son sank into mental illness. Stadler variously told me that Neil had been committed to Patton State Hospital due to seizures, or that Neil was gaming the system, getting free room and board from the state, or laying low, hiding out from the classless cocksuckers who were out to kill him. He told Neil's mother that her son was suffering from cancer. She had been institutionalized in the early sixties, and remained so when I spoke with her, a therapist on the line monitoring the call.

After Neil was taken away, maybe Stadler, now alone and bitter, began to suffer from the isolation of his living conditions. Wonder Valley had an unusually high number of single-person households— white males over fifty years old predominantly, according to the Census. These men lived alone, often cut-off from each other and society, yet they could see one another, this flat treeless landscape making the comings and goings of your neighbors apparent. I imagine, in those conditions, you might begin to string together a narrative to the random actions you see, you might begin to assign motives and motivations to your neighbors where there were none. I was thinking of the Naborly Road feud, but Stadler had lived even more isolated than my neighbors had. I think maybe Stadler, in refusing to be a victim, refusing to accept those things beyond his control, his son's mental illness, his own poverty and disease, came to convince himself that he was under attack, his mind giving faces to the random forces, the just plain bad luck that had so devastated his life, creating of them tangible villains he could fight, Jack

McConaha, Ted Meyers, the crooked cops, until acting out defensively against those villains, he began to suffer in actuality the hostility he had before only imagined, because, in the end, he was right, they had been out to get him.

But what the hell do I know.

I called Stadler's veteran's advocate again. I wanted more information, to see more of his records, maybe bounce my new theory off him. I figured I should do what I could to help with his case and maybe get Stadler the treatment he needed. The advocate's outgoing message said he was on medical leave until further notice and gave an alternate contact. That mailbox, however, was persistently full. His boss told me he'd look into it, then his boss's boss told me the same, then his boss's boss's boss. I never heard a word from them again. Stadler told me he could no longer reach them either. He thought it was a conspiracy; they were fucking with him again. It didn't matter how or why, but it looked like Stadler's ball had again been dropped.

The irony was that now that Stadler had located some of his medical records, he might have been able to recover some of the disability income he was denied for all those decades, income owed to him—some $250,000 by his own estimation—the lack of which resulted in his homelessness. Of course, he'd likely never see the benefit of that money. The appeals process could take years, and with his veterans' advocates MIA, his chances were slimmer yet. And then there was the unsettled issue of his shooting at the meter reader which renewed cries to get rid of him, to arrest him, to put him away for good. His cabin up by Nutty Ned's was condemned and there was a notice of tax default filed on the singlewide he was squatting in. He had only a couple of years there at best, then he'd have to go, though I suspect that when they finally come to get him, they'll have to bring the SWAT team, the helicopters, the whole fucking shop, because nobody fucks with George Stadler.

Chapter 9

I laughed out loud as I pulled through the gate of this particular homestead compound, the open dirt lot sprawled with a dozen or so cars. It wasn't all the cars that made me laugh—cars scattered around a Wonder Valley cabin was completely unremarkable—but these cars were different. They had all their tires, for one thing, all four. They were all clean, too. And just looking at them you knew that with the slightest twist of the key each would fire right up.

I parked amid the cars and got out of my truck. I had arrived uninvited and hesitated a beat before starting for the cabin. LA people were staying there, Hollywood actors and musicians, a morphing group of friends I'd met earlier in the week, thirty-somethings, who came to Wonder Valley to marvel at the changing colors of the desert sunset, the wide-open skies, the limitless stars, making for themselves a kind of Wonder Valley summer camp of campfires and guitars.

As I walked up to the house, one of the girls, an actress with stunning green eyes, strode out from under the saltcedar trees in a towel. I don't know why, but I imagined she was naked under that towel, making her way to the house from the hot tub where she soaked under the warm sun of the Mojave autumn. The actress gave me a smile of casual recognition and entered the house as another actor exited.

"They're inside," he said, pausing to shake my hand. I rapped on the open door with my knuckles, then went in, twirling the joint I brought in my fingers. I'd stopped by Jill Davis's on the way and she'd given me the joint, and I, not wanting to visit the Hollywood actors and musicians empty-handed, planned to offer it as a sort of gift to the house.

Nobody noticed my entrance. The singer with the booming voice was shoveling food and beer into an open fridge. The TV was on. I stood fidgeting for a moment, rolling the joint around in my fingers. As I walked to the house I had stuck the joint in my pocket, then lipped it, both ends, stuck it in this ear, then that one, but finally twirled it in my fingers so that when the Hollywood singer with the booming voice finally looked up and said, "Hey, look who's here!" sticking out his hand to shake, I had to switch the joint from one hand to the other and missed the hand the singer offered. It didn't matter. The singer grabbed me and pulled me into a hug as his girlfriend brightened at the sight of me, giving me a genuinely welcoming "Hey there!" She offered baby carrots and hummus, a fresh supply of beer. "Want one?" she asked. I handed off the joint.

This group of Hollywood actors and musicians came to Wonder Valley every year and they always rented this same vacation rental. The house and guesthouse sat in a clump of saltcedar trees on a sandy knoll near Whitefeather's rock cabin. There was a hot tub and swimming pool—except the swimming pool was really the hull of an old boat sunk into the ground. The day I visited, it had no water in it. The property was owned by the Sibleys, Mary and her kids, the family who also owned The Palms. I'd met the Hollywood actors and musicians there a few days before.

I had been at the bar with Whitefeather and Pizza Richard when the singer with the booming voice and his friend, a classically trained guitarist, stopped in. They ordered beers, beers chosen from among the row of dusty bottles along the top shelf of the bar, beers The Palms would have liked to stock and even maybe sometimes did, but they were out of the particular brand the Hollywood musicians had chosen, as well as their next choice, and the next. In fact, Tonya had just found a compromise for them when Whitefeather walked out of the bathroom drying his hands on his soiled jeans. He had been in town with Pizza Richard all day—in the back of Richard's pickup with the cooler and the beer—and was sufficiently drunk to lean awkwardly into their personal space pushing them back against the bar with his approach and come-on. Whitefeather insisted they come to Pizza Richard's, drink some beers, smoke some smoke. It was a Thursday, though, and Pizza Richard didn't like to have anyone over on Thursdays. He had to work the next day, had to get up at four in the morning to make the long drive down the hill. On Thursdays, he just wanted to relax, drink a few beers, get to bed early. But the Hollywood musicians had acquiesced to Whitefeather's persistence.

"These guys are coming over!" Whitefeather announced. Richard rolled his eyes with a distinct displeasure.

The two musicians brought beer and guitars to Richard's rock guesthouse and stood talking, then playing and singing and after an hour or so left, but apparently had a good enough time they accepted my invitation to come to my cabin the next night. They arrived with more actors and actresses and musicians and beers and guitars. They took pictures of the sunset and the mountains and the charred remains of my asshole neighbor's burned-out commuter bus. They smoked a joint under the gaze of the cabin's infrared cameras.

The pinnacle of their stay in Wonder Valley was to be their own performances at a concert at The Palms the next night. The concert was the finale to a weekend art event where the artists of the area opened their studios to visitors from down below, setting out plates of cubed cheeses and round crackers and talking about the inspiration they found in the desert. Ann was coming out for the weekend and we were to tour the studios together.

On the day of the concert, we visited the studio of an artist who displayed a canvas she'd painted of Ricka McGuire's 1950 Wayne school bus. In the painting, the bus sits on Nutty Ned's parcel way up there at the northern edge of the valley. The artist called the painting "Vega" for Ned's dead red car next to the bus. She said she'd painted the canvas from a Polaroid snapshot she'd taken on a foray into Wonder Valley. It was part of a series of Wonder Valley paintings she was working on, paintings that depicted the "*remnants and relics of this quasi ghost valley settlement.*" A blurb about her said her work "*eulogizes abandoned habitats and domestic landscapes.*" Ricka McGuire died in that bus, I told her. Of course she didn't know this. The expediencies of her work, she said, were such that she painted the scenes as she encountered them, then learned the backstories later, if ever. Yet all of the places she painted had backstories, I said, the story of a mid-century homesteader proving up the land at least, and others coming later, living a life there before abandoning it. Or not. Nutty Ned still lived in that old school bus. Other places in her paintings were lived-in too.

I was a writer, I told the "Vega" artist, trying to seem relevant. She didn't read much she said, painting consumed her time. What I wanted to tell her was that, for me, Wonder Valley was all backstory, it was the way it is because of the way it was. For me, this place was alive, changing, evolving still, informed by its unique history, but by no means a "relic." Ned's place, for instance, now bore no similarity to the one depicted in the painting, he was always busy moving this here and that there and dragging the bus from one corner of the parcel to the other. But I guess that static quality was inherent to her medium. I'd encountered other artists' work out here, paintings of the desert sunsets or the sepia mountains, even some, like this artist's, of the tumbledown homestead shacks, stripped bare or boarded up. But those paintings were vacant, lifeless, flatlined. Hers, at least, looked lived in, not abandoned. The scattered debris in them gave her art a pulse, and while that pulse absent the people lent her paintings a sort of voyeuristic feel, like she was going through Ned's underwear drawer without his knowing—as if Ned had an underwear drawer—to me that was the appeal of it. At the same time, however, it felt slightly exploitive, as though she were taking something that wasn't hers, taking it without Ned knowing. I thought about that story I wrote about Nutty Ned and Ricka and wondered if I could be accused of the same thing.

But I genuinely found the people out here compelling. I was

fascinated by their individual stories: How did they get to Wonder Valley? What keeps them here? People like George Stadler and Whitefeather and Nutty Ned. Even Pizza Richard. Their stories were raw, at times life or death. Survival out here was not simply a matter of economics—as with Ricka McGuire, if you failed here, you could die. I don't think there is any amount of paint or canvas that can capture that. You can't make short forays out here to really get this place, you can't just pass through, stopping only long enough to snap a Polaroid of a shack, a landscape.

The painting of Ricka's bus and Ned's Vega hung along with a price tag of $9,500.

"It's a good investment," the artist said, "it will surely go up in price." That price already approached the average annual income for someone in Wonder Valley. It was ten times what I was paid to write about that bus. She was also working under a grant, she said, and was using it to rent a place in town and wanted to paint more Wonder Valley. I offered to show her around, but she was heading off soon, had a fellowship and showing on the East Coast, and asked for a raincheck.

§ § §

On the artist's encouragement, Ann and I attended the performance art exhibition at The Palms that evening. The open studio weekend culminated on the weathered plywood stage behind the bar, lit by lights strung up on the steel skeleton of the inverted halfpipe. In the art performance, a man with a Charles Manson look and a prison jumpsuit writhed like a snake on the stage while pushing a guitar in a plastic grocery bag around with his head. He rose occasionally to adjust the levels on the guitar's amp. Simultaneously, near the bar's rear entrance, two men in dervish trances raked up sand and drained it through their fingers, drizzling it in arcs on the ground and on themselves. The artists and hipster visitors watched the performance in silence from the church pews and an assortment of chairs scrounged up for that purpose. At one point, Whitefeather, seeing a friend in the doorway of the bar, inadvertently wandered between the sand-pouring men, and noticing them, stood staring, slacked-jaw and baffled. Finally, Diana, the bartender for the night, broke his trance. "It's supposed to be art!" she bellowed into the quiet. That scene alone made my night.

Throughout the performance art exhibition, the Hollywood actors and musicians sat inside drinking beer as they waited for the Sibleys to finish up as cooks and take the stage as a band. Sibley siblings James and Laura sang bubble-gummy pop songs before the singer with the booming voice took the stage and sang, most notably an a cappella of "Hallelujah," then the other Hollywood actors and musicians joined him and played mostly in ensemble bands and mostly for one another. They sang "Won-der, Won-der Valley! Won-der, Won-der Valleeey!" a song they had written over the weekend at the vacation rental. They later retired there to watch the sunrise from a hill above the house.

When I arrived at their rental with the borrowed joint the next day it was nearly sunset. Ann had gone home and I was again out here on my own. Behind the rental the Hollywood actors and musicians were gathering. A clutch of new arrivals harmonized over their guitars as others debated the math surrounding 'shrooms. The classically trained musician was dividing an ounce of psilocybin mushrooms into teabags in preparation for that night's "experience." There were eight eighths in an ounce, one eighth was a dose. They counted participants. "You in?" they asked me.

"Umm, uhh, sure, I guess, just a taste," I stammered in response.

"That's what I like about you," the blond actress said. "You're open to anything! I guess it's because you're a writer and into *experiences*."

That was true, I suppose, I was into experiences. In my youth, I had wandered the world nomadic, an amateur explorer. I had crossed the Equator, battled 40-foot seas, been chased by that orangutan, yadda, yadda, yadda. And I was here, now, in fact, immersing myself into Wonder Valley. At that moment it occurred to me that all my life I'd collected experiences like they were merit badges, things to be checked-off and openly worn. I felt like they would one day count toward something, that they were units earned in preparation for something, something big, something to come, but I never knew what. I always figured I'd find out, that it would come to me and I'd be ready. But as I stood there, middle age had overtaken me, and nothing had come to me. I was still waiting.

"We ate mushrooms the other night," the singer with the booming voice said to me. He clapped me on the shoulder. "Ando took half a dose and still had a good trip. Take half of a half of a dose. It should still be pretty good."

Soon, the discussion turned to which was the best hill to watch the sunset fast approaching. Ando was for the rocks above Whitefeather's rock-walled cabin, Mount Ando, he'd dubbed it.

"It's not just a name, it's a suggestion! Up there you get a 360-degree view of the valley," he told the newcomers as a means to sell his idea. "It feels like no one has ever been there before, like you're the first, the trash and broken bottles placed there by God."

The quickly setting sun soon vetoed his idea, however. They passed the joint I brought and debated the knoll to the south but settled on the hill to the west, the one with the rock cairns they'd erected at sunrises and sunsets over the past week. Walking to the hill, a newcomer asked me how I knew the Hollywood actors and musicians.

"I live here," I said. "I'm a writer." I blushed. Every time I said that, it felt like a lie. People around Wonder Valley had already started calling me Writer Bill or Reporter Bill, but I hadn't been writing. The homeless magazine had lost its funding and Tim, the editor, was looking to move on and I was beginning to suspect that "writer," for me, was just a euphemism for being unemployed, my sniper lie, nothing more than a face-saving ruse.

"Oh," the newcomer responded, noticing my awkwardness. "Well, it must be wonderful living in such a beautiful place!" I nodded and looked away, not sure what to say.

Up on the hill, the sun broke into rays, its orange orb disintegrating into the horizon. The singer with the booming voice played guitar and sang. The others turned into silhouettes haloed by glowing aureoles.

"Look at the mountains," another newcomer exclaimed, one in cowboy boots and a denim miniskirt. "Oh my God, they're beautiful! Look, look! They're purple!"

As the colors changed, I walked down off the hill and back to my truck. The Hollywood actors and musicians would be returning to LA in the morning, and from my truck I watched them, shadows against the orange glow of the horizon. They chatted in groups, danced, and sang. I wouldn't stay, wouldn't take the half of a half of a dose of mushroom tea. The Hollywood actors and musicians would have their *experience* without me. I felt out of place among them. This was a different desert to them, a different place than the one I'd found, the one I was experiencing. They saw only the beauty of the desert, the sunsets and stars, the purple mountains majesty. They saw the decrepit cabins and litter of detritus out here not as signs of decay and degeneration, but as art and inspiration, divinely placed, without source or backstory. I think they had no perception of the specters who haunted those cabins, the people who lived there around them. It was as though their Wonder Valley existed in a reality parallel to mine, an Eden to my purgatory, a place I'd never see. I started my truck, and in the failing light drifted away, across the valley and up Naborly Road to my bleached-bone cabin.

A few weeks later, the "Vega" artist called to take me up on my offer to show her around. I drove her to Bartender George's place where she painted a picture of George's boat, a tiny, fast-looking mother with no cover on its motor nor wheels on its trailer. Desert Dave had given George that boat as repayment for money he borrowed. Later, the "Vega" artist would give me the painting she made of it as repayment of a favor. I cherish that painting still, a painting of a boat used to repay a debt, used to repay a debt. To me, Wonder Valley was all backstory.

Chapter 10

A couple weeks later, I was driving around the valley listening to the local radio station when I heard the news: Some guy named Fred Harris had stabbed Bud and Natalie Barber at The Palms the night before. I didn't know Harris or the Barbers, and when I asked around the bar that afternoon, it seemed not many people did either. The stabbing, however, was all anyone could talk about. Those who were there said the stabber, Fred Harris, was a skinhead, a white supremacist. The woman he stabbed was black.

When she entered the bar, they said, everyone noticed her. She was striking, not like other Wonder Valley women. Everyone sniggered as they told me this, about how her alabaster teeth were straight and all present and accounted for. And her skin, the color of oiled mahogany, was smooth and unblemished. She was tall, too—nearly six-foot—and fit, with strong hands and toned biceps well-defined. She wore a clean, fashionable Western shirt, the nape of her chocolate-brown neck and her Adam's apple shaded under her strong chin and the broad brim of her coordinating cowboy hat. She covered her mouth as she laughed a nervous laugh, and seeing her, they said, your eyes might have drifted, your peripheral vision scanning her, following the line of her taut leg up from the boot to the hollow of her tight black skirt, where you might have suspected, the regulars winked, hidden up there, tucked up in that little shimmy of charmeuse, hung her penis.

"She was a man!" George crowed. He delivered the news like a punch line. "The lady was a man!"

In addition to being black, I realized, she was also transgender.

My first thought was, what the hell was she doing in a place like this? Caucasian nearly to a man and as conservative as the '50s South, this was not a place you'd expect to see a black trans woman sidled up to the bar. But Wonder Valley was also close enough to LA and on an established enough byway that of course The Palms saw its share of hipsters and day-trippers who regularly stopped by to take pictures and maybe grab a burger and a brew. Holiday weekends, like the art event a couple of weeks before, brought a parade of passers-through and consequently bar regulars were pretty tolerant of outsiders, often teasing them good-naturedly and laughing together about them after they left. Thinking about it now, that someone was stabbed for being different was actually pretty shocking to me. I pieced the story together gradually.

It occurred the day after Halloween. Just after seven in the evening, Natalie and Bud Barber arrived at The Palms for a drink, taking places at the bar. As usual on a Sunday night, George, with his brillo of beard, was bartending.

Apparently, it all happened very quickly. Taking a break from playing pool, Natalie joined Bud out front for a cigarette. He was out there with the skinhead Fred Harris. There, Harris started up some shit with Natalie, called her a nigger. Bud stepped between them and urged her to go back inside.

In there, she grumbled to a regular, the one with slicked-back hair and a white Fu Manchu. "Fuck that fool," she said. "Fuck all this Wonder Valley bullshit." Then Bud's screams resonated through the bar, "You motherfucker! You motherfucker!" Natalie leaned over to the regular and told him she was going to take care of the situation, whatever it was. She was going to regulate. That skinhead motherfucker didn't scare her. She strode back outside.

The moon hung full, heavy overhead. It cast a gray pall over the parking lot, washing the color from the few remaining cars and leaving a void of black in the shadows. Out there, Natalie found herself alone. She called for Bud. Nothing. She stepped out of the warm glow shining from the bar's front door and into the cold light of the moon. A floodlight colored the peeling paint of The Palms' sign and its splintering plywood buffalo. Natalie walked around Bud's truck, parked where he'd left it. She looked around the other cars, too, no one. She shrugged and turned to go back inside.

Fred Harris crept out of the black void. As Natalie swung around, she found herself face-to-face with him. He smiled. Then, with a quick flick of his Buck knife, he slashed her throat.

Her severed artery fountained to the beat of her heart. She shrieked and grabbed her neck, sinking slowly to her knees, down into an ever-widening pool of her own blood, black as tar in the moonlight. Fred Harris, into the void, once again disappeared.

This was a fascinating story, I thought, made all the more so because it happened in my bar, witnessed by people I knew. I pitched the story to Tim, my editor. I knew the magazine could no longer pay me, but I volunteered to do it anyway. Tim, however, balked. No depth to it, he said.

"A skinhead slashing a black transgender woman's throat is a hate crime," he said. "It's news-worthy, maybe, but not magazine material. Besides, we don't want to sensationalize this kind of thing, give spotlight to this kind of behavior."

"But Fred Harris wasn't being charged with a hate crime," I told him. "Perhaps there's more to the story. In fact, maybe that is the story. Maybe it shows the profound institutionalized racism of this part of the country where a known white supremacist can stab a trans African-American woman and not be charged with hate." I had heard that Bud Barber had been warned about Fred Harris, he was a racist, people told him, Natalie might be in danger around him. Still, Tim wasn't interested.

I drove out to the place where Bud and Natalie lived. The Ostrich Farm, as everyone called it, was a maze of six-foot fences, pens, and whitewashed stalls sitting by itself up on the northern edge of the valley. The ostriches were long gone. Tumbleweeds grew in the sand of the corrals.

Records showed that when the Barbers bought the Ostrich Farm it was the cheapest property in all of California with five acres and a well. Natalie got it with money from a settlement or something, the finalization of a divorce from the woman she'd married. A foreclosure, the place came with a squatter. The old man who had homesteaded the land and built the cabin, raised the ostriches and over-leveraged his investments had simply stayed on when the bank took the place from under him. Evicted and bankrupt, the Barbers dragged him and his trailer and his junk to the expanse of desert to the north, and there he stayed, supplied with water and power by them, until, at 85, he died.

Other than that old squatter, however, Bud and Natalie were slow to meet people in Wonder Valley, surrounded as they were by mostly open desert punctuated by only the occasional abandoned homesteader's shack. Homes, actual lived-in properties, were few and far between. Bud at least got out, though. He pounded sand looking for work as a handyman around the valley and even went to The Palms occasionally in the afternoons. Pizza Richard and others knew him. Natalie, on the other hand, stayed home. She occupied herself fixing-up their cabin and trying to make a few bucks on internet schemes—difficult when all she had for access was dial-up. She stayed out of sight mostly, worried about the reactions she'd receive in such a conservative area. She had been to The Palms only a couple times before, once the morning before being stabbed.

I dug up what I could about her background. She had grown up a dark-skinned boy in white suburbia, son of a Dutch engineer and an Indonesian mother. She wasn't actually African-American at all, it turned out, though raised by immigrant parents in a mixed-race neighborhood of LA's hinterlands, she, as a boy, fell into the diction and mannerisms of those around her, began to identify with the image projected upon her by others. And that boy grew up to be quite the player. In fact, her brother told me that, in those days, that young man could have had any woman he wanted. Women, he said, found him exotic and attractive. He hopped chick to chick, bed to bed. Maybe he had something to prove. He married young and had children. I found his wedding pictures through a Google search. They show a debonair young man with slicked-back hair in a brat-pack tux with the sleeves rolled up, a cigarette draped from his mouth. He looked cool, polished, suave, someone I'd have liked to have known—not a woman trapped in a man's body or whatever the cliché for that phenomenon is.

I read about gender dysphoria, the sense that one's gender identity was at odds with one's physical body, and I found it just baffling. I looked at those pictures of Natalie as a dude and wondered how it was that he came to realize or conclude or admit that he was really a she? And a black woman at that? I was sure she legitimately considered herself a woman and I had no problem accepting that as a broad fact, but I was curious as to the process, the mechanism of that realization, the timeline. Clearly, she as a young man must have been conflicted. The first marriage didn't work and before long they divorced. Soon, though, he wed again— an older woman this time, more a business partnership than a marriage, it seemed. It was during that time that he began his transition, the sex reassignment counseling and soul searching. Then, with doctor-prescribed hormone therapy and psychiatric oversight, that dapper young man became Natalie.

As part of her transformation, Natalie played the tranny scene in the bars of LA. She dated men with the same abandon she, as a young man, had dated women. She split with the older woman and eventually settled down with a German man, moving to his apartment in the San Fernando Valley. It was through him that she met Bud— he was the man's best friend. Eventually, she and Bud began an affair together and developed a bond. She was returning home with Bud one afternoon, in fact, when they discovered their friend on the floor of his apartment. Of a bad heart, he had died. Natalie called for help, but the police locked her out of her home. She wasn't married, not on the lease, the landlord wouldn't vouch for her. She lost all her things. She and Bud had remained a couple ever since.

Bud's biker looks, his goat's tuft of beard, his hair pulled into a knot behind his head were what had attracted Natalie. He reminded her of her brothers, all of whom had been in jail, one, for murder, in prison. Natalie, though, eschewed the drugs and crime, the gangster affiliations and associated violence that her brothers had fallen into, but still, that life fascinated her. Despite Bud's bad-boy looks, however, he was clean, had never been in jail, had no criminal record. He hadn't even had a speeding ticket in years.

Fred Harris, on the other hand, was the real deal. Natalie knew his type when she first saw him through the Ostrich Farm's dark windows. He sat on the front porch of the decrepit cabin across the road drinking beer, throwing the empties into the bare sand of the yard. Right away she recognized that prison yard build, his skinhead tattoos. And through the window as she watched him, she felt a certain attraction. She knew his kind, but she also knew there'd be trouble.

§ § §

The last time Fred Harris was in The Palms, he sat at the bar and leered at the other customers over his beer. Roger, the ruddy Marine I met there, saw him come in. "If you had seen him," he said, "you'd have wanted to look at him, have wanted to eye him up and down, his shaved head was tattooed with flames, but you could feel those menacing eyes of his, like Charles Manson's, and you'd do anything not to meet them."

Harris, though, didn't go to the bar much—at least not inside. He'd stop out front on occasion and wait in his car for someone to bring him beer or cigarettes or whatever it was he wanted. He didn't go in much, I'm told, because, for one thing, the terms of his parole prohibited him from entering drinking establishments. He could be returned to jail just for being caught inside. Beyond that, however, he had been banned from The Palms in particular for pulling a knife on Mark Bennett, the bartender, angry that the bar had run out of whiskey. It took Bennett's baseball bat to convince him finally to leave.

And that wasn't the last time he caused trouble in the bar, either. Sneaking around back onto the patio sometime later, he flicked knives into the picnic table, taunting bystanders to pull them out. He picked up Loretta, Diana's younger sister, by her throat, squeezing her windpipe. Bystanders stood by, mouths agape, sure they were witnessing a murder. With a pistol, Roger compelled him to stop, encouraged him to go. I'd heard this story from Roger, but I hadn't until now put two and two together.

This type of behavior seemed to be a recurring thing with Harris. He flashed easily to anger, his knee-jerk emotion hate. In his forty-seven years, he had racked up a string of priors that included assault, battery with gross bodily injury, witness intimidation, Latino bashing, and felony possession of narcotics. It was the hate crimes and felony stalking, however, the threatening and harassing of his neighbors that got him his most recent time in the pen. He thought the neighbors were Jewish. He blared blinding lights through their windows all night, blasted anti-Semitic hate songs at them until their children knew the words by heart and sang them for the judge in court: "*We're taking down the ZOG machine Jew, by Jew, by Jew. The white man marches on.*" The fact that the neighbors weren't Jewish didn't save him from a three-year stint in the joint. Upon parole, he found the decrepit cabin across the corrugated road from Bud and Natalie way out there in Wonder Valley.

Natalie was hanging laundry in the Ostrich Farm yard when Harris first came over. In a hot summer's twilight, she'd been out in a bikini top—out of sight, she thought, unaccustomed as she was to having neighbors. Walking back to the cabin in the deep dusk, she heard him over at her gate. He called to her, had brought a carton of beer, the half-filled remains of a 12-pack. He handed her one over the fence. In the gloom, she noticed his smile.

Natalie was immediately taken by Harris's charm. She also found his danger thrilling. The intensity in those eyes, like a wild animal's, instilled fear. But Natalie was a lion tamer, she knew she could control him. She flirted with him, giggled at his jokes, covering her mouth with a hand as she laughed. In the days after Harris first met her, he began coming over regularly, crossing the dirt road with a 12-pack. At first, Natalie avoided being alone with him. Slowly, though, he gained Bud's trust. After a short while, he moved from the decrepit cabin to a single-wide down by The Palms, but they all stayed friendly. One night, Harris even took Bud and Natalie to a restaurant in town, then to a bar to shoot some pool. Harris paid for everything. Returning to Wonder Valley, they went to The Palms— Natalie's first time there. By this time, they were all well drunk. This was the night, as it happened, that Harris grabbed Loretta by the throat on the patio—Natalie thought he was going to kill her. When the gun came out, she intervened and convinced Harris they should leave. The three went back to his place.

At Harris's, Bud and Natalie fought. It was late and Bud had to work in the morning, a handyman job. But Natalie was drunk and testy, she didn't want to leave. When she was like this, Bud knew, she was beyond reason. He left her curled up on Fred Harris's floor.

In the dark, Harris melted. Through the night, he told Natalie of his childhood, the violence and abuse he suffered. Then he kissed her. Fred Harris, she knew, was under her spell. In the morning, they lay entwined together, Natalie's burnished body in Harris's white arms.

"What are we going to do about Dude?" he asked her.

"What are we going to do about Dude?" Natalie let go a nervous laugh, but she saw the cold seriousness in his eyes. He thought she was his now, she realized, and Bud was in the way of his claiming his prize.

Over the following weeks Harris got ever more serious. For her it was just sex, she told herself, for thrills, but he had fallen in love with her, had turned into her kitten, was no longer a tiger. Still, he prodded her to leave Bud. "What are we going to do about Dude?"

They were nude together in the saloon of the Ostrich Farm one afternoon when Bud returned home unexpectedly. He fumed but Natalie laughed it off.

"Motherfucker drank himself impotent!" she said after Harris left. "Could hardly get it up anyway!" It was nothing. She had just been bored. Being caught in the act, though, Natalie broke off the affair. Bud agreed he should spend more time with her at home. They began to put their relationship back together.

A few weeks after Natalie ended the affair, though, Harris started calling, late night calls imploring, cajoling her to come back to him. Then came the threats. He'd kill Dude, he said, how would she like that? He'd kill them both if she didn't come back to him. She unplugged the phone. Then, two weeks later, the night after Halloween, Harris found them at The Palms.

Bud and Natalie were at the bar finishing their beers when Harris entered. Neither of them could meet his gaze. Harris, though, mad-dogged Natalie as he walked across the room, pulling up a stool a few down from Bud. The bar fell silent. Natalie leaned into Bud, "He keeps staring at me," she said.

Jesus, Bud thought. He and Natalie were just about to leave, and now he wanted to grab Natalie by the arm and just get the hell out of there. But Bud knew Harris, he knew he preyed on the weak. He worried that their leaving in the face of his arrival might embolden him, that he might take their leaving just as he walked in as a sign of fear, of weakness, that he might follow them out and there might be trouble. He feared that if he didn't disarm the situation, they'd forever have to watch their backs. Bud sighed and ordered another beer.

Trying to remain casual—nothing's wrong, everything's cool— Bud challenged Harris to game of pool, just like old times, like nothing had happened. He suggested doubles, he and Harris versus Natalie and the bar regular with the white Fu Manchu. Bud racked the balls and Harris broke; he was affable and friendly, the charming neighbor they had known. The regular took his shots, then

Bud. It was Natalie's turn, but she was still back at the bar talking. Bud and Harris waited, then gave up and stepped out front together for a smoke. Natalie soon followed.

Outside, Bud rolled her a cigarette. They smoked under the light of the moon. Natalie, with a couple beers in her, got mouthy. "Man, don't be calling me at home, fool! I told you, this shit's over!" She mocked Harris for his impotency. Harris flushed. "Nigga, you're just a pussy!" she said, laughing at him again.

"*Nigger?*" he screeched, flashing to anger. "Who are you calling a nigger? You're the nigger!" He pushed up into her face. Bud squeezed between them. "Go back inside!" he told Natalie. Grumbling, she went back into the bar. Bud watched her go.

As he was turning back around, Harris's hand came out from behind his back, the chrome steel of his Buck knife flashing white in the moonlight. He lunged. Bud, more out of reflex than reaction, axe-kicked the knife from his hand. It clanked to the ground at their feet. Harris stared at Bud in stunned silence, his nostrils flaring with each breath. Bud took a step backwards.

"We don't want no trouble, man," he said. "Come on." He again tried to disarm the situation. "Let's just go back inside and finish our game." Harris crouched down like an animal leering up at Bud as he fumbled for his knife. Bud watched him return it behind his back to the sheath. He pushed open the bar's door, but Harris didn't follow. He had softened, though, his tone changed. He seemed courteous, apologetic. From just outside the warm glow of the doorway he called to Bud.

"I need to talk to you," he said.

"Talk to me in here," Bud replied from the threshold. Harris smiled a sheepish smile. Bud backed into the bar further, but Harris implored him.

"Come on, man. Come here for just a second." Bud stepped back outside.

I'm puzzled still as to why Bud went back out there. But then again, few people I talked to thought Harris would actually stab anybody. Most figured his psycho skinhead hater-thing was really just a bunch of horseshit.

"Come on," Harris said again. "Come here for just a second." He smiled that smile of his, a naughty boy's self-conscious smirk. Then his eyes went cold. He sprang. Bud felt the buck knife's polished steel slice painlessly into his throat, piercing his esophagus, his larynx, his trachea. Harris pulled the knife back as quickly as he'd jabbed it, its blade now candy apple crimson in the warm light of the door. He held Bud's gaze for a heartbeat, then fled into the void of darkness.

Bud grabbed his neck. "You motherfucker! You motherfucker!" he screamed. Anger and adrenaline surged through him. He pushed through the bar's door and strode back inside. Duped, he wanted Harris brought to justice. Blood frothed up in his mouth as he panted. Seeing him, someone grabbed a t-shirt from the sale rack and pressed it to his neck. "Call 911!" they yelled to George behind the bar. George just stood and stared, immobile.

At the other end of the bar, Natalie was agitated after her exchange with Harris. Standing with her back to the door, she was bitching to a regular about all the Wonder Valley bullshit. She heard Bud yelling, but when he burst through the door, he passed behind her. Distracted as she was, she somehow missed him coming back inside. Hearing Bud yell, however, pissed her off. She leaned into the regular, told him she was going to put that Fred Harris in check. Then she went outside. Moments later, everyone heard her shriek. By the time Bud reached her, she was slumped down to her knees, painting the cracked, sand-covered asphalt with her blood.

Bud ran back into the bar. His heart throbbed in his ears as he grabbed a handful of t-shirts. "Call 911!" he screamed again, his chest bloodied by the flow from his neck and the drizzle from his mouth. Adrenaline surging and clearly unaware of the extent of his own injuries, he ran back outside to help Natalie. George fumbled with the phone and stammered confused instructions to the emergency operator. At the operator's insistence, George handed the phone to another at the bar, who then passed it to another. "And people wonder why you don't hang around in bars," the operator quipped. Minutes ticked by before the operator dispatched paramedics. In the meantime, George slammed the bar's heavy wooden front door, sliding a timber through steel loops across it, locking the victims with the perpetrator outside.

It took paramedics forty minutes to arrive on the scene. By then, the regulars had gone. Deputies cordoned off the parking lot, strung up crime scene tape, measured blood stains, took pictures, got a description of the perp for the wire. They wouldn't let anybody in or out of the bar.

Now, The Palms sits at the geographic heart of Wonder Valley, in an area of open desert interspersed with distantly strewn shacks. That isolation and long response times give a man ample time and multiple options to flee a crime. I figure Harris could have dropped into the wash behind the bar, for example, skirted the one or two inhabited places until he came to the highway, then jumped a ride to the state line. Or he could have bee-lined south over the mountains and miles of uninterrupted desert to Mexico. But he did none of that.

Hours later, as deputies wrapped-up their investigation, a homeless drifter's little dog yapped and yapped at the bar's banged-up dumpster. Gathering his pet, the drifter found Fred Harris sitting behind it. He still had the bloody knife in his hand.

Harris died in prison a few months later. The news reported liver failure as the cause of death; it was the second Centinela Prison death in a week. There'd be an investigation into prison conditions. Shortly thereafter, if you'd gone to the tobacco store in town, you might have seen a coffee can on the counter with Harris's picture on it. Family members were asking for donations. They were taking a collection for his funeral. Rumor had it Fred Harris didn't want a prison cremation. It was his last request, the rumor said: he worried his ashes would be mingled with those of niggers.

§ § §

Natalie didn't much leave the Ostrich Farm after that. When she talked to me about Fred Harris, she touched the nut of brown flesh at the base of her neck, her scar, the location of her stab wound. "I loved him," she told me.

When the ambulance arrived at The Palms that night, they found Natalie stabilized, the blood flow stopped by the t-shirts Bud used as compresses. She called family from the ambulance. At the hospital, a nurse thought she must have come from a Halloween party, that she was masquerading as a woman, her Western wear a costume. A helicopter airlifted Bud to a hospital in LA for surgery, then to ICU. Harris had severed an artery; it had been hemorrhaging into his throat, filling his stomach with blood. As he attended to Natalie's wounds, he nearly bled-out. He was not expected to live.

At The Palms after the stabbing, I sat with the regulars as they talked about the he-she, that *thing* that was stabbed.

"*She* was a man, the *woman* was a *man!*" George had said to me. "An *it*," he sniggered.

"What was *it* doing messing around with a guy like Fred Harris anyway?" someone else chimed in. "Arguing with that guy?"

"*It* was asking for it," another said. "*It* just needs to learn how to keep *its* fucking mouth shut." Clearly, in the minds of the regulars, blame for the attack was hers. I wanted to stand up for her, to remind them that being mouthy or transgender or having an affair with a guy like that didn't justify her getting stabbed. Being stupid or obnoxious or just different doesn't warrant the death penalty. But I kept my mouth shut. It wasn't my place to correct them, not my place to attempt to explain Natalie's gender and racial identity to others. Not that I could have, not that I'd even know. As a middle age white man that would have been overstepping, I told myself. Or maybe I was just afraid the others would turn their judgements on me.

I again pitched the story to Tim. "It's not what you think," I said.

But he was even less interested in a bizarre love triangle than a hate crime.

I, however, was fixated. My interest in Bud and Natalie began to feel voyeuristic. I started hanging out with them after Bud recovered under the guise of writing their story, going over to the Ostrich Farm sometimes in the evenings with a box of beer and eventually developing a friendship with them that would cause a rift between me and the Sibleys, the owners of The Palms. Even while we became friends, however, I studied Natalie like a lab specimen. To me she seemed to drift across gender lines like a shapeshifter, sometimes fully woman, other times male, but most often something else, a third sex, a mélange, something in-between—yet comfortable with who and what she was. I remember the time when she first leaned over to me and whispered, "I used to be a man." She then sent me nude pictures of herself and invited me to have an affair with her.

My initial shock embarrassed me as much as her proposition. I had always considered myself culturally aware, but this tested my ability to overcome my white, middle-class, suburban upbringing. I dwelled on it. I imagined us having sex, lying in the saloon of the Ostrich Farm. It seemed natural, but then again it didn't. I thought about Bud and Fred Harris, men in love with a woman with male parts. How did they see her? I read that men attracted to gynandromorphs—trans women—are heterosexual, which is consistent with what Bud told me. "I'm not gay," he had said. But Fred Harris, falling in love with not just a trans woman, but someone who racially he professed to hate, was another thing altogether. Maybe Natalie gave him plausible deniability, though: she wasn't African American, she just acted like it, having assumed that culture as she had her gender. Maybe all that freed Harris of some of his congenital prejudices and knee-jerk animosity and bigotry. Maybe it allowed him to act on some of his closeted urges. Who knows the abuse he suffered as a child, abuse that informed his sexuality, cementing his abhorrence or attractions to particular deeds or acts or creeds or people. Whatever she was and whomever she might resemble, Natalie was none of the things Harris had learned to hate, and maybe that gave him license to love, though ultimately being jilted by a black trans woman was probably more than he could accept. Maybe that's why he stabbed her. Who knows? It's not my place to speculate, I realized. Besides, Natalie didn't believe Harris was trying to kill her. Her wounds, she said, were non-life threatening. Bud's stabbing, on the other hand, was attempted murder. That, she reminded me, was what Fred Harris always said he was going to do about Dude.

Chapter 11

I had heard about Larkin McAllister before I ever met him, about his on-going squabbles with county code enforcement over the garbage dump at his property, the escalating fines. He was a bit of an odd duck, people said, obviously queer, a fairy, gayer than a purse full of rainbows. "Why would you ever want to meet him?" they asked.

I didn't know why I wanted to meet him. I guess meeting and getting to know Natalie whetted a fascination with those who didn't fit the norm of Wonder Valley. Not that there could be anything considered normal out here. "Odd duck" was a relative term. Nutty Ned surely qualified as one, as did my asshole neighbor Craig who still dragged the road by my place to create dust. George Stadler was obviously one, too, and others who I'd only ever encountered while working on the Census, those who lived cloistered from the world behind thicket walls of scraggly trees, who'd run you off at the barrel of a rifle, whose mummified remains go unfound for months like the old woman from over on Betty Lane or the guy whose outline stains the floor of a place out by the Sheephole. But Larkin seemed different. He wasn't a recluse. Everyone knew him. Yet he was an outcast here even in this land of outcasts.

He lived on Boom Boom, up near the Marine Corps bombing range. I entered his compound through a gap in the hedge of used tires that surrounded his place. A terracotta statue of the Virgin Mary stood in demure silence beside a collection of Mercedes Benzes. I pressed past her, deeper into the parcel, making a large loop around the homestead cabin at its center, the garage and a little camper next to it, around mobile homes, a dozen of them, lined up together like tractor trailers unloading. As I drove, I circled limos, Caddies, yachts, an old Corvair and an English Cortina, a few trucks, water trailers, commercial appliances, ovens, freezers, washing machines, dryers, wheels and tires and parts, a trailer stacked with oriental rugs, a sea of housewares and bric-a-brac, chandeliers and sconces, patio furniture, tables, chairs, wooden beams and French doors, and sundry stacks of windows.

I stopped my truck and got out. A path to the cabin threaded through stacks of ornamental iron, used lumber in graded piles, commercial heating and air conditioning units, and feet upon feet of old ducting. The cabin, I could tell, was unlivable. The windows were blocked with stacks of stuff, the breezeway filled to the rafters with boxes of books and magazines and *objets d'art*. Nothing stirred. The wind swayed lamps swagged from a tree in the yard. I paused. "Hello? Anybody home?"

From under the camper next to the garage pitbulls swarmed out at me like hornets from a hive. They growled savagely, circling me, the ones behind nipping at my ass. I spun around trying to keep them at bay. The standoff lasted more than a minute before the door of the little camper sprung wide and Larkin appeared in the opening.

"Oh hush!" he hollered at the dogs. He wore a pair of boxers and some slip-on shoes. His body was smooth and hairless, deeply tanned, his skin stretched taught over his bulge of belly. "Can I help you?" he asked me.

"I'm looking for Richard McAllister," I said using Larkin's given name. "I thought he might be interesting to talk to."

"Well," Larkin replied, "you've come to the right place."

§ § §

It was in the *San Francisco Chronicle* that columnist Herb Caen suggested Larkin McAllister trade the John Spencer House, the Victorian mansion where he lived, for the intersection of Larkin and McAllister Streets, the location of the seat of San Francisco government. Larkin understood that as a call to run for office.

Caen, however, might have been referring to Larkin's unconventional use of John Spencer House. He may have been drawing a parallel, perhaps, between Larkin's flamboyantly gay lifestyle and his Machiavellian manner of attaining his goals with the antics and politics of San Francisco Mayor George Moscone and openly gay Supervisor Harvey Milk.

You may have seen Larkin's house. If you happen to be an aficionado of a certain kind of movie, in particular those that featured performers with one-word names like "Angelique" and double entendre titles like "The Filthy Rich," you might recognize Larkin's Queen Anne mansion. In fact, if you could tear your eyes away from the action, the writhing bodies in the foreground, you could see Larkin in the background of one such movie playing the piano. Unlike the other actors, Larkin is fully clothed.

"I get $1,000 a day," Caen quoted Larkin explaining why he would debauch such a beautiful residence. "And besides, I get to watch."

It wasn't just the movies that raised eyebrows. Larkin's parties were legendary, the porn stars and politicians, actors and musicians snorting blow off his glass-topped Louis XV desk. All the beautiful people attended, and Larkin would invite everyone to sleep with him. "Why don't you stay over tonight," he'd say. "You can all share my bed." Many would accept. He was young and fit, then, a vegetarian. In the morning, he might even show up to breakfast nude, no matter who was there—the women working for him, the boys from the night before, the trick or two he'd picked up over on Polk Street, his construction crew, it didn't matter. With Larkin, it was expected.

He still slept nude, he told me, here in Wonder Valley—if it was hot, that is—a fan blowing the heavy stale air of his little camper over his tan, round body. He slept alone, now, though, on a futon on the floor. He was lonely, he told me. Most days he saw no one at all.

Some days he didn't even go outside. When the wind was up, its force could be staggering. The wind often buffeted the little camper, threatening to shake it from its stands; it roared and whistled, ripping at everything, tearing at the roof hatches until they finally gave way. It found entrance through the smallest cracks, carrying dust as fine as talc that maddened Larkin's sinuses. The wind in Wonder Valley could blow for days without cease, or it could come lightning quick with a tornado force, dust devils strong enough to knock you to the ground, to fling your things about. It ripped Larkin's swamp cooler from his roof.

The floods had been worse, he said. The slightest rain could yield a tremendous flash flood that washed through his property, undermining the camper, carrying away or burying belongings and leaving his homestead parcel a muddy wallow. The barrier levee of used tires lining the perimeter proved an inadequate defense.

After that first visit, I returned often to talk to him. We'd sit and chat under the shade of a mesquite tree, chandeliers hanging from its branches. There, he fanned himself with a piece of wind-blown cardboard. It offered little respite from the heat. During the summer, everything crackled in the Wonder Valley inferno, but it seemed especially hot at Larkin's. The metal of the cars and the chairs and the housewares and the appliances radiated the desert, impossible to touch, the white sand as blinding as the sun. When no one was around, Larkin sat nude in the shade of that mesquite tree, he told me. And if he had water, he poured it over himself, over his sparsely thatched blonde head, his gray stubble of beard, his slick, hairless body.

He seemed to enjoy my visits. He suffered to remember the past. He worried that his mind, like so much else, was slipping away from him. "Memory is precious," he said. "It's all I have left."

In San Francisco, years ago, the John Spencer House was only one of Larkin's properties. It is now the grandest of the "Painted

Ladies," on the National Register of Historic Places, regularly voted the most beautiful home in the city. It sits on three lots across the street from Buena Vista Park. When he bought the home in the seventies, however, it was derelict: weeds and sapling trees obscured the view of the house from the street. He leveraged his Edwardian apartment building, his other Victorians, to afford it. I verified all this through public records. He'd acquired those buildings by buying the unpaid mortgages, then foreclosing on the deadbeat owners. Larkin had a genius for going through the tax rolls, had an eye for hidden beauty, paying as little as $2,500 for what are now, because of him, national treasures. But he paid a relative fortune for the Spencer House: $258,000. Like the others, however, he transformed it—everything it is today, Larkin made it.

He told me about his life in San Francisco in a syrupy southern drawl. It was in Spencer House that he threw his most lavish parties, had the most beautiful boys around him, and girls too, he made love to all of them, singly and all together, not knowing where one's parts ended and another's began. "You wouldn't believe it," he said, wouldn't believe how markedly, how astonishingly, his life back then contrasted with how he lived now.

"Out here, it feels like I'm in a constant tug-of-war with these people out here! They broke into my cabin, they stole all my jewelry, my antique furniture, my paintings and china. They stole the radiator out of my Chevy truck, they took the wheels off the Ford and the lug nuts off a boat trailer!" He said people came shopping, Wonder Valley shopping, walking and dragging and driving off with whatever wasn't nailed down.

"I recovered my pick-up from Denise Reynolds's garage and a Mercedes from the water delivery guy. I found my trailer on the other side of the valley! The cops do nothing. They don't care. No one is arrested. No one is ever arrested!" Because of this, Larkin worried about his security, his stuff, worried himself sick, grinding his jaw at night until his teeth shattered, chipping and falling from his mouth until so few remained he couldn't eat a proper meal.

"As if I could get a proper meal, with what money?" As he said this, he smiled a tight grimace, his shards of shattered teeth like the porcelain of broken teacups, artifacts of fatter times. Dental care was beyond his reach: the dentist wanted two hundred dollars a tooth to pull each of the broken stumps, then thousands more for a bridge of acrylic dentures. The wire rims of his glasses were bent and misshapen, too, the prescription for a younger man, a man of brighter times, not the destitute senior whose bulb of a nose supports them, whose small, wet, gray eyes see only an impressionistic, insensible world though them.

By contrast, Larkin had been immersed in beauty in San Francisco. He had a wonderful sense of aesthetics, an old friend of his told me, the eye of an artist. Beauty was his passion, pleasure his devotion. He hired workers, formed crews of starving writers, artists, musicians to remodel his properties. Many of them had gone on to great success. A renowned writer and philosopher, once Larkin's painting foreman, told me he owes his career to Larkin. Larkin was tolerant, he said, flexible, and he paid his workers in cash.

"He'd ask us how many hours we worked and pay us in hundred-dollar bills." When Larkin ran out of money, he'd go to the bank. He was gregarious, colorful and engaging. The bankers always gave him more. He shopped exclusively at Saks Fifth Avenue and I. Magnin back then, drove Cadillacs, Mercedes Benzes, some of which he still had, oxidized under the brutal Wonder Valley sun. He went to the finest restaurants, attended the opera, took his entire crew of twenty-five to the San Francisco opening of "A Chorus Line." He also spent his evenings in the city's famous bathhouses.

"There were the most beautiful boys there," he told me, a grin sweeping across his face. "Everyone walked around nude—I walked around nude, because, if you've got it, flaunt it." Larkin told me about his nights in those bathhouses, about the special rooms where men undulated together in pleasure, their bodies as one on mats on the floor.

Friends remembered him bringing young men home with him, home to populate the emptiness of Spencer House. He begged them to stay forever. He offered them money, jobs, if they needed work, like that one boy, so sweet and innocent. Larkin implored the foreman to let him work for the painting crew. That boy climbed the scaffolding to scrape paint wearing the fireman's helmet and tutu he'd arrived in the night before. By lunch, however, he'd had enough and he, like the others, went away.

Larkin had years ago left San Francisco, though, and moved to Southern California. The liability of Spencer House had exceeded his income, interest rates had skyrocketed into double digits and the bankers no longer took his calls—a story that rang familiar to me. The money well had dried up. He lost the house. Besides, he had married, he said, to a woman, Marja. She had ended up at Spencer House, stayed after a party, maybe, just showed up, Larkin couldn't remember. She became his project. He would leave San Francisco, he decided, leave the gay lifestyle. He would settle down. He could no longer afford that city anyway. He went to Palm Springs, an investor's dream. But after a number of failed real estate deals there, the money grew scarce and the cocaine stopped flowing. Marja found another source for both and left him. Eventually even Palm Springs priced Larkin out.

Seduced by ever cheaper real estate and a yearning to reestablish himself, Larkin pressed further east, up into the Mojave. He found five acres and a cabin here in Wonder Valley, a probate sale, a gold mine at that price. He bought it. He acquired single family homes near the Marine base, too, and trailers in a trailer park farther west, leveraging one to get another. But then, deployed to war, his Marines Corps tenants left them vacant. The bank took them back. The houses were gone. The mobile homes he dragged back and lined up like tractor trailers next to his Wonder Valley cabin.

Back then, his mother lived with him. He had set her up with a bedroom of her own, a TV. There was still, in those days, space in the cabin to move around. With the water tank out front, water still ran, the toilet still flushed. Larkin slept on a couch. But things weren't going well for him, the money had run out, those foreclosures had taken his real estate in town. In despair, he increased his drinking, vodka and gin from half-gallon plastic jugs mixed with whatever juice he got from the food bank giveaway. His mother's health had been failing, too, and she quietly slipped into dementia. She got a check, though, Social Security from her years of service as a schoolteacher. She got Meals-On-Wheels. Rumors circulated Larkin tied her to the bed when he left her.

"Nonsense," Larkin retorted when I asked him about it. Regardless, one day while he was in town, something happened to her. "I came home to find her out of bed, a bloody mess. Perhaps a dog bit her. Or she fell, or I'd grabbed-her arm—not hard, it didn't have to be hard, you know how tissue-paper frail a woman's skin is at that age." He took her to the ER. After they returned home, deputies came by, investigating. In the cabin, they found Larkin's mother on a futon on the floor. "She liked it there, I told them. She could have lain down on the couch if she wanted, but she chose that futon on the floor. She liked to lay there and watch TV." After the deputies left Larkin thought everything was fine, but they came back later and arrested him, charged him with elder abuse. He spent the night in jail, fought the charges for months. The authorities took his mother to a home in town. She could no longer live with him, the court mandated. Larkin eventually returned her to her house in Mississippi, where, that winter, alone, she died.

Winters had been hard on Larkin since. Thoughts of his mother ate at him, as did the cold. In winter, he said, he slept in a stocking cap, a knit mask that completely covered his face. He wore layers, sweatpants over sweatpants, socks over socks, jackets over sweatshirts over sweatshirts. His breath billowed in white puffs. He was often too cold to sleep.

On warm winter days, I sat in the sun with him, out of the wind, if we were lucky. While we talked, he wore that stocking cap, pulled up to his forehead to reveal his face. He welcomed my visits, he said.

"You're my only friend." I came to consider him a friend too.

He had tried to maintain other friendships out here over the years, most recently with Gladys and her husband who he'd met through his mother. They lived on fifteen acres across from the abandoned jojoba farm, below George Stadler's singlewide. Larkin's mother had been quite close with them, and though they were considerably older than him, he found them comforting to be around after his mother died. When Gladys's husband passed away, Larkin became like a son to her. Elderly and alone, she had gotten herself in trouble with the county after she brought the entire inventory of junk and stuff from her defunct thrift store home to her property. Neighbors wanted it all removed. Code Enforcement inspected, they cited. They issued a clean-up mandate beyond what she, a woman in her nineties, could do, followed by fines above what she, on a fixed income, could pay. Larkin felt for the poor old woman. He brought her meals. He offered her advice. He had an idea.

If Gladys transferred title to her properties to him, he told her, it would render the enforcements against her moot. He would borrow against the properties and give her $10,000 for the lot—the fifteen acres by the jojoba farm and the other five over by the airport. She could live there the rest of her life, he said. He'd take care of her. Just as she signed the papers, however, she died.

Titles in hand, though, Larkin took Gladys's place to the bank. The real estate boom of the early 2000s was on. Without appraisals, without proof of income, without documents, the bank gave him a line of credit equaling hundreds of thousands of dollars. With that cash, he bought commercial appliances and carved wood beams and carpets and bronzes and art and antiques at auction to outfit the house he planned to build. He carted home the best of Gladys's junk, bought cars and boats and recreational vehicles, as he amassed a piecemeal collection of the accoutrements of the good life, the life he once had, the one he knew, the one he longed to remember.

County Code Enforcement started proceedings against him for

the condition of Gladys's place almost immediately. Then they began on Boom Boom.

With the money he'd borrowed, Larkin hired an employee to live in Gladys's place, clean it up, remodel it. This employee was a trusted friend, they had worked together in his San Francisco days, but now he lived in Las Vegas and was down on his luck. It was a handshake deal—there'd be something in it for the employee, Larkin promised. But when the employee arrived, he came with a wife, Denise. Denise, Larkin said, all but ruined him.

"She came here stealing with impunity," he said, "She took my flute, my ceramic figurines, one of a set of cushions! Who steals one cushion? She even broke apart my stained-glass windows to scavenge materials for crafts!" He grew frantic as talked. He waved his arms in stunned disbelief. "She stole my truck—police recovered it from Gladys's garage where she lived. She took the wheels from another truck, and the radiator from another one. She has a taste for meth, everybody knows that. That's why she steals, she steals to get money for drugs." Finally, the employee friend became ill, a brain tumor, but he left his wife, Denise, behind at Gladys's.

"When I finally got Denise out," Larkin said, "the place was worse than when I got it. And just to spite me, she encouraged people to dump their trash there, too."

I had seen Gladys's place before, on a ride-along with county volunteers—my dad, actually. They took me to the dump, as he called it, a fifteen-acre homegrown landfill. Happy to be back in uniform, my father volunteered with the Citizens on Patrol, a sheriff's auxiliary organization that visited seniors and shut-ins. Gladys's was on my dad's tour of Wonder Valley sites, proof positive, he believed, of the squalor and degeneracy of the area. At Gladys's, garbage formed piles, couches, carpet, tree limbs and lumber. Plastic bags hung dense from the creosote scrub like withered fruit. The cabins sagged, destroyed, buried to the windows under the waste. Recently, somebody scrapping metal torched what was left of them.

There was beauty in Wonder Valley: the mountains at sunset, the stars at night. Even the derelict cabins were not devoid of charm. Gladys's place, on the other hand, was a blight. It was more than a spectacle, it was a lesson. How could people who have nothing find themselves so buried under *things*? It had become a prison for Larkin. It mired him in his situation, not able to leave it for fear of losing his *stuff*. Yet his coveted possessions had all but decomposed before his eyes under the harsh Wonder Valley sun. It was worthless. He had nothing. As he and I had become friends, I hated to see what all this stuff was doing to him. He could have been—should have been—just another retiree out here. Or he could have formed bonds with the area artists and musicians—in his past he'd run in those circles. But because of his junk, he'd been shunned. Many found his living conditions inexplicable, inexcusable even. He had a hoard of luxury goods rotting into the desert but wouldn't sell it for what he could get to lift himself from his mire. His junk was his prison, yet he was the jailor.

Clearly, Larkin failed to see the situation he was in. Because of the trash dump at Gladys's, his code enforcement fines now exceeded $30,000 dollars. Twenty-five dollars a month towards them kept him out of jail, but five years without paying taxes and his properties would go on the block for auction. He planned to bid on them, he told me.

"The tax default will strip away the mortgage debt. I'll buy them back for next to nothing." I wondered where he'd get the money. He had already borrowed hundreds of thousands of dollars against the properties, yet destitute, he couldn't make those mortgage payments. The bank had begun foreclosure proceedings.

"It doesn't matter," he said, "the cost to clean up these places up far exceeds what they're worth. The bank can't afford to take them back." More likely, however, the county would get them by default. Taxpayers would foot the bill for clean-up, and he would finally be homeless.

Larkin had a house in Mississippi, though, his mother's house, his childhood home. He could abandon his sea of rotting rubbish and move there. "Or go visit friends in San Francisco," I suggested.

"But the thieves out here would rob me blind!"

The tragedy of Larkin's isolation was that he craved company. He was a gregarious socialite, after all. But many people found his unrestrained, flamboyantly gay demeanor and his penchant for touching and caressing off-putting. These eccentricities led to gossip and conjured rumors suggesting he had proclivities for pedophilia and even bestiality. These were nonsense, of course, but believed enough to get him further spurned. The threats of violence that followed him made him unwelcome at The Palms.

Still, Larkin took in drifters down on their luck. I don't know how he came to find them, but he often had one or two living on his land, holed-up in the odd travel trailer or, as with Fluffy, Dingy's boyfriend, in a cabin cruiser beached behind Larkin's garage. Larkin fed these guys when he could, as well, and got them drunk. But then, so often, he got familiar, a little drunk himself, maybe he touched them—a hug, a squeeze—innocent, meaning nothing, it was just that he was affectionate—and lonely—but these men would lash out against him, call him names, a fat fucking pedophile faggot. Or like that one drifter-guest, stab him, jab him in the throat with a steak knife in his own kitchen.

The man fled the cabin. Rumor says Larkin chased him, barreled after him across the creosote scrub in an old limo. Larkin, however, insisted it didn't happen like that. He said that after the man stabbed him, he ran, but quickly returned, apologetic. He'd take him to the hospital, he said. Driving Larkin's car, they headed to the highway and through town as he bled into an old t-shirt. When the man drove past the ER and back into the open desert, though, Larkin panicked. He opened the passenger side door and bailed out, tumbling down the sandy shoulder of the highway. "Help! Help!" he screamed. The man sped away in Larkin's car, but returned to Larkin's home where he was later arrested.

During the time I was visiting him, another man arrived to stay in one of his trailers, a mean-looking man with Nazi tattoos. Larkin told me that he and the man had been drinking together, and that the man stole one hundred dollars from his purse. When Larkin demanded he leave, the man returned the money.

"Jesus," I said. "Why do you let him stay?"

"He has nowhere else to go," he said.

I just shook my head. Larkin had me baffled. I imagined him in some parallel reality, living unremarkably among friends in San Francisco or in that house in Mississippi or even in a mobile home park on LA's fringe somewhere, rather than out here in the dirt and the dust and the disharmony. He was so out of place here, a species unto himself, I thought. But Wonder Valley was the place for the displaced. He was just another castaway on this desert island after all.

We sat together in weathered patio chairs out in the sunshine, Larkin's pitbulls lounging at our feet, soaking in the sun. The desert that day was weightless. Contrails streaked the cerulean skies. As we talked, I dug my hand into the sand, absentmindedly picking out a small stone. I tossed it at one of the lounging dogs. Larkin slapped my hand.

"Meany," he rebuked. "You can't bear letting sleeping dogs lie!"

We both laughed, but then fell quiet. I was prying into his life for my own gain, we both knew, dredging up his memories, refusing to let his sleeping dogs lie. That's why I was there.

We sat in an awkward stillness until he sighed and pulled his stocking cap from his head. "Do you mind if I take a shower at your place?" he asked. He blushed, then smiled. "I can't remember the last time I had a real shower."

"Of course," I said. I stood and dusted myself off, then helped him into my truck. Seeing him struggle up I again imagined him in that parallel reality. He had nothing here, but in that other reality, at least he had a shower. I slipped the truck into gear and threaded it slowly around Larkin's little camper and the cabin cruiser, past the sea of housewares and bric-a-brac, the mobile homes, the limos, the collection of Mercedes Benzes. The terra cotta statue of the Virgin Mary stood with her back to us by the gap in the low hedge of used tires. The truck creaked as I eased it over the berm and onto the road towards my cabin and through the heart of Wonder Valley.

Chapter 12

It was a Thursday. I know because my dad showed up at my place while Larkin was taking his shower. He arrived riding shotgun in a county-issued vehicle, Sheriff's decals on the doors, lights on top, Fangmeyer, my landlord, in the driver's seat. Neither of them lived in Wonder Valley, of course, but they made their assigned Citizens on Patrol rounds out here on Thursdays, came out from town to check on the elderly and infirm as well as the cabins left unoccupied by artists and weekenders.

As usual when he stopped by on patrol, my dad and I exchanged pleasantries over the fence, discussed the weather, related gossip. Patrolling out here had given him a sense of area expertise, and stopping by, he always related what he'd seen or heard, so-and-so told us something about something or other. His information was usually dated, the product of the telephone game, but I thanked him, nonetheless. He never got out of the county-issued vehicle and he never stayed long.

In fact, they were just backing away when Larkin walked out of my cabin with a towel around his neck. He stopped them with a wave and shook my father's hand through the passenger window. "So glad to finally meet you," he said in his syrupy drawl. "I need your services immediately! The low-lifes out here, they're all thieves, they'll steal anything that isn't nailed down! Can you believe these people?"

"Oh, I believe it," my dad said. "Maybe they should pay a visit to that nut on Boom Boom! You've seen all the junk he has? All the tires and junk and boats and stuff. The county's after him now..." He

141

was gossiping to Larkin about Larkin. I leered at him to shut him up and sent him on his way.

I doubted Larkin got the gist of what my dad was saying—the smile never left his face. I'm sure he sensed none of the tension between my dad and me, either. We'd had decades of practice whitewashing our public rapport. We remained staid and polite with one another, each hoarding our resentment and acrimony behind the wall we'd built between us. We didn't talk, he and me. He might ask about Ann and I'd say she was fine. I had never told him about getting fired or losing a fortune, nor why I was out here so far from Ann and home, and he never asked.

As with my parents, I'd told very few people that I'd been fired from my job or that I'd lost everything in a bad real estate deal—but then again, I hadn't needed to. From the outside, nothing in Ann's and my life visibly changed. I was out here working on my stuff and Ann still had her job. The bills got paid. Only we knew those bills were oppressive and the stress of them was taking a toll on Ann's health. Outwardly, we showed no signs of trouble.

We were essentially not much different from so many other American couples, I suppose: in debt up to our ears, trying to keep our relationship together and just make it day to day. But we had never been that couple. We had always been best friends. We'd been very conservative with our spending, too, discussing everything and making decisions together. Ann had been especially averse to investment risk. I avoided bankruptcy after my real estate debacle by simply walking away from the property I'd wrapped all our money into, but because of that, Ann's credit crumbled. And though we had no plans to borrow any more cash, I knew it pained her that my credit score was nearly perfect—over 800—while creditors considered her a risk. She felt betrayed. She didn't say so, but I knew. I could tell. Around friends and family, she blushed when asked how we were doing. She hated being forced by decorum to cover for me, to repeat my justifications for why I wasn't home. I saw this, what I was making her do, how I was making her feel, and it made me feel diminished in her eyes, like we were no longer equals in our relationship. My embarrassment, frustration, humiliation, this sense of disgrace turned to resentment, then anger—my knee-jerk reaction—anger at the world, at her.

"Why don't you want to be with me?" she would cry. I didn't know how to answer that. I did want to be with her. I loved her. She was my best friend. I just didn't want her to want to be with me, I guess. I wanted her to be angry, furious, to leave me, divorce me, tell me to fuck off, but she didn't. She was incomprehensibly understanding, like a mother to a child who had just peed the bed. And that pissed me off. I knew I had been wrong, I knew our financial ruin was my fault, and I knew I deserved scorn, but she was never anything other than outwardly supportive. "We'll get through this," was what she'd say.

Looking back, though, I'm sure she felt herself treading a minefield. I had become explosive, the smallest thing setting me off. I had started drinking, too, drinking myself to sleep to counter the anxiety attacks that woke me most nights. I got into therapy, began taking anti-depressants. Nothing helped. Ann worried I would kill myself. I fantasized how I would do it. I'd been cavalier, reckless, and I just couldn't seem to recover from the disaster that resulted. I just couldn't seem to pick myself back up. The stigma of having been fired had left me besmirched, tainted, unemployable in the highly competitive job market I'd found myself in. It was over a personality conflict, not performance, but that wouldn't matter to prospective employers. It tainted me, nonetheless. I felt I shouldn't have had my future destroyed over something like that, minor missteps.

Making matters worse for me, I lacked the qualifications on paper for the few jobs available, those jobs growing scarcer and paying less, as the economy, favoring capital and automation over people and labor, created work for robots and offshore, but not here. In my industry, for example, corporations were relocating their call centers overseas at a frenzied pace, sending them to India and elsewhere to exploit cheap labor, meaning jobs like the one I lost had largely left the country. I'd been raised to believe in the American Dream, to believe in a system that rewarded hard work with success, one favoring aggressiveness and competitiveness over congeniality. And I had worked hard, played by the rules as I understood them, but I got sidelined anyway. The system failed me, that's what it seemed like to me. Rather than floating all boats, this globalized economic model was scuttling those previously buoyed. I felt I'd been robbed and that overwhelmed me with bitterness. And I now sat idle.

In the months after losing my job I regaled Ann with sanctimonious rants, filled as I was with this righteousness and indignation. I was a victim I told myself. I had, of course, always known that rich white men had had their thumbs on the scale for centuries and I knew this meant that, as a white man myself, I had been vested in and benefited from that unequal system by default. I knew it meant I got to eat at the table first. But I was raised to believe that duty and responsibility mitigated male power and privilege—at least partly. This was the social contract. It was my duty as a man to provide and protect, for example. It was my responsibility to be fair-minded and compassionate. As quaint and outdated as this sounds now, it was the ideal of the American male I grew up immersed in. These masculine narratives, repeated and strengthened over centuries, saturated me, a relentless stream of messages from television and school, my father and every bit as much my mother. Big boys don't cry, my mother instructed. She deemed me Man of the House during my father's months-long military deployments, conferring upon me at six, eight, ten years-old the vague responsibilities of guardian and mediator and protector. I was the one expected to answer the door, the phone. I was the one to keep the family safe, to take a bullet in my father's absence—or so I felt. I didn't at the time understand this as the purely symbolic role my parents surely intended it to be, a tactic employed to assure I'd behave myself without my father as disciplinarian. On the contrary, I felt it compulsory, a duty I obliged as the eldest son.

As an adult, of course, I came to recognize these gender ideals as laughable, outdated notions. But these obsolete ideals of manhood endured, if repressed, within me as ineradicable chimera in my reptilian brain. They hissed subliminal accusations to my subconscious. I had shirked my responsibilities, they murmured, it had been my duty to provide and protect, my failures chinks in the armor of my masculinity, so while I *knew* in my head that these ideas of masculine duty and responsibility were outdated and irrelevant, that reptilian hiss deeply shamed me anyway. I was ashamed I couldn't live up to those ideals while simultaneously humiliated that I couldn't just fucking let them go.

What I found particularly frustrating during these times is that I felt I was getting no help or support. To Ann, my internal demons were incomprehensible, my struggles with them bordering on silly. "Just get over it," she'd say. She didn't understand because she didn't have these demons. Her lot, like most American women's, was improving—at least relatively. Like me, she'd had her coming-of-age during a time of cultural transition, but she and women like her had benefited from the support of a vast community, one that swaddled girls and young women in positive affirmations of confidence, of strength, of capability. I, on the other hand, found myself wrestling internal conflicts while at the same time fending off a barrage of social negatives, bombarding me constantly with reminders of my inherited privilege and insistence that I'd only ever lost what I hadn't really earned. I understood the social backlash, the spite and hostility, the "well, now you know how it feels" retorts men hear when bemoaning their struggles, but that doesn't mean the struggles weren't real, weren't legitimate. I felt this backlash was mocking me for internalizing a lifetime of social conditioning, a conditioning that to a large extent had been reiterated and reinforced by the women in my life. I felt derided for my inability to redefine myself and my masculinity in the face of a new narrative that insisted that who I was was wrong but offered me few clues as to who I should be to be right. I knew and agreed that the Father-

Knows-Best model of manhood had no place in a more inclusive, egalitarian reality, but a new model of man hadn't yet emerged. And yet the pressure to reinvent myself went unabated, creating an irresoluble conundrum within and outside of me, a conundrum these same cultural pressures insisted I face with the same old masculine strength and stoicism now being otherwise maligned. The contradiction was inescapable: I was expected to redefine myself by myself, alone, with no support, no crutches, no examples or models, and without a community—the very idea of middle-age white male solidarity being an affront to everyone, including most middle-age white men. Uncertainty in men still seen as weakness, I felt expected to find my path to reinvention resolutely, yet quietly and emotionlessly, to resolve this contradiction unaided, my feelings of distress unexpressed and unacknowledged, admonished by everyone, my wife, even other men, to man-up, to get over it. But I couldn't get over it. I didn't know how.

§ § §

Contradiction is by definition irresolvable. Its result is negation, not transformation, the opposites canceling one another out, leaving nothing. In Wonder Valley I saw an entire landscape of negated men around me, their former identities as valued employees and providers for families nullified by contradictions unresolved, their identities supplanted by anonymity. "It's their own doing" was the narrative, an accusation. Blame assigned. They were weak. They had failed. They couldn't adapt, couldn't reinvent themselves. They had made mistakes, been cavalier, and now negatives—alcoholism or drug abuse or mental illness or bitterness—defined them. They lived here in stop-time, withdrawn from an outside world moving on without them, leaving them their beer and anger and rage as the only means by which to cope.

I, too, felt negated. I'd been cavalier with jobs and investments both because I thought I could afford to be and because I thought I had to be. I had promises of prosperity to fulfill as well as expectations to live up to. And I had something to prove, too, I guess. I'd hate to admit what I ended up proving, though. I had bet everything I had, my life savings, my home, my marriage on a throw of the dice. And I lost it all and more. I lost myself.

I sometimes imagined what life would have been like if I'd succeeded, had kept and advanced at that job or better yet built and sold those condos and walked away with a few million in the bank. My life would have been pretty good in my imagination. I'd have my beautiful home and beautiful wife as they had been. The successes would have bolstered my self-esteem, my self-confidence. I'd have something to show for my success, too, something I could hold up and say, *see, I did this.* And I'd never have to do anything like it again. I'd never again have to put my whole life on black and spin the roulette wheel just to prove something, just to prove I could be the man I was raised to be. It would be obvious to everyone.

Hindsight is 20/20. In hindsight I see I should have listened to Ann's council and approached opportunities that came to me more soberly, more thoughtfully. I should have moderated my own expectations, too, and reexamined what I felt was expected of me. If I hadn't been so driven to prove myself maybe I could have accepted the consequences of my actions along with the outcomes beyond my control without so much regret and anger and bitterness. I thought of George Stadler. Bitterness at how the world had failed him drove him mad. Maybe that same kind of bitterness was keeping me down, too, was keeping me from picking myself back up.

I felt myself at a crossroads. I could stoically bear up to my failures or I could withdraw to Wonder Valley, to a clutch of men who silently, unquestioningly understood one another—and I was at the limit of my stoicism. No one here was asking me to man up.

I thought about Ann. She had broken glass ceilings her whole life, a female geologist where before her there'd been few, and a mentor now to young geologists, female virtually to a man. I'd saddled her with the responsibility to provide—having a deadbeat husband was not the ideal of womanhood she'd aspired to, I'm sure. But, like women of her generation, she'd been raised to nurture, which was why she paid the rent on my cabin without complaint, I suppose. She was patiently mothering the child that had pissed the bed. She even came out here on occasion to check on me. Together we'd go on long walks, enjoy the sunsets and the stars at night. The desert was a special place for her, it always had been, and I was glad when we could share it.

Larkin and I stood at my front gate that Thursday and watched my father and Fangmeyer back away to resume their COP patrol. "It must be nice to have your parents so close," he said, waving good-bye. He looked at me for some sort of response. The reality was, having my father this close dredged up things I'd rather suppress. Seeing him reminded me how so completely he had shaped me, how I was pulling myself asunder trying to both meet his expectations and repudiate them, this contradiction resulting in my negation. Seeing him so frequently also laid bald the pate of irony that my inability to reconcile this contradiction was what was putting me in such close and continual contact with him.

I leaned against the fence and sighed. "I wouldn't be in Wonder Valley if it weren't for my parents," I said somberly. Larkin took that as something I hadn't meant, and he smiled.

Chapter 13

I'd been more than a year in Wonder Valley when a little yellow cabin seemed to magically appear on the parcel to the north of me. It was a classic homestead cabin—one hundred and ninety-square feet, no plumbing or electricity—one of the originals. It was so striking with its canary yellow façade, its bright white door, its modern vinyl window and flouncy lace curtains, that I wondered how I'd never noticed it before. I walked over to it. The door was locked, a detail I found strange because while the door and the modern vinyl window and flouncy curtains as well as the siding and paint on the wall that faced my cabin were indeed new—brand new—that was it. The other three walls weren't even walls. They were just bare, weathered studs, the same bare studs that had been standing there on that cracked concrete foundation since the fifties. I squeezed between them. Sun poured in on me through the open roof, wind tussled the flouncy curtains from the wrong side. I opened the front door and stood in it looking out at my place a couple hundred yards away.

I had been around Wonder Valley long enough by this point that few things surprised me, but this was just plain weird. Who did this? And why? It might have been some sort of art project or a prop for a photo shoot or something, but I had seen no one around taking pictures or admiring the work. I concluded my kooky neighbor Brian had done it during a particularly manic bout of paranoia. He'd posed mannequins and cut-out silhouettes around in the trees on his compound to make it look like he had an army in there guarding him. This one-sided cabin, I assumed, was another of his loony security schemes.

149

A few days later, however, some guy showed up with a load of lumber and supplies. He'd bought the place for back taxes, he said, $2,500, and planned to do a quick fix and flip. He had spruced up that one wall first to get a photo up on the internet.

I'd seen this happening all across the valley: land speculators snapping up properties at the annual tax sale like this guy had, five acres and a cabin for just a few thousand bucks. Like him, there'd be a flurry of activity, hammering and painting, walls thrown up, windows reinstalled. Over the course of the day he was there, this guy sided and painted the other three walls and, leaving the roof open to the elements, stuck a for sale sign in the sand and left. The sign lasted a month until the wind took it. No one ever returned to right it. And the little yellow cabin weathered and faded back into the creosote scrub out of which it seemed to so miraculously arise until I'd completely forgotten about it.

Then Paule arrived. Jack McConaha had come by on his weekly security patrol and together we stood at my front gate looking north at the little yellow cabin. Pup tents hugged the dirt around it, the white crown of a party tent poked above its eaves. Bicycles leaned against one another. As we watched, someone pulled plastic sheeting up and over the roof.

"Nice to see the Boy Scouts out here again," Jack said.

Paule, it turned out, was no Boy Scout.

He was in his forties, thin and loud, with kelly-green hair spiked up and a matching beard shaved into two horns.

"Damn glad to meet ya," he said, wrenching my hand in a construction worker's grip when I introduced myself. He told me his story in rapid-fire New Jersey slang. "I'm a Katrina survivor. Been homeless for the last seven years, yadda yadda and such and such."

He grew up in Atlantic City, had worked in restaurants, became a stripper in Miami clubs, then a carnie based in New Orleans. He was on the road when Katrina struck, but the subsequent flood took everything he didn't have with him. I couldn't follow how he got to

Los Angeles from there or how he came to live on the beach, but he said he lived there homeless until diagnosed with PTSD and paranoid schizophrenia. With that diagnosis, the Social Security Administration deemed him disabled, so mentally disabled, in fact, they forbade him from managing the monthly money they gave him for survival. They appointed a ward, a charity that doled his cash to him in dribs and drabs. It took him a few years, he said, until he got the crazy dialed in, got the balance right, learned to be just the right amount of insane: not so much he had to have a ward, so to speak, but not so sane he didn't get any money either. Yadda yadda, such and such. Once settled, however, he gained access to the money he'd amassed and bought the little yellow cabin from that photo on the internet, his first real home in a decade. He told me all this with a self-assured tone designed, I was sure, to convince me he was gaming the system. No one meeting him in person, however, could ever begrudge him the money.

Instantly I worried for him. He reminded me a lot of Nutty Ned who had arrived in Wonder Valley under similar circumstances. Ned's parents had bought his place for him, sight unseen, then they packed him up and shipped him out here. But by the time I met him, Ned had been here for decades. He knew his way around the desert. Paule, on the other hand, had never even seen the desert before moving here, knew nothing about it. Already the weather was unnerving him.

"The wind out here, Jesus fucking Christ, man," he said. "It was like a fucking gale or something, pardon my French." The wind we'd experienced was nothing unusual for Wonder Valley, I told him, nothing like we get, with windstorms blowing dust that blackens the valley, reducing visibility to feet.

"Winds in one storm last spring reached hurricane force," I said, "gusts to seventy miles an hour. Dust wheedled itself into everything." The winds Paule had experienced, however, had shaken his tent mercilessly and sent his new solar-electric system flying, shattering its glass front. It also tore the plastic from the roof of the cabin. Paule was in a hurry to repair it, he said, before the rain came.

"Any rain," I said, "will be isolated to the coast. Rarely does it make it over the mountains to the desert. All we'd likely get was that wind." Paule gave me a dubious look.

"You don't understand, man," he said, "I've been living on the streets of Venice Beach for the last seven years, okay? I take the threat of rain seriously, so to speak and such and such."

"Most of the rain we get comes in the summer," I explained. "Thunderstorms." I showed him the gullies etched by flash floods across his property. "Last August," I said, "thunderstorms stomped across the valley once a week, pummeling us with rain that scoured down the barren hills, turning virtually every road into a river." One night, taking Curtis home after a rainstorm, I found myself up to my bumper in fast-moving water. The water rushed out of the mountains with such astonishing speed that within minutes it had converted the valley floor into a mud river as wide as the Amazon. I couldn't drive forward, and trying to back up, my tires spun. Rats and snakes, tarantulas and scorpions scurried up into the creosote shrubs sticking above the floodwaters, dissuading me from getting out of my truck. Out in the darkness, however, I noticed a man standing on a high spot next to me. I lowered my window.

"That's my car," he said, pointing down the road ahead. Slowly a car turned toward me. Spinning in the current, it drifted away.

"I spent that night there in my truck waiting for the water to recede," I said to Paule, "Curtis slept on his cabin roof as water bore through his place."

Paule nodded. He'd heard all about these floods. Brian, our mutual neighbor, told him all about Wonder Valley.

"He seems like a nice enough guy, so to speak, yadda yadda," Paule said of Brian. Brian had been nice enough to me, too, I replied. On the rare occasions we spoke, he had been cordial, talking about the weather or ranting about the other neighbors—Red and Gary, primarily—as well as the crime in the valley. Other times, however, I'd see him hiding in the saltcedar trees of his compound with a video camera recording my movements. At night, he kept his place lit up like a correctional institution with hundreds of lights strung along his perimeter as well as crisscrossed through the trees. I called his place Wonder Valley State Penitentiary, a prison with only one inmate. I'd see him patrolling his compound through the wee hours shining a searchlight-strong beam around. I sometimes heard him screaming obscenities at the silence.

Because of Brian's lights, it was daylight-bright at Paule's at night. I asked him what he thought of that.

"I don't mind the lights," he said. "I don't mind them at all. I'm from the city, you know. Living on the streets, lights are comforting, so to speak. It means safety, you know, yadda yadda. Besides, I've got no electricity, it's nice to be able to come outside at night and see." I asked him about the night sky out here, about the stars that hang close enough to touch anywhere else in the valley. He just shrugged.

Brian had given Paule access to the dumpster on his property to dispose his trash. He also gave him a wood burning stove and a propane range for his cabin. Even that asshole Craig behind me, the guy who hated everyone, was being nice to Paule. He had driven him to town and took him to the free food giveaway and to get drinking water from the spigot in the national park. They had also taken these opportunities to tell Paule about the Naborly Road feud, telling him stories about me and Gary with the basset hound and Fangmeyer and Red, versions of events that conflicted markedly with my experiences.

"You know, Craig flips me the bird every time he sees me," I replied. "He films me through my kitchen window from his van. Worse, he drags a goddamn chunk of carpet up and down the road just to create dust. You'll see. And Brian over there spies on everyone from that thicket of trees—in fact, he's there watching us right now!"

And yes, Fangmeyer kept the pot stirred by coming out from town weekly to clean and reposition the security cameras that shined toward Craig and Brian's properties. Arriving, he'd stand out in the dirt yard and wave his hat at Brian hiding in the trees and scream an exaggerated, pseudo-friendly "howdy neighbor" at him as he did it. He later installed a cardboard cut-out of himself waving that hat for the times he was not around to do it personally. He also hung a bullseye on the power pole near the road. "It's for Brian to shoot at rather than shoot at the cabin," he'd said.

Someone had shot a hole through my kitchen window when I wasn't home one day. It had shattered the window, piercing the roll-up blind and the frilly lace curtains before passing over the kitchen table to mark the far wall with a small black dot. I hadn't seen it but Fangmeyer noticed it immediately when he next came to review the security recordings. He lined up a laser between the hole in the wall and the one in the window. "And guess what?" he said. "The laser points straight to goofball's cabin." He sawed the wallboard around the hole to extract the slug while we waited for the cops to arrive. "I always wondered what would happen," he said, examining the wall wound. "For a bullet to fly straight it spins, the rifling in the barrel causes it to spin. I thought it might stop when it passed through the glass and everything, but it's wound up tight in the insulation. I had to cut it out. That means it was still spinning." This was a point of evidence to Fangmeyer who inked a mental note of it for some final Scooby-Do showdown with Brian.

The showdown never came. Brian told the responding deputy he didn't do it. He said he'd heard the shot, that two kids were walking by when it happened.

I found his story dubious. I knew Brian well enough to know that if he had heard a shot, he would have called the police. He called them on me the day I moved in—in fact, he made up a story about gunshots. I had been sitting on the front porch drinking beer with Whitefeather when the tear light of a Sheriff's cruiser lit us up. A neighbor had reported gunfire coming from my place, the deputy said. I didn't own a gun I told him.

"You don't know your neighbor over there?" he asked, pointing to Brian's. "You will," he said. "He calls us a lot."

And he did call a lot. Even though he knew me, he called the cops anytime he saw me walking in the desert. I kept a scrapbook of the incidents clipped from the weekly Sheriff's Blotter in the newspaper. "Man seen prowling," they typically said. I knew, therefore, that if he had seen kids walking near his property, he would have called the police, even if they hadn't fired shots.

The thought of my neighbor taking potshots at my cabin spooked me. I could stand in the path of that gunshot and imagine the bullet hitting me right between the eyes. I called Jack McConaha and hired him for security.

Jack came over and did a reconnoiter. He walked my cabin and the perimeter pointing out the potential for breaches. He gave me paper signs, *Wonder Valley Community Watch*.

"Put these in your windows," he said. "Nobody will mess with you. Don't worry, we're on the job."

Having Jack come around weekly worked somewhat to put me at ease. He carried that handgun on his hip—even if I knew the gun wasn't loaded—and I wanted Brian and Craig to see that, to see Jack roll up in his Jeep, a big gold star on the door, him in his crisp camouflaged fatigues, *SECURITY* in big bold letters on his back, and know I was taking action. I showed Jack the bullet hole through the window.

"Do you have a weapon for protection?" he asked, planting a hand on the grip of his own pistol. I told him I didn't really think Brian was trying to shoot me.

"Well, there's some son of a bitch trying to kill me!" he said, clamping his mouth closed tightly. He wasn't wearing his lowers, so his chin mashed flat making his head nearly perfectly round.

"Old George Stadler has a .44 Magnum," he continued, repeating back intel I'd supplied to him months before, "but I hear he's trying to get a rifle. If he wants to go long, I'll go long. I'm going to mount a rifle in my rig. The sheriff doesn't like it, but I'll be damned if I'm going to go down without a fight!"

When I saw him next, he had, indeed, mounted an assault rifle in his Jeep, a 9mm carbine. He kept it covered in plastic like a saran wrap prophylactic. The gun remained in Jack's jeep even after George Stadler died. Heart attack.

I had stopped visiting Stadler and only heard from him once since when he called to gloat about how he'd finally shot some son of a bitch or other who had come onto his property, someone he said had been tormenting him for years. I dismissed it as the ranting of a lunatic, but then a few hundred yards down the road from his place a returning snowbird discovered a man's raven-picked, coyote-eaten remains slumped between a couple of cars. Seems the dead man had gotten his car stuck in the sand over the summer and walked for help. The news report surmised that he had been overcome by the heat, but I wondered if he hadn't wandered up to Stadler's singlewide and, taking him for some phantom out of his past, Stadler shot him. I envisioned the man staggering away for help and, reaching the neighbor's, slumped down and died. I wanted to ask Stadler about it, but never got up the courage. I'll admit, I'd been avoiding him. He frightened me. And now he was dead. I told Jack all this again, but he wasn't hearing me. That George Stadler was gone didn't seem to lessen his fear of him, as if even in death Stadler was a threat.

After hiring Jack, he made his rounds regularly, stopping by to chat over the fence. And, once, after Craig stepped up his aggression with me, he intervened. Ann had come to visit in her clean, white car, and Craig, seeing it, how nice it was, decided I was some kind of fraud taking advantage of him and others out here for personal gain. He started following me and confronting me in public, sticking his camera in my face, baiting me and making threats. He even came onto my property to tamper with Ann's car parked outside the gate while she was there alone. He had stabbed both Gary's and

Fangmeyer's tires before and I assumed that was what he was up to. I showed the security camera footage of the incident to Jack.

"Oh, I know Craig," Jack said, reviewing the video. "He's an asshole. I'll go talk to him." I don't know what he said, but after that Craig ceased his overt harassment and mellowed out considerably, so that by the time Paule arrived, he largely left me alone.

Brian eased-up on his spying and cop calling, too. He came out of his trees when he saw me at Paule's, sometimes walking over to talk. Gary often stopped by to offer Paule favors, too, and he and Brian actually acted civilly toward one another. I introduced Paule to Bud and Natalie, Pizza Richard. I invited him down to the bar. Because of Paule, things on Naborly Road almost got neighborly.

I think this was because we all recognized how horribly unprepared Paule was for his situation and we felt a responsibility for him. First, he was an East Coast guy, unfamiliar with the desert. And he'd bought the very cheapest plywood shack he could find and moved into it, sight-unseen. That little plywood shack had no roof, no insulation, no electricity or running water, no septic or toilet or mod con of any kind. It didn't even have an outhouse. Paule wasn't stupid, he was just cocky, sure of himself, underestimating, I thought, the impending summer heat.

"How bad can it be?" he said. "I've lived in Miami, I've lived in New Orleans and such and such. It gets a hundred degrees there with one hundred percent humidity. I love the heat. I worked in kitchens down there, it'd be 120, 130 degrees on the line, so to speak."

"But the heat out here is relentless," I said. "It will be over a hundred degrees day and well into the night all summer. And in your situation, there's no escaping it."

"I'll get an air conditioner," he said. "I'll run it off a generator." The point he seemed to miss, however, was that he was twenty miles from his water source, twenty miles from food, twenty miles from the gas for that generator he'd have to run day and night to power an air conditioner he didn't even have. And he had no car.

I worried for Paule. But I'd worried for Nutty Ned too when I first met him. He lived in similar conditions in Ricka McGuire's old school bus with no electricity or plumbing. I visited him regularly during that first summer, just to see if he was OK. I remember going over there once and he was sitting on a huge block of ice.

"What are you doing?" I asked him.

"Rejuvenating," he said. I still laugh thinking about that.

"Bill, man," he continued after a pause, "I'm going to sell ice out here, man. That's what people fucking need, man, ice!" But what you really need out here is water, something Ned had long before learned. Paule was another matter.

"But I've got water," Paule interjected. He pointed to the half dozen five-gallon buckets that Craig had taken him to fill at the national park. That amount of water had given him a false sense of security because it had lasted him almost the entire first month he was out here—January.

But he'd be OK, I told myself. Craig was helping him get water and Brian took him to town for food. Bud brought over a couple of loads of firewood. We weren't going to let anybody die out here. Those that had died from the heat were anomalies, I told myself. Paule would be fine. Then, a week later, Gary and Craig showed up at Paule's place at the same time. Craig had tried to stop Gary from driving on his road by running him off it, then was suing him for the damage his van incurred when Gary refused to stop. They exchanged words: fuck you, no fuck you, and suddenly any armistice on Naborly Road was over.

Confronted with this new reality, Paule had to choose. When he accepted a ride to town from Gary, Brian stopped taking his calls. He had cast his lot with the enemy and burned his bridge to Craig and Brian forever.

The point was hammered home days later when a county Code Enforcement inspector arrived. Under county rules, an inspector can only open an investigation if someone—a neighbor, for example—files a complaint. They cannot initiate anything on their own. Once a complaint was made and an action started, however, they had the entirety of county building code to enforce. That building code, the inspector told Paule, mandated all residences have hot and cold running water as well as a functioning toilet and septic system. More than that, if Paule wanted to live in the little yellow cabin, he would need to enlarge the living space, bring in electricity, install more doors and windows, all subject to inspection, then apply for an occupancy permit. His shack was considered a recreational cabin, never intended as a residence. Therefore, until the upgrades were made, the cabin was considered uninhabitable. As the inspector read his laundry list of requirements, Brian video recorded everything from the saltcedar trees of his compound. After the inspector left, Paule screamed a tirade of obscenities at him, told him he would call the code man on him, too, see how he liked that! "It's war now!" he screamed. Brian called the police.

The escalating hostility on Naborly Road spilled back onto me, too. Craig confronted me a short time later, walking with Ann on the road west of his cabin. On our walks together, Ann and I would stick to the dirt roads for the most part, though, like I said, we did enjoy exploring the abandoned shacks, too. On the day that Craig confronted us, we'd been walking on Raymond Drive, the side road that ran in front of Craig's property. My bleached-bone cabin sat on that stub of road too, though, right at the intersection of Raymond and Naborly. In fact, my place had a Raymond Drive address. Craig had years ago closed the road to traffic by dragging an old steel water tank across it west of his place and dumping nails and debris in the ruts, effectively making the road impassable. But that section of dirt road was actually *our* road, a fact Fangmeyer reiterated the day he hitched his truck to that old steel tank and dragged it out into the desert. Truth be told, on the day Craig confronted me, Ann and I had been walking that route on Raymond to see if the tank was in fact gone—it was, but Craig had re-blocked the road with the bedframe and piece of carpet he dragged behind his van to create dust. He pulled it around by a towline he connected with a couple of large carabiners to his hitch. It would have been easy, if one had been so inclined, to unclip the carabiners and discard the towline deep into the desert, effectively, if temporarily, disabling that goddamn drag and granting oneself a reprieve from its dust—which is what I might have done if at that exact moment Craig hadn't turned onto Raymond and headed straight for us.

Trying to be nonchalant, I gave Craig a friendly wave—I was still pretending we were cordial. Craig, however, was hostile.

"What are you doing prowling around my property?" he sneered, his camera trained on us. "I'm tired of you prowling around here!"

"I haven't been..." I started.

"You have!" he bellowed. He dialed the police as he screamed. "I can see it! It's the same boots!" He pointed to my boot prints in the sand. I had no idea what he was talking about. We were a couple of hundred yards from his parcel on a remnant of government land. I knew better than to go anywhere near his place. There was no way he could say I was trespassing on his or anyone else's property. Still, I was alone with Ann and it seemed Craig might turn violent, so we turned and high-tailed it, down Raymond toward my cabin. Craig followed on our heels, no doubt filming us from behind.

Back on his own property, he sat in his van for the next couple hours. He raced his engine and blared his horn and shined his headlights through my back windows. The police never came.

"Why don't you call code enforcement on *him*," Joe, a neighbor from up the road, said when I told him about the altercation. "Get him thrown out of there." The fact is, if Paule's living arrangement wasn't legal, neither was Craig's: his cobbled together cabin had no electricity or running water either, and I suspected none of the work he was doing on the place was properly permitted. Besides, it looked like a junkyard with the burned-out hulk of bus, abandoned cars strewn about, piles of scavenged castoffs. When the wind picked up, partially burned pages of spy gear catalogues blew across my land plastering my creosote shrubs like paper mâché. Then there were the remains of his spite flags, tattered by the wind and helped to that end by the BB holes Fangmeyer shot through them on the occasions he visited.

I made a formal complaint against him. This property has been abandoned by the owner, I typed into the online county Land Use Services complaint form. He has left numerous vehicles including cars, boats, and a burned city bus. Trash and junk litter the property and the wind blows it into my yard. I have picked up more than a dozen trash bags of paper in recent months. I mentioned that he had no plumbing, no functioning well or water source. I even told them I suspected he defecated in a bucket and dumped it in the desert. On a roll, I filed a complaint against Brian as well, for all those goddamn lights. Hundreds of them were strung along extension cords around and through his property. I wrote, This is an extreme hazard as the property is covered with junk as well as dead and dying trees.

The next week a Code Enforcement officer came and went from Craig's to Brian's. Maybe some of Brian's lights came down, maybe they didn't. There were still a lot—too many. As for Craig, he told the code officer that the remains of the burned-out bus and the fortress wall, the charred spy catalog pages and tatters of spite flags were parts of a crime scene, an arson investigation. He couldn't touch anything until the investigation was complete. Nothing, the Code Enforcement officer told me, could be done about it.

"That is all a lie!" I snapped back. "That investigation is long over!" The investigation concluded that the extension cords Craig ran to the spite lights he shined at my bedroom windows had melted through causing the fire. "It's time for Craig to clean up that mess!" I said.

"Your neighbors have been reporting one another for years," the inspector said. "I've dealt with Craig before, there's nothing I can do. He won't do anything unless I take him to court, and then he'll just drag it out." With that, he closed the case.

Paule, unlike his neighbors, however, was trying to address his code violations. "I called the county," he said to me one afternoon a few weeks after the initial citations, "I called them and asked about all these ghost stories and such and such that everyone's telling me, like you'll never get power hooked up to one of these old cabins, like you have to have a well, and the code man says they aren't true."

What I tried to explain to him was that the work the county was requiring would cost him tens of thousands of dollars, many times what he paid for his place. And they wouldn't let him live on the property while the work was being done. I suggested he find another cabin to buy, one with water and electricity, then walk away from the little yellow one, away from that asshole Craig and Brian and his lights.

"But I kind of like it here," Paule responded. "The place has grown on me, so to speak." All I could do was roll my eyes.

Chapter 14

Pizza Richard would punch-out on the pizza parlor time clock around eleven Monday mornings, and with that, he was off until Friday. He'd load the leftover buffet pizzas he'd accumulated over the weekend into the back of his truck, throw in his cooler, roll up his sleeping bag, and head toward home. He didn't drive straight to his cabin, though, he had his stops to make: the tobacco shop for tobacco, the liquor store for beer, the drive-through for fast food. He then made the rounds through the valley delivering his pizzas, trading them for cash to those who had it, or for pot or promises to those who didn't. At Desert Dave's, he might leave some frozen chicken wings, some toilet paper at Slim's.

At each stop on his rounds, he'd grab a beer from the cooler in the back of his pickup, offer one around to whoever was there, pass out pizzas, shoot the shit, anything to avoid going home, home to the rock-walled guesthouse. That's because Whitefeather was undoubtedly there, sitting at Richard's formica table, smoking his cigarettes, drinking his beer. If he dawdled long enough, however, the beer might have overtaken Whitefeather and he'd have gone home to sleep.

It had become a problem. Whitefeather was always at Richard's. When Richard woke on his days off, Whitefeather would already be sitting there, drinking beer at the formica table and watching *Let's Make a Deal* on his television. And every afternoon, when Richard made his beer run to town, Whitefeather would join him. Others would want rides to town, too, Curtis maybe, and Desert Dave. They'd offer him money for gas or a T-bone purchased with food stamps.

They'd load themselves into the back of the truck. Whitefeather rode up front, though, in the cab of Richard's rattle-trap truck. Richard kept Whitefeather up front to keep him away from the cooler and the beer in back, but still, Whitefeather would have already had a few before they left, then he'd pop one in the supermarket parking lot, another at each of the other stops, and once they were back on the dirt roads of the valley, one or two or three more up there in the cab of the truck, so that by the time I'd see him sitting at Pizza Richard's table in his own big leather desk chair in the evenings, he'd be glassy-eyed and belligerent, gritting his teeth as he spat his hare-brained prophecies about God and the Angels, Satan and the demons, or Nostradamus and the Mayan prediction of the imminent end of the Earth.

When he was like that, I felt myself on a powder keg. I avoided looking at him, careful not to trigger an explosion. As Pizza Richard's landlord, this was *his* house, he felt, meaning provoking him in any way could get you kicked out of Richard's home, banished by Whitefeather from the property. You'd have to beg your way back in. I once saw him throw Dingy out for reading the newspaper while he pontificated. He pushed another out for suggesting he get his cats fixed. He kicked Red off the property, too, more times than I can remember, usually for something Red said, Red's miscomprehended response to something he'd misunderstood. Red was deaf—or damn near—and hated his hearing aids. Sitting there at the table, he'd see Whitefeather's lips moving, knew words were coming out, then fill the silence in his ears with dialogue from his own beer-addled brain, adding sentences never said to a conversation never uttered. Red's responses would be loud, too, echoing with the Elmer Fuddian Rs of the hard of hearing. He'd point his thick calloused finger at Whitefeather and boisterously make an irrelevant statement that Whitefeather would take as criticism or a threat. Whitefeather would then bark something back at him, "Shut up!" or "You don't know what you're talking about!" each man having his own private argument, two monologues spit hostilely at one another that grew in intensity until Whitefeather sprang up from his black leather desk chair, sending it skidding across the room. Bodily, he'd throw Red out. Richard, afraid of Whitefeather, would say nothing.

I'll admit, I was surprised by Whitefeather's behavior. Before Richard moved in, I hadn't known him to be the explosive, domineering, drunken lout he was proving to be. Eruptions that threatened violence were common out here, disputes over simple things often, beer as often as not. But anyone acting like Whitefeather would have been ostracized. Whitefeather lived here, though—well, next door technically, but he clearly saw no boundaries. The thing is, Whitefeather had often held the role as arbiter in past disputes, mediating them. He had always had the least of anybody and had had to rely on others for his food and housing and beer. When I'd take him to The Palms, he'd drink the beers I or others bought him slowly, and never more than two or three, while casually chatting with whomever. But now he had an unlimited supply of beer and weed owed to him, in his opinion, rights he exercised to the extreme now that he was *landlord*, that title elevating his stature still further, empowering and emboldening him, turning him into an authoritarian, a tyrant—an often violent one. He'd drink himself to a stupor at Richard's table, sit hunched over in his own leather desk chair, brooding, eyes-closed, head hung, his lips murmuring as if in prayer, a beer and weed-addled holy spirit coursing through his veins. But then something would spark him. His tirades typically started out as a mumble that grew ever more intense, confrontational, until that inward-focused aggression turned outward, pointed, looking for a target forcing everyone else to sit there on eggshells, avoiding eye contact. Pizza Richard's rock guesthouse would fall silent.

One evening, after one such blowup, Whitefeather pushed Red out the door, admonishing him not to come back unless he brought his own beer. "I'm tired of Red," he announced, slamming the door. "I'm tired of him drinking all Richard's beer." He grabbed a fresh one from the fridge and popped it open, shaking the foam from his fingers. Richard, both frightened of Whitefeather's explosive violence and exasperated by Red and the bickering over *his* beer, again said nothing.

Kicked off the property, though, Red stewed. He felt he had rights to that beer, too. He was Richard's mechanic, after all, he repaired Pizza Richard's rattletrap truck for free. Whenever anything happened to it, he was there—he was the only reason Richard could get to the store to buy beer in the first place! And when Richard lived at the one-room cabin out by the Sheephole, it was Red who fed the Chihuahuas while Richard was away at work. He'd drink beer while he was there and take a few in his pockets for the ride home— Richard left it for him.

But Whitefeather had that beer now. That was part of the deal, Red knew, rent plus the electricity and beer. But why couldn't he stop in on the weekends and get a beer or two like he used to when Pizza Richard lived at the one-roomed cabin? He was his mechanic, they had an agreement, too. With resolve, he staggered into the next Taco Tuesday already drunk. He'd brought his own beer. Whitefeather sat at the formica table, head hung in a trance.

"I've been coming to Taco Tuesday for years," Red said to Richard. "I don't see why I have to bring my own beer when nobody else does. Besides, this is your place, Richard. You rent it, you have the say in who stays and who goes, not Whitefeather."

Hearing Red rant, Whitefeather popped awake. He slammed his hand down on the table. "Yeah, Richard rents the place, but that doesn't give him the right to have just anyone over to the property he wants! And now you think you're somehow entitled to beer?"

Red started to speak, but Whitefeather screamed at him. "Shut up!"

"No, you shut up!" Red screamed back. He had had enough. "You shut up, I'm talking to Pizza Richard." He turned his back to him. "Whitefeather's selling your beer when you're down the hill," he blurted to Richard. "Did you know that? Bud saw him do it."

Bud looked down at his hands. Since recovering from their stab wounds, he and Natalie had become regulars at Taco Tuesdays. He'd told Red he'd bought beer from Whitefeather but now wanted nothing to do with the confrontation. Whitefeather, however, exploded. He sprang up from his leather desk chair, sending it skidding across the room.

"Off the property! Now!" he screamed at Red.

"No!" Red bellowed. "This is Pizza Richard's place. He rents it. You leave!" Whitefeather's nostrils flared. Richard looked away, covered his face, said nothing. Red turned to face Whitefeather, his chin jutting forth in defiance. "You'd better be careful, someone might call the county about all your cats!"

Whitefeather flushed with anger. He hit Red with two jabs to the face. Red staggered back but shook the blows off. Whitefeather landed another punch, one that sent Red reeling out the screen door and tumbling flat out in the desert dirt. He struggled up, cocking his fist, but Whitefeather was on top of him, landing one punch, then another. He pummeled Red, pulping his face and shattering his teeth. Bud and Desert Dave fought to pull Whitefeather off him. Red lay in the dirt motionless. A folding knife, blade open, dropped from his hand. Fuming, struggling, Whitefeather wrenched himself free. He kicked Red in the head, landing his steel-toed combat boot against Red's temple. Red twitched, then was still. His breathing stopped.

Whitefeather stared down at the man, panting. The others backed away. Panicking, Whitefeather seized Red's arm and heaved, straining to drag him, his eyes darting man to man, searching for someone to help him. "We got to get him out of here!" he screamed. He had to hide Red's corpse, lug it out into the desert, up into the rocks behind the cabin where the ravens and coyotes could pick his bones clean and no one would find it. "Somebody help me!" he roared. Everyone backed further away. Whitefeather tugged harder,

Red's body shuddering and gasping with the exertion. He came to, then sputtered blood and drifted out again. Seeing him alive, others ran to his aid. They grabbed his arms and hauled him to his ATV, heaving him across it. Whitefeather slipped back to his desk chair and his beer while everyone else attended to Red until he could make his way home.

Pizza Richard didn't have Taco Tuesday much after that. And that was the way Whitefeather liked it. He could now spend his evenings in his leather desk chair watching the movies he picked up at the library in peace. He'd sit at Richard's table and smoke weed and drink beer until he slipped into his trance. Then maybe Richard could take the TV remote, watch what he wanted or listen to music.

"It's supposed to be my place, man," Richard whispered to me, leaning in close so Whitefeather couldn't hear. "I mean, come on!"

"Clyde Eddie has a cabin for rent," I told him. It was in the middle of the valley, close to the bar. It didn't have a shower or water—the well was down—and there was currently no heat or swamp cooler, but Pizza Richard agreed to let it immediately, paid Clyde Eddie three month's rent in advance, $900, anything to get out of there and away from Whitefeather. They made the arrangements in secret, Richard whispering the news to me through cupped hands while turned away from Whitefeather who sat head hung in stupor. He figured he'd still have to buy Whitefeather beer, tobacco, give him a ride to town, even after he moved, he was that afraid of Whitefeather.

"Dude, I just don't want any trouble. *Exactly*."

The power company cut-off Whitefeather's electricity soon after Pizza Richard moved out. After that I'd see him occasionally pushing his bike through the desert, a sack of foraged cans tied to the handlebars. He'd wave, but I'd pass him without stopping.

Chapter 15

While driving home from Pizza Richard's shortly after he moved to the new place, I found Curtis walking in the desert. That was nothing unusual, Curtis walked everywhere, summer and winter, barefoot often, his pockets filled with body-warm beers that he drank one by one, tossing the empties over his shoulder leaving a Hansel and Gretel trail of cans as he went. As it was common to see Curtis out walking, finding him that day was only noteworthy because he'd gone missing several days before. He'd walked away from Pizza Richard's place while Richard was away at work and no one had seen him since.

Curtis had moved in with Pizza Richard and had been living there only a couple weeks, but he'd had to leave, he told me as he climbed into my truck, because while Richard was away, someone stole his ATV.

"I woke up in the morning and it was gone," he said, "and Richard's Chihuahuas didn't bark or nothing and Richard had asked me to watch the place and I knew he would be mad, so I took off a-walking." He'd been sleeping in the wash, he said, because he couldn't go back to the shack he used to live in because Crazy Carolyn was there now. I had no idea what he was talking about. I drove him to The Palms.

I'd met Curtis the first time I went to The Palms, now years ago. He'd come up to me, thrown his arms wide and spun around, "Hi, I'm Curtis," he'd said. "I'm the Wonder Valley drunk." He then bent forward and with a finger traced the scar across the top of his head so I could feel the fused crack in his skull from when at fifteen that boat on that lake sent his nose through his brain and crushed his forehead flat.

"I'm a dead man walking," he'd said, throwing his arms wide again for me to take him all in.

What actually happened to Curtis is murky. He told me he was a teen waterskiing on a reservoir in Texas when friends slung him into a dead tree or a dock or a dead tree and a dock, the impact concaving his face at the bridge of his nose. Curtis, though, only knew what he'd been told, and at the time no one owned up to anything. More likely, the boat hit him, his friends messing around, gunning it at him as he floated in the water so that the bow came down on him with a thud, crushing his skull. Upon impact—whatever it was—he lost sight in his eyes, grew disoriented, acted funny. Curtis said his friends thought he was faking. They dragged him into the boat, then to the shore, and then they took off and left him. Forgot him. As he lay in the sun his brain swelled. A Samaritan found him hours later, in a coma, near death.

Doctors removed his shattered forehead to relieve the pressure. That chunk of skull would have to remain out for most of a year if his brain were to heal properly, doctors told his mother. He'd need to be hospitalized for most of that time, too, under constant care, chalking up a medical bill that would reach into the hundreds of thousands of dollars. But Curtis's family was poor, his father long out of the picture, his bartender mother couldn't care for a son with his brain on display. To fit him back together doctors sliced off parts of Curtis's frontal lobe and grafted his forehead back in place. He was home from the hospital thirty-two days after the accident.

If you asked Curtis's mother, she'd tell you she found him hard to manage after that. Shattered by that boat and with that slice of his brain missing, he lost sight in one eye, his sense of smell, of taste, as well as his short-term memory, his ability to weigh risk and reward, to plan, to make decisions. Gone also was a normal person's inhibitions. Kids around town would put him up to stunts. He threw up the live tadpoles and guppies they made him swallow and joyfully pissed on his fourteen-year-old sister when she changed his catheter. His mother decided to move the family to Wonder Valley—her mother was here, they relocated to be near her so she could help with his care.

Even here in Wonder Valley, though, Curtis was unruly. He pushed his mother around and went to jail for it. He did more time for smashing the hood of a caregiver's truck. He racked up some drunken-in-public arrests, others for possession of drugs and paraphernalia. He did time for computer fraud: a neighbor used his aunt's credit card to pay for porn, a crime Curtis took the fall for. He contracted hepatitis, rumor has it, from a man who made Curtis sodomize him, a man some say later died of AIDS. They say Curtis put porno mags on the man's back to help him perform, but Curtis told me the man only had magazines with pictures of naked men in them.

When I met Curtis, he lived in a beat-down shithole shack on the rim of the wash, but that was until the flash flood jumped the bank and bore through the cabin, filling it with mud, waterlogging his mattress and unsticking the pages of the porno mags that littered his floor. After that, Pizza Richard took him in.

He had asked me to help him move, but I just stood around while he stuffed some dirty clothes into a trash bag, gathered up a few cans of food, and chucked the porno mags out into the desert. Pizza Richard didn't help him either. He was kneeling near his truck fretting over a weathered chunk of siding stuck to his tire.

To get to Curtis's shack, he had followed a short cut Curtis recommended, a beeline across the desert, the route Curtis walked when he went to the bar or his sister's or to town. The route, however, turned out to be completely unsuitable for wheeled vehicles because, amongst other things, it cut directly across the remains of a cabin, shattered and crumbled, chunks of lumber studded with nails strewn over the sand.

"Goddamn it, Curtis!" Richard grumbled looking at his tire. He pulled the siding loose and air gushed from the wound with a loud hiss. He didn't have a spare. I lent him a can of Fix-A-Flat from my truck. Its white goo hemorrhaged from the hole in the tire as he sped off with Curtis and his clothes and his cans.

Pizza Richard gave Curtis the second bedroom in his new cabin, but only until Curtis pissed the mattress so thoroughly that urine ran clean through to the plywood floor beneath. He then evicted him to a motorhome Slim had found abandoned and Desert Dave dragged over. Curtis was to sleep in the motorhome at night but could use the cabin during the day to watch TV or cook food as long as he didn't piss anything or touch Pizza Richard's beer. The hundred dollars a month Richard charged him expressly did not include beer. Curtis could buy his own beer, Richard said, he had his own money, money his sister gave him every Friday. Curtis's perpetual problem was, however, that he owed the money his sister gave him every week to those he'd borrowed from the week before, meaning he always had to borrow more money to buy beer until the following Friday. It was a cycle that more than once got him thrown out of the bar for being a beggar and a pest, forcing him to find other means to satisfy that particular need.

With the ground rules thus established, though, I thought living with Richard was going to be good for Curtis. Richard made him shower, for example, and wash his clothes. He wasn't drinking so much and got enough to eat. Then Crazy Carolyn showed up.

I was at The Palms when Curtis came striding up to me flinging his arms wide open, "I'm getting married," he said, spinning around so I could take him all in. He fixed me with his one good eye. "My ex moved back in yesterday!"

Curtis's "ex," Carolyn, was a long-time Wonder Valley resident who had spent some time with him a couple of years before in the burned-out shell of her father, Dutch's, block cabin. They slept together in a heavy wood-framed bed that Carolyn had hauled over from her estranged husband's place. She left Curtis and the bed within a day or two, though, and walked across the desert to someone else. Now, it seemed, she was back. Curtis returned to his old shack with her, lugging his waterlogged mattress back inside and gathering up his scattered porno mags.

"Me and Carolyn fucked all night last night," he said to me in the bar, stepping back and throwing his arms wide again. "I'm God's gift to women!" Carolyn was waiting for him out in the desert, he said. He was just in there for an 18-pack to go, then they'd go back to his shack to fuck all night again. I shook his hand and returned to my beer while Curtis bumped person to person down the bar with the news of his impending nuptials until someone finally lent him the money he needed.

I hadn't seen Carolyn in months. The last I'd heard, she had been living happily with Biker Richard in a well-kept cabin at the head of the wash. But then, Biker Richard said, she dumped her pills down the toilet. They were toxic, she told him. Someone was trying to poison her, she said. Soon after, Carolyn launched herself onto him, waking him from a nap by pressing a butcher knife to his chest. "I'm going to kill you," she seethed. Grabbing her by the wrists Biker Richard forced her out the door. Carolyn then walked the desert miles to Pizza Richard's.

At Pizza Richard's, she sat herself down in front of his TV and smoked his cigarettes as fast as he could roll them. All night she talked and argued with her dead father, her estranged husband, with Sonny Barger of the Hell's Angels, and with Charles Manson himself, as well as others only she could see, to whom she spoke coyly or lashed at in anger or cried to or shrank back from in fear. She invited them to dance with her, to go down on her, to fuck her.

I hadn't always known Carolyn to be so unhinged. When first I met her, she was stable on her meds and living with her husband, Frank Keene, a wheelchair-bound old man with one leg missing. Around them they had collected a gathering of guys, keeping them in beer and cigarettes, and in Tom Whitefeather's case, letting him do odd jobs in exchange for the sacks of cat food they'd buy for him in town. Carolyn loved animals, loved her fat little dachshund, Sassy. She'd even taken in some of Whitefeather's kittens before they could be destroyed by the county. They were proof, Whitefeather had told me at the time, of how healthy the kitties were.

In those days, Carolyn would curl herself up in a chair in front of the TV, lighting Marlboro 100s one off another, their smoke cupping her face and wisping through her teased-up bottle-blond hair. I never knew her age, but guessed at it variously, taking stabs between forty and sixty, the sum of her years seeming to ebb and flood depending on how the day was treating her. She doted on Frank, fetching him beers, but never said much except to comment on something on the tube or speak up about an animal rights issue she'd come to hear about.

She had been in Wonder Valley since her teenage years, had come to live with her father in his white-washed block cabin just off the paved road. It was the homestead cabin that originally bore the sign "Wonder Valley," the one that lent its name to the entire valley.

From her father's, Carolyn bumped man to man around the valley. Before Frank, she lived with a guy named Miguel, the guy who smacked her around in The Palms until Roger clocked him so hard it sent his glass eye flying. After he was deported, Carolyn moved in with Frank. They married in Las Vegas with Whitefeather and others in attendance. Whenever I was around, they seemed a happy couple.

I had heard rumors, though, that all was not right with her. Slim, for example, told me he came across her lying across the dirt road in front of her and Frank's place, naked and dazed. He and Desert Dave had to drag her out of the road to get by. Others had also seen her walking the desert nude, too. I heard stories of her raging and railing at Frank, as well, beating him with whatever she could lay her hands on. In a fury, she'd once kicked the old man so hard she left him with a festering, open wound on his leg that would never, for the rest of his life, heal. Whitefeather had to restrain her, forcing her out of the cabin and into the desert until he got her calmed down.

Fearing for his safety, Frank got a restraining order against her, one she violated with impunity as the psychotic episodes escalated. Finally, the cops caught her locked in the bathroom of his cabin. Legs spread, she pissed on them when they broke down the door. She went to jail, then to an institution and some recuperative time with her daughter out of the area.

Once stabilized on medication, she returned to Wonder Valley, living first with Biker Richard in a little travel trailer and then moving with him to the well-kept cabin with a carport and a fenced yard at the head of the wash. I'd see Biker Richard at the bar sometimes where he'd have a quick beer before going home to his cabin and Carolyn and her dachshund, Sassy, and a pit bull named Sable and his dinner.

After she dumped her pills down the toilet, however, people again saw her walking the desert nude. Then she pulled that knife on Biker Richard, and, at a loss as to how to handle that, he pushed her out the door.

"What are you doing here?" Pizza Richard asked her repeatedly when she showed up at his place that first night. Carolyn, though, just talked and argued and bitched and ranted at invisible people. With Carolyn seemingly incoherent, Richard went to bed, pointing her to the spare mattress in the back room that Curtis had slept in and pissed on before being relocated to the motorhome. In the middle of the night, however, Richard awoke to Carolyn spooned-up nude against him. In the morning Curtis took her, talking and arguing as she was with her estranged husband and Sonny Barger and Charles Manson, to his old shack. The next afternoon Curtis walked into the bar and threw his arms wide and announced to all who'd listen that he was getting married, that he was God's gift to women.

It was a couple weeks later that I found Curtis walking in the desert and brought him to the bar. He had moved out of his shithole shack and had been back at Pizza Richard's, sleeping at night in the old motorhome. But then someone stole the quad, he said, and he felt he couldn't go back there. Nor could he return to his shithole shack because Carolyn was there ranting and raving and cooing and seducing and talking all night long even in her sleep. Besides, she drank all his beer and jonesed ceaselessly for cigarettes so that Curtis had to trudge the ten miles to The Palms to scrounge butts from the dirt.

"That bitch is crazy!" he said to me on the way to The Palms.

Pizza Richard was at the bar when we arrived. Seeing him, Curtis grew quiet and morose.

"Cheer up buddy," Richard said. 'You're better off without Carolyn. And don't worry about the quad. Donny probably came and got it." Richard had asked his friend Donny to work on his ATV while he was down the hill and figured he had come and taken it. He bought Curtis a beer. Then Donny walked in.

"I don't have your quad," Donny said. "I haven't had time to get over there to get it." We all turned our attention to Curtis again. He retold his story: he woke up Monday morning and it was gone, the Chihuahuas hadn't even barked. By now a crowd had gathered around.

Mary, the owner of the bar, overheard the conversation. "What was all that talk about a quad on Sunday?" she asked Curtis. "There'd been a kid there that day," she said. "He'd come to fix the jukebox, but he didn't know what the hell he was doing. Curtis started talking to him, and they left together. They were saying something about a quad."

Diane piped in. She lived in the roofless block shack behind The Palms and was there frequently to use the electricity to charge her phone. "Mary asked me to pick someone up and bring them to the bar," she said. "I went up to the cabin across the road from Pizza Richard's, and the kid was there, the one trying to fix the jukebox. He wanted me to haul an ATV for them." They loaded a quad into her truck. "I asked Curtis. He said it was OK. I brought them and the quad to the bar." Someone came later and took the quad away.

"Curtis told me the quad was his," she said. "He traded it to the kid." Traded it, it turned out, for beer.

§ § §

Desert Dave recovered Richard's quad. The kid had taken it apart to paint it, but Donny would reassemble it. Curtis moved back into the old motorhome behind Pizza Richard's but could still sit inside as long as he didn't piss anything or drink Richard's beer. Inside that night, his eyes closed, he swayed back and forth to the classic rock loping from the console stereo while muttering the lyrics in his throaty croak a half second behind the songs. He tipped back his beer and crushed the empty mid-swill, drizzling beer down his chin and onto the couch.

"Goddamn it, Curtis!" Pizza Richard grumbled. Curtis ignored him.

Carolyn faced the stereo. She pulled the hem of the nightie she wore up to her thighs and danced seductively to the music on the radio, glancing furtively at an invisible someone she cooed to. In an eerie moment, she bent to my ear and whispered something I didn't catch, calling me by name. In that instant she seemed her old self—she knew who I was—but that instant was fleeting. She glided back to the stereo to resume with the characters conjured by her psychosis, swaying and teasing and enticing them. "Which one of you is going to fuck me?" she screamed suddenly at the shadows.

Pizza Richard and I quickly pointed at Curtis, who sat rigidly still, shaking his head, an anxious grimace showing through his strawberry beard. Neither of us laughed. I found seeing Carolyn so haunted, so possessed, disturbing, even frightening. We didn't know what to do with her.

"I wish she'd just get out of here!" Richard whispered to me through cupped hands. Not only was she murmuring and screaming and whispering and cooing so incessantly, she smoked Richard's cigarettes one after another, taking them from his fingers as he lit them. The rent Curtis paid barely covered the food he ate and the beer he snuck and the special diligence required to keep him out of trouble. Carolyn, however, was not part of the bargain. To make matters worse, Clyde Eddie had raised Richard's rent to counter the damages he knew Curtis would cause. If Curtis left, Carolyn would follow him, but Richard figured he couldn't very well kick Curtis out. Curtis had the mind of a child—he wasn't stupid, could read and write, do math, it's just that, mentally, he was a ten-year-old, a ten-year-old who could legally drink and loved to smoke pot and would do just about anything anyone put him up to. Richard was concerned for him—we all were—and watched over him like an orphan.

Carolyn, however, was on her own. After Curtis left her at his shithole shack, she had wandered the desert until taken in by men who obliged her demand for sex until they too could tolerate her no longer, then they'd forced her back out into the desert. She found herself back at Pizza Richard's a week later and hung around there until the next day when guests pushed her out of the cabin and sent her walking barefoot out into the night. Every time she returned, they ran her off again.

No one seemed to worry for Carolyn, though, I was sure she would be found dead. Temperatures were dipping below freezing and she was wearing nothing but that nightie.

Denise later showed up at the bar and delivered news: Carolyn had been picked up and taken to jail. She said Carolyn told the police that Curtis and others had assaulted her while she was incoherent and now the police were coming for them, coming for Curtis and all the guys who had taken advantage of her. In actuality, Carolyn had been found disoriented by a passer-through and taken to the bar. Mary had them bring her to the firehouse. A deputy returned her to Biker Richard with a warning to take better care of her.

It was Curtis who went to jail the next week. He had thrown his arms open to some guys at The Palms, took them to a burned down cabin where there was metal to be scrapped. Someone saw them loading the junk and called the police, a deputy just happened to be driving by. Curtis had said the scrap was his, the scrappers told the

178

cops. He had traded it to them for beer. The deputy let them go but hauled Curtis to jail. He was out after a few days and walked the hundred miles back to Wonder Valley. While he was gone my father and Fangmeyer found Carolyn disoriented in the desert again while on their rounds as Citizens on Patrol. An ambulance took her to the medical center in town. There they got her cleaned up, stabilized on her medication, and sent back to her daughter up north after that.

§ § §

In the weeks that followed, Curtis missed his court appearance for the scrapping incident. I had offered to take him, but the date slipped by and I'd forgotten. Now, he had a warrant issued for his arrest. When I told him about it, he just shrugged, not understanding what that meant. "It means they're going to come looking for you," I said, "and if they find you, they'll arrest you."

Carolyn returned to Wonder Valley, her hair shorn and dark, no longer the brassy blond she had kept it. Seeing me she thanked me for rescuing her. She remembered nothing of the episode but heard I had found her and taken her to the hospital. We share the same name, my dad and I, senior and junior. I never corrected her. She hugged me figuring I'd helped her, when in fact I'd stood aside and watched her passed around, abused, discarded. I wasn't at Pizza Richard's the evening they cast her out shoeless into the freezing desert night, but had I been there, I don't know what I would have done. Knowing what I know now, I would have taken her to the fire station, but I doubt that would have occurred to me then. My dad had known what to do, though. I was proud of him. His quick, decisive action saved her life, making my own inaction, by contrast, seem all the more reprehensible to me.

Curtis, though, didn't have much to worry about, I thought. He'd lived his whole life out here flying under the radar. It would take some pretty serious sleuthing for the cops to track him down. That thought made me feel better about forgetting to take him to court. It had been a fluke that he'd been arrested in the first place—it's not like deputies patrolled out here.

At Richard's, Curtis cracked another beer from his thirty-pack at his feet. He stood. "The bar's open," he said. It was three o'clock. Richard grabbed a fresh beer, handing one to me, too. I stood and followed them outside. They climbed into Richard's truck while I loaded into mine. Setting my beer in the cupholder, I led the way to The Palms.

Chapter 16

Although I'd never met her, Sarah's name came up frequently. Richard or Natalie or Dinghy talked about having just seen her, or she just left, or she arrived right after I'd gone. I was beginning to wonder if she existed solely on another parallel plane, in some Euclidian space that never intersected mine, when, out of the blue one evening, she showed up at Pizza Richard's. She burst through the tattered screen door suddenly, well after dark, breathless and panting. Desert Dave thrust a plastic jug of Black Velvet at her. She waved it off. Richard passed her a joint, which she just held while she caught her breath.

"I got stuck," she said, huffing for air. She had buried her ATV in soft sand and had been wandering the desert for an hour trying to find us, cawing like a crow. She cawed for us again, demonstrating the technique. We were to have responded in a manner that would have led her to where we were, I suppose, except none of us had heard her. We were inside under the whoosh of the swamp cooler listening to a Bee Gees reunion concert on TV and talking and drinking.

The sound of the Bee Gees revived her. She began dancing along with the concert. She didn't sit the entire evening, but instead shimmied to the music and sang at full volume, fluent, it seemed, of every word of the Bee Gees songbook. I found her singing voice captivating. I drank beer and watched her like she was part of the show. Between songs she talked about the Bee Gees and music and the alignment of the cosmos and fate. And of love and hugs and trust. She was curious about me too, in a friendly way, asking me where I lived, how long I'd been there. She gave me a great big hug when she left a couple hours later.

She showed up at my cabin the next morning, waking me by cawing outside. I was hung over. I stumbled out to her sitting on her ATV in my front yard.

"I'm glad to have met you," she said again. She had gone to Pizza Richard's the night before because she wanted to check out my vibe. She had come to see if I was legit, to see if I could be trusted. "I'm a good judge of character," she said. "I'd know if you were FBI or CIA or some kind of spy for the man. People think you're a cop or something, but I can tell you aren't." She laughed as she said this, brushing her salt and pepper hair aside and looking up at me. She had make-up on that morning, lipstick—unusual, I thought, for a woman of this desert.

"But I'm not like other women out here," she said. "I'm not a degenerate. I don't do drugs—not speed or meth at any rate. You can test me, do a hair follicle test to prove it." She tugged at her short-cropped hair as she sat on her ATV, a quad with bald, mismatched tires, a plastic milk crate bungeed to the back. She had filled the crate with rope and oil, a pinwheel, a gas can, bubble soap. She gave me a tiny ampule of bubble soap and blew bubbles from one of her own as she talked. She wore a short, flowered skirt that rode up as she sat on her ATV exposing the crotch of her corn-yellow cotton panties. I was surprised, I'll admit, to see that she wore panties.

She asked me that morning to have an affair with her—not a one-night stand, I gathered from her tone, but a torrid, passionate affair. We'd lie together on the roof of her cabin in the moonlight, the place where she wrote her songs, played her guitar, smoked her weed. We would fall in love.

"Would you like to have an affair with me?" she asked.

"I don't know," I said.

"I'm not like the other women out here," she reiterated. "I never trade favors." She never took groceries or handyman work or lines of methamphetamine for a quickie, she assured me. "In fact, I can't even remember the last time I had sex—or I can, it was years ago, with a man I'd met at an open mic who turned out to be married." She found out from his wife. "But we would be different," she said. "I can tell. Besides, you could write about it, it could be part of the story. Don't you ever write about yourself?"

"I could write about myself," I said, "but surely my wife would read it."

She dismissed the affair idea instantly, seemingly as quickly as it came to her. That wasn't why she was there. "Would you give me a ride to town to get gas? You're the only one I can ask that has a running vehicle."

On the drive to town, Sarah chattered about Wonder Valley. "When I first came out here, I felt like a rock star," she said. "I had a new record out, an album of original folk songs with a pretty impressive lineup of backing artists." She quickly became a mainstay at the area's open mics; everyone wanted to play with her, hangout with her, write songs with her. After a while she started bartending at The Palms. "You should have seen it" she said. "I'd park Althea out front." Althea was her VW hippy van. "I had covered her with hundreds of stickers of bands and places and things I'd seen. Passers-through would stop on their way by just to see her. Bikers took pictures of her next to their hogs. It became kind of a tourist attraction!" She quickly integrated herself into the community, she said. She gave singing and performance pointers to James and Laura Sibley, the children of Mary, The Palms' owner, and later, she produced a couple music festivals of her own there, brought musicians from all over the country to the big sandy field and stage in the back of the bar where attendees camped, played music, had drum circles, juggled and hula hooped.

"I loved working at The Palms. I especially loved the old timers. I wish you could have met Miss Lillian. She was a dainty old woman in her eighties. She would ask weekenders and passers-through if they'd seen her mouse tattoo. She'd then lift her dress and make a gasp. The tattoo was gone! 'I guess my pussy ate it!' she'd say. Oh my god, everyone would howl with laughter every time." Other than the old-timers, though, Wonder Valley was full of degenerates, as she called them.

"My first day working at The Palms I had just put my coat and purse down when I heard voices from people on their hands and knees crawling on the floor. I didn't know any of them—yet. Anyway, a woman popped up and yelled 'I found it!' Then some guy scrambled out from under the pool table." She began laughing. "The guy snatched the object from the woman's hand and put it into his mouth. He rolled it around a couple of times and then spit it into his palm and popped it into his empty eye socket! It was his glass eye! That was my introduction to Wonder Valley!" She laughed again, swiping a tear from her eye. "Oh my God! Can you believe these people?"

§ § §

A few days later I visited Sarah at her home on Rainbow Road, a road marked by a rainbow-colored road sign, a sign Sarah had painted herself. Her sign had been altered, though. It now read "Rainbow BRoad."

She was nude in her cabin when I arrived. This I know only because she told me. I beeped my horn, then banged on her door and waited. She called to me from inside, "Just a minute." When she came to the door she wore jeans and a t-shirt.

"People are bothered by my nudity," she said. "Would you be bothered?" I told her no, but I wasn't sure my answer was entirely truthful.

Sarah lived on fifteen acres in what appeared more like a proper house than a Wonder Valley cabin. It looked south over the low dune field in the center of the valley toward the Pinto Mountains in the national park. It was cluttered, like Wonder Valley places were, but not trashed like so many others. In fact, I recognized her place when I drove up—this wasn't the first time I had been there. I'd come once before with Whitefeather; he had wanted me to meet Sarah so she could tell me about his kitties. It was Sarah's uncle who sold the Cat Ranch to Jan, the German artist. He was the one who had let Whitefeather move his camper out front of it, him and his two kittens, the one male and one female. Nobody was around the day Whitefeather and I visited, and I hadn't been back until now.

Out front, Sarah again said she was really happy to have met me. She could tell I was honest, reliable, sincere. She was lonely in the desert.

"Things haven't been going my way," she said. "I've had a falling out of sorts with the valley."

She pulled me across the yard, there was something she wanted to show me. Half a dozen dogs—pitbull mixes and desert mutts—followed us to a covered carport, where, wedged in a jumbled mass of boxes and parts was her VW hippy van, Althea.

"The engine's dead," she said. "It was her seventh." Sarah said she'd put eight hundred thousand miles on Althea while touring and traveling. As a musician, she had gained quite a following, she had played with and opened up for some blues and rock greats like Huey Lewis and the News, Bonnie Raitt, and John Lee Hooker, earning as much as $2,000 a show. But now she couldn't afford to fix the van. It sat dead in the toothpaste-green carport of her toothpaste-green house. Recently, though, someone had smashed a window and gotten inside it. "They trashed it," she said. She teared up as she told me this.

She slumped against the van, deflated. "Wonder Valley has betrayed me. I'd tried to be part of the solution, to help people out of such a rut of a place, to spread a little hippy kindness and love in a place so desolate and dead-set in its dysfunction." She began to cry, a mournful, moaning cry, like one cries for the loss of a loved one, her face, flushed and lined by the sun, crushed into a grimace, columns of spittle stretched across her open mouth like prison bars. I shifted foot to foot. "It was the bar," she said. "The Sibleys, they've done this."

Sarah had been working at the bar the Sunday Bud and Natalie came in for breakfast prior to their stabbing. "I remember it very clearly, Mary hadn't bought any eggs, so there were only hamburgers. Well, I saw Natalie there that morning and was immediately drawn to her. Without even knowing her I worried for her. Natalie was so elegant, not like anyone else out here." Sarah never spoke to Natalie that morning—she was just coming in to start her shift as they were leaving—but she thought about her thereafter.

The ambulance that would rush Bud and Natalie to the hospital screamed past Sarah as she headed to town with a friend later that evening. "I didn't know the ambulance was for them," she said, leaning back against her hippy van. "I had no idea they'd gone back to the bar, but I felt something ominous was happening. On my way back from town I saw the flashing lights and the police there. A pool of blood covered the parking lot." Later, George called her and told her the he-she had been stabbed, told her he thought the he-she had died. George said Fred Harris, the man with the prison-yard build and the flame tattoos, had done it.

"But Mary had specifically banned Fred from ever coming back to the bar. I had personally kicked him out three times before. But George let him in and served him. And he stabbed those people and they nearly died. After that, I tried to do what was right. I went to meet Natalie, to offer her help, but I'd been naïve. Now Wonder Valley is killing me, and if I don't get the hell out of here I'm going to die." She leaned into me for a hug.

§§§

Three times in one year, when Sarah was a child, she got called to the principal's office at school. "Three times that year," she said, "a sibling of mine had unexpectedly, mysteriously died." Her mother suffered depression, as well as other mental illnesses, including, Sarah since concluded, Munchausen-by-proxy syndrome—she deliberately induced illness in her children. Sarah believed her mother over-medicated her and her brothers and sisters to the point that three of them perished, poisoned. Even then, as a child, Sarah knew something was going on.

"I knew my mother was sick, I knew she was dangerous, but I didn't do anything to stop her." Sarah felt she could have saved her siblings if she'd been more attentive, had tried harder to protect them. This had eaten at her all her life. As the eldest of six, she believed she was only alive today because she was complicit in covering up for her mother's madness, hiding it from the rest of the world. "My mother needed me," she said, "so she let me live." Sarah was ten.

She got her first guitar a couple of years later and taught herself to play. She made up her own songs, songs about fate and love and hugs and trust. As her home life worsened, she sank deeper into her music. At eighteen she finally met her biological father, the man her mother had erased from her life when she was only four. She tracked him down from pictures and snippets of information and got to know him on the sly. Her mother had told her he was an uncaring, vicious man, said that she had saved her from his tyranny. But the person Sarah found was tender, loving. He also understood her mother, knew about her mental illness. Sarah could talk to him about her. She told him her suspicions about her siblings' deaths.

"My mother grew furious when she found out about my father. And it caused a rift with my stepfather, too. I loved that man, the only dad I'd ever known, but he always sided with my mother, not wanting to make waves, going along blind to my mother's crimes. But he had to have known—how could he not have known?" Feeling abandoned and betrayed by all sides, Sarah also felt torn, pulled three ways, ripped apart. She suffered a breakdown. She had to free herself of this quagmire, to restore her sense of identity and distance herself from her dysfunctional family. As part of this process she changed her name. She lopped-off her last name, the name her stepdad imposed on her when he adopted her. She dropped her first name, too, the name picked for her by her biological father. She kept nothing but Sarah, her middle name. She became simply Sarah. Or sometimes Sarah Sarah or Sarah [Legal Single Name] to those agencies and others who struggled to fill empty blanks on forms.

Just as she fought to heal emotionally and come to grips with her family issues, though, ovarian cancer struck. She was still in her twenties, delivering singing telegrams and gigging around Marin County when she got the diagnosis. Again, it came back to her mother. The cancer, Sarah felt, was caused by her mother over-medicating her as a child, from her smoking and drugging while she was pregnant, as well as the stress and abuse of an unhappy childhood. Chemotherapy was hard on her, too hard, she said, so doctors took her ovaries and fallopian tubes, her uterus and her cervix. Because of the hysterectomy, she would never be able to have a family of her own, the one thing she desperately wanted.

While she was recovering from surgery, an aunt found her mother dead on the kitchen floor, overdosed on barbiturates, suicide.

After that, Sarah left Marin. In Althea, she set out on the road following the Grateful Dead and Phish as well as hitting the festival circuit where she played the guitar and sang or sold the hats and purses and bong covers she sewed on the machine she carried around with her.

"Traveling around I felt I'd finally found my people, my tribe, you know?" She stayed on the road through the season, returning home to Marin in the winter to pick up work as a waitress or bartender and build a stake to hit the road anew in the spring. Her biological father died while she was on the road. While absent another year, a remaining sibling committed suicide. Then her stepfather passed away. After that she never returned to Marin.

"I could have spent the rest of my life on the road, it was the only place I felt at home, but I had a boyfriend," an aspiring glass blower twelve years her junior. "Two years of traveling with me was enough for him. He wanted to settle down." Sarah was approaching forty when she came to Wonder Valley with her boyfriend, attracted to the area by friends she met at a retro-hippy commune near San Diego. She found the desert beautiful.

She and her boyfriend eventually settled into the toothpaste-green house out by the dune field. He blew glass, she hit the open mics and worked at The Palms. Then Mary fired her. "I was never really sure why," she said. "Mary just called one day and left the message, 'We won't be needing you anymore.'" Tonya took Sarah's shifts.

After Mary let her go, Sarah couldn't find steady work. She picked up a few hours a week as caregiver for Curtis until he smashed the hood of her car and went to jail. She had other problems too. Her boyfriend had fallen deeply into meth and become violent. He bashed Sarah's face into a table, breaking her two front teeth. He left her for another woman shortly thereafter, Sarah's best friend, before leaving Wonder Valley for good. Then Althea blew her engine, forcing Sarah to limp around the valley on that ATV with mismatched tires, all bald.

When a couple years later Tonya went to jail for a parole violation, out of the blue Mary asked her if she wanted her old job back.

"When I went back to The Palms, though it wasn't the same. The atmosphere had changed; all the old-timers were gone. And I was still pissed off that Mary had fired me for no reason."

When Tonya got out of jail and returned to work, Mary again cut Sarah's shifts, so that by the time of Bud and Natalie's stabbing, Sunday was the only day she worked, leaving her struggling financially again, and bitter at Mary and Tonya. The stabbing weighed heavily on her, too.

"It should never have happened," she said. "Fred Harris wasn't even supposed to be at the bar. Something has to be done. This valley can't continue to function like this." Sarah rode her ATV out to the Ostrich Farm and cawed like a crow until Natalie came out. Bud was still in intensive care.

"I told Natalie how I worried about her since I saw her in the bar that Sunday, how as soon as I saw her I knew something bad would happen. These degenerates out here are animals! They destroy what they don't understand!"

She told Natalie about the spatter of blood in the cracked asphalt parking lot. "It stretched twenty-eight feet long," she said. "I measured it." She told Natalie that Mary had made her throw Fred Harris out of the bar three times in the past, and how on the night of the stabbing, the Sibleys couldn't even be bothered to come over from their home next door. "They knew what was happening, they had to, but they didn't care. It was the bar's fault they were stabbed. It was negligence. I told Natalie that if she sued them, I'd testify on her behalf. Something had to be done. This valley can't go on this way."

Soon after, Sarah quit her job at The Palms. Rumors had been circulating that someone with a key had let themselves in through the back door and left with the cash box through the front, leaving the door wide open. "I heard that Tonya told Mary she saw me do it. I heard Mary planned to fire me, so I just quit."

Quitting turned out to be a smart move because when word got around Sarah was helping with the lawsuit, people turned hostile toward her. "Everyone thought it was my fault Mary raised the price of beer!" Hers and Bud's and Natalie's. "The Sibleys sent spies around, too, I'm sure of it. And someone smashed Althea's window and trashed her."

Men came around with meth, she said, and tried to get her into compromising positions. "And people think you're a spy," she said to me, "a mole or a private investigator hired by the Sibleys to dig up dirt. They'd do that, you know, they're smart and ruthless. They've turned the whole valley against me and Bud and Natalie."

I knew it was true that Mary was upset about the lawsuit. She resented Bud and Natalie for it, and Sarah as well. Mary banned me from the bar briefly for standing up for them and remained cold to me after discovering my friendship with them. She harped on about the lawsuit to anyone who'd listen, too, but she didn't appear to be plotting revenge, at least as far as I could tell. Talk of spies and moles and private investigators seemed overly melodramatic to me. Still, I could see Sarah was genuinely frightened by what she saw happening, adding to her distress over her financial situation and current living conditions.

"I'm literally starving," she said. "I've lost fifty pounds." Since quitting the bar, her only income came from a house she cleaned on the other side of town, one day a week, fifty bucks. But the house was forty miles away, one way, a trip she had to make on her ATV with the bald, mismatched tires off any paved road. That fifty bucks went mostly to gas with little left for food and necessities.

She needed help, assistance. Her problem was she owned that toothpaste-green house and another cabin next door and because of that she was ineligible for any government program. Unemployed, however, she could no longer pay her mortgage. Predators came by, one man with a bag of groceries and some dog food. "They were mine for a blowjob, he told me. But I had yet to fall that low. So he took the groceries and left, leaving me only the dog food for my dogs."

§ § §

A few days after we spoke at her cabin, Sarah came to my place and told me she was leaving. She'd called a musician friend from her touring days: he was going to get her out of Wonder Valley. She apologized to me as if her leaving was some sort of weakness, a feebleness of spirit that would leave me here in this valley alone.

"I came to Wonder Valley to spread a little hippy kindness and love," she said. "I came to be part of the solution. But Wonder Valley betrayed me. And now if I don't get out of here, I'll die."

I didn't really understand this sense of betrayal, but I did know the feeling of being suspect. In all my time out here, I hadn't met many of the artists or musicians or retirees. I had heard, however, that many of them had cast me as some kind of crime kingpin because of my association with the so-called degenerates. At the same time, I struggled to overcome suspicions from the others that I was FBI or CIA or some kind of spy for the man because I was too clean-cut. In Sarah's case, I suspect her association with Bud and Natalie had in some ways alienated her from the artists and musicians—her tribe—in Wonder Valley. But beyond that, her worsening economic situation and deteriorating lifestyle further disconnected her from them. This fit with the theory about Wonder Valley that gestated in me. There were separate, overlapping and often competing communities of like-minded people out here that very much kept to themselves. You had the retirees, on one hand, the living embodiment of the original homesteaders, besieged by nature, fighting against it to turn these vast God-given wastes into man-made gardens of Eden. These, by and large, were the old-timers Sarah remembered from the bar. They lived on fixed incomes, but generally had the means to support themselves. On the other hand, you had the artists and writers and musicians. They were younger people typically, who tended to embrace nature and the beauty of the desert, the mountains and stars. This was Sarah's tribe, the kind of people who had attracted her here, the ones at the open mics and weekend music festivals. Finally, there were the others, the "degenerates," the "feral people," the "low-lifes," as they were called, those who just sort of found themselves here, the marginalized economic refugees, having fallen through the porous sieve of American society.

These "others," as well as the snowbirds and retirees and the artists and musicians, existed out here all but unintelligible to one another, like separate and distinct subspecies of humanity, as different as dogs and cats are from coyotes. The artists look at the retirees with snarky aloofness and the retirees the artists with bewilderment, while they both struggled with the degenerates and their squalor, their machinations for survival, or, in the artists' case, willfully looked past that poverty or even incorporated it into their art, creating *assemblage* sculptures as Jan had from the desert's junk and cast-offs without regard to its origin. The marginalized others out here were often the scapegoats for the problems the other communities saw in Wonder Valley, as though their poverty were a disease, communicable and infectious, making the feral families and degenerates vectors of ills to be shunned and avoided. This shunning, in turn, fueled a hamster-wheel cycle of fear and isolation, and the coping through drinking and anger and rage.

Sarah, it seemed to me, had fallen out of her community and found herself marginalized, on the outside. This snubbing occurred subtly, though, slowly, without deliberate malice, as she became a liability, needy, a burden that fed the general anxiety in Wonder Valley, the broad disquiet, the unsettling sense that we were all just one misstep away from finding ourselves like her, mired in poverty, no way to boot-strap our way out of it. She was on a one-way trip, a downward spiral from artist to other. This fear festered, a systemic neurosis, one not just isolated to Wonder Valley. The media and political rhetoric fed it so that many people I knew in and outside of the desert lived with a deep, unending unease—myself included. What if Ann lost her job? What if she got injured or sick? Her mother had died of cancer in her early fifties, a very few years older than Ann was now. In addition to losing his wife of thirty years, Ann's father then lost his home to the medical bills. And it had gotten worse since the economic crash, a great uncertainty had pervaded, leaving people across America with the sense that should we fall, we may never get back up. Charity seemed in short supply, too, as we worried those flailing others could drag us down with them. We retreated to our own, distrustful of those not like us, the country balkanizing to the point we lost any faith in our nation, our government, the media, exacerbating the sense that we were in this on our own.

This stress was amplified further in Wonder Valley by its remoteness from the rest of society, the sheer distance in miles as well as the cultural separation. So many people out here—artists, retirees and especially the others—lacked reliably functioning cars. Fewer still had computers, the internet was expensive and slow, so that apart from limited broadcast television, many Wonder Valley residents lacked any regular, meaningful contact with the outside world.

I've thought about this a lot. I've called Wonder Valley an island, a desert Galapagos, because it felt to me like a petri dish for the state of the country to come, a country that felt to be on the verge of apocalypse. To me, Wonder Valley was a laboratory for America after the meltdown, the meltdown that seemed to loom imminent, where family and tribe and community would be all that we could count on.

Newcomers were changing the character of the valley, too, spilling out here at ever a faster pace, moving into the derelict cabins, fixing them up, some, or just making do in others. And while many would tell you they came for the changing colors of the desert sunset and the limitless stars, most ended up here for the same reasons as those who came before them, the affordability of the place, maybe, or as a reaction to society at large. Some came searching for a sense of authenticity, an alternative to the American Dream that had proved so nebulous and unattainable. They wanted bedrock, the real deal, life and death and heat and grit, not the inescapable Hollywood renderings portrayed as reality. Others came for a freedom no longer available elsewhere or to escape the conformist pressures of mainstream America. They were coming hedging bets against an imminent collapse or just looking for a place to hunker down and wait for times to turn. The newly arrived artists and retirees and downtrodden each found their tribes here, took to their own communities, limiting themselves to members of their own group, avoiding and even rejecting as invalid the lifestyles of the others, which created a dichotomy of cooperation and competition that fostered a unique, contradicting blend of social Darwinism and socialism, where the fittest thrived on the backs of the weak, yet anyone with anything to trade could get by.

I thought of Sarah's proposition, her asking me to have an affair with her. Out of her depth and panicking, I think she recognized me as safe, as one of her own, and clutched for me like a life ring. A single woman, alone without family or tribe, Sarah, at her most vulnerable, had found herself reduced to an object, a commodity, allowed only one thing to offer in trade. But not only had she refused to allow this as a fact of her life, she struggled to accept it as a reality. Her melodramatic theories of moles and spies and G-men were her attempt to understand the situation she had found herself in, that as a woman broke and destitute in Wonder Valley, her vagina was the only barter she possessed.

The irony was that Sarah had inherited a trust. Her stepfather had left her a sum of money but wanting her to make her own way in the world, restricted her access to it until retirement age. She could only get her money if she lived to fifty-nine.

§ § §

A few days after I saw Sarah last, her friend sent some people down and they took her away. I later visited her, living in the mountains above LA. I needed to know how her story concluded. I found her saddened, wounded.

"It wasn't supposed to end like this," she said. "I'd wanted to make a difference in Wonder Valley, to do good. I just wanted to make people happy, to sing my songs and make people happy."

Bud and Natalie had sued The Palms for 1.2 million dollars, but they settled for thirty-three thousand, paid out in monthly installments, $400 a month. And the attorney got half of it. Sarah got nothing. Not that she expected anything—that wasn't why she did it—but she was hopeful.

"All I got for trying to help was to be terrorized. I suffered nightmares, awoke screaming and sweaty and scared and shivering with fear, but the Sibleys got off easy and nothing in Wonder Valley changed. Nothing ever changes.

"Who's going to be stabbed at that bar next? Someone has to do something." She told me she called the California Department of Alcoholic Beverage Control. "I didn't tell them who I was or what bar I was calling about, but just asked questions in general about the procedures for filing a complaint and for making a report." The bar she was calling about, she told them, had employees off the books, they weren't paying fair wages, taxes, they sold cigarettes without a license. "I also told them the bartender—I didn't say who—was selling meth from behind the bar."

I went to The Palms shortly thereafter and found the bar closed. It remained closed for two weeks. When it reopened, things had changed. They had a license to sell cigarettes, a computer and cash register to record transactions. A video camera monitored motion in the bar. And George was gone. So was Tonya. Mary called them and told them they would no longer be needed.

At a bar in the mountains above LA, Sarah downed the last of her whiskey and diet and stared out the window at the gray day outside. It looked like it might snow. Her friend and former partner had gone back east, back to whence he came, and left her alone on that mountain. Before he left, though, he got her into counseling, onto medication for the depression and the symptoms of PTSD. And he took her to Wonder Valley one last time to get her things. She found the doors of her toothpaste-green house kicked in and the place looted, everything she cared about stolen. Then Desert Dave moved in. She didn't know how she would get rid of him. Althea was still there, though, engine blown, at a neighbor's she hoped she could trust.

"It wasn't supposed to end like this," she murmured as she stared out of the bar's window. "This wasn't how it was supposed to end."

Chapter 17

I had never been to The Palms on a Sunday morning, and entering for the first time, it seemed an entirely different place than the bar I frequented. Sunlight filtered through the east side windows and onto the pool table and across the floor. At the bar, the owners of the art gallery with the glass-walled outhouse occupied the stools where Pizza Richard held court in the afternoons. The retired gold miner from out near the Sheephole was at the other end where the regular with the white Fu Manchu sometimes sat. An area artist famous for her restored homestead cabin "sculptures" filled the backroom booths with her entourage, while people I didn't know— weekenders and overnighters from the bands that had played the night before—wandered around taking selfies in front of the stage and Instagramming the distant mountains. I felt awkward and out of place.

I found Jill planted on a stool looking like she'd just rolled out of bed. I took a seat next to her and waited for Mary to notice me. Eventually, she shuffled over and greeted me with a tired smile, her hair in disarray, her oversized flannel shirt lopsided, buttoned up crooked and draped over her fatigue-slouched frame. There was a menu back behind the bar somewhere, she said, a laminated card with a few simple options, though she couldn't find it.

"But you know," she said, we just have eggs and bacon and waffles and stuff. And we can make you an omelet though it's not on the menu."

She wrote my order on a little receipt pad—ham and eggs over easy—then took it to Laura in the kitchen. James, Laura's brother,

197

was working back there with her. Time was, Sundays were the only days the Sibleys worked at their bar, Mary alongside her kids in the kitchen. But since the stabbing and lawsuit and the problems with the Department of Alcoholic Beverage Control, and since she fired Tonya and George, Mary now worked behind the bar every day.

"I'm not a very good bar owner," she had said to me once. "I'm not a bartender. None of us are. We hate it and would rather be doing anything else." Back when they had Tonya and George and Sarah and others working for them, they were free to come and go as they pleased. Sure, Laura had to cook—she'd drive over to the bar when someone placed an order—and they all worked on Sundays, but they were behind the scenes for the most part, where they felt the most comfortable.

"I've got a million other things to do rather than run this bar every day," Mary had said. It just wasn't a priority for her. Her rental cabins consumed her time now. She had a dozen or so cabins that she rented to locals—Biker Richard and Carolyn, and Carolyn's estranged husband Frank and others—but those weren't a problem. Those tenants came in and paid their rent over the bar and were largely responsible for their own cabin's maintenance. If they broke a toilet or smashed a wall or the roof leaked, that was on them to repair. It was the other cabins, however, the vacation rentals, that wore Mary out. She spent the hours before the bar opened washing sheets and towels and changing beds before the arrival of weekenders and out-of-towners.

"They can be so demanding," she complained. "They expect everything to be perfect." They wanted the washing machine to drain somewhere out of sight and the windows to keep the dust out and drinking water that was actually drinkable. James was responsible for all that stuff. While Mary and Laura did the cleaning, he was the maintenance man. Before his afternoon shift at the bar began, he ran place to place, patching plumbing leaks, fixing broken appliances, shooing rattlesnakes off patios. He also did much of the heavy construction on the new places Mary purchased.

After dropping my order at the kitchen Mary returned balancing an overfull cup of coffee, carefully setting it in front of me. She then slid onto a stool up against the waterbed headboard shelves and hugged a cup of tea to herself, arms tight against her oversized, lopsided flannel shirt. She sucked on her lower lip and rocked gently to the music of her own thoughts. She'd never figured out the music player, so the bar had only the chatter of its guests until James, bringing me my breakfast sometime later, turned the music on.

Biker Richard came in and hung his cane on the edge of the bar. Mary slid off her barstool and slowly ambled to the cooler. She withdrew a beer and held the can to her cheek to check its temperature before bringing it to him, taking his money, and resuming her place on her stool.

"He's never any problem," she said to me. Other locals straggled in as the morning progressed. Scruffy Eddie ordered a beer. "He doesn't ever bother anybody." Desert Dave slipped into a booth to have a margarita with his breakfast. "Dave runs a tab, but he always pays his bills." Dingy and Fluffy took Bloody Marys out back to the patio. Mary liked it that they preferred to drink outside. She had an opinion of everyone, and as the morning progressed, it occurred to me that she was making this accounting of the bar's regulars for me, holding each one up in comparison to those that would bother other patrons or invite violence to the bar or sue her in its aftermath. She was letting me know that she knew exactly what was going on. In case I had any doubt, she was letting me know that she knew better how things worked around here than I did.

I had seen the deference people paid her, too. As unassuming as she seemed, everyone knew she called the shots. She was also probably the area's biggest land holder with dozens of homestead parcels under her control, though on paper she owned nothing. She'd spread ownership of the bar and her rentals among family members as well as some limited liability corporations and holding companies. All Mary had to her name was thousands of dollars of medical debt.

"Contracting cancer without medical insurance would be a death sentence if the hospitals had their way," she'd once said to me. I assumed she was referring to the breast cancer that had taken her breast. A private person, I had to extrapolate what I knew about her from small comments like that. But because of her reticence, rumors and stories about her and The Palms circulated Wonder Valley unchecked. She'd been married to a musician, her kids' father, that much I knew. He had been a trombone player in the Air Force Band, then the Salvation Army's. She'd lost a breast to cancer, her husband to a new Asian bride, and their home to debt, not necessarily in that order. Struggling to get by, she moved her children from LA's hinterland to Pioneertown, a Western movie set turned actual town with a saloon as its centerpiece that featured rock bands and barbeque. They lived with a man there, the story went. He was simply a boarder, maybe, or a trusted friend or Mary's lover, I never could figure out which. She invested in real estate with this man until he went to prison for sexual abuse, then, it seems, Mary liquidated the properties. At some point she'd heard about a bar for sale way out in Wonder Valley, an old roadhouse like the one in the kitschy Western movie set. She herself told me she left the decision to buy The Palms up to James and Laura—they were just teens then. They moved to Wonder Valley together, at first living behind the bar in the vintage silver-sided motor coach the man they'd lived with had owned, before buying the cabin next door.

The Palms, at that time, had been vacant, neglected, run down. Mary had told me that the hardest part for her had been finding people she could trust to do the renovation work. That problem plagued her still. "I always have work if I can only find someone to do it," she said to me on one occasion. "I can never get anyone to show up when I ask them to or finish anything they ever start. They mess things up and break things. And they all steal. Tonya stole from me. So did Sarah, probably." Though nobody had ever let themselves in through the back door and left with the cash box through the front, as Sarah thought. It was nickel and dime stuff, skimming off the day's receipts, taking liquor home, pilfering food. "Probably the only one who didn't steal from me was George, but what a mistake he turned out to be." George and the stabbing were subjects she seemed to inevitably circle back around to.

"George should have been looking after the place better. He should have handled the situation better. He couldn't even get the 911 call right! Then that he-she sued me? She came to the bar with Fred Harris as far as I know, that he-she brought him here! That man Fred Harris had never been any trouble before. He'd just come to buy beer to go. It wasn't until that he-she showed up that there was trouble. Besides, it happened outside, not even inside the bar!" But the bar had had no insurance. To pay for her defense and settlement, Mary had to raise the price of beer from a dollar to a dollar twenty-five to a dollar fifty. Customers got upset. "We could have won that lawsuit, I know that," she said. "We had no liability, it wasn't our responsibility. But it would have cost me more to fight it than we ended up paying out in the end." She called the monthly settlement payments her extortion money. "I sometimes forget to send it," she said. Bud and Natalie had told me she forgot a lot.

After the lawsuit, Mary felt herself under siege. "I'm not about to lose everything again," she had said to me. Agitated, she paced away down the bar hugging herself, but returned and stood before me, her jaw clenched. She felt betrayed. She spoke about Bud and Natalie and Sarah and others with disgust, revilement, calling them *those* people, a term of derision that I took to include many of those who hung out drinking at her bar in the afternoons, only exempting the few she considered "Never any trouble." I wasn't sure which group she lumped me into. I think she came to consider me a threat, something she wanted to avoid, yet felt she needed to keep an eye on. When she first resumed operating the bar after she fired Tonya and George, however, she and I talked often. I think she saw in me a vestige of her past life, someone from the outside world, normal, safe. Someone who knew what it was like to lose everything. I became a confidant of sorts—as much a confidant as she would ever allow, I suppose. But then, learning of my friendship with Bud and Natalie, she at first avoided me, then, once triggered, she exploded in anger. She banned me from the bar. "He's a horrible person!" she yelled, screaming at the person sitting next to me at the bar, refusing to look at me or speak to me or acknowledge me. I let her cool down, then apologized and begged my way back in. She remained cold to me after that, however. She felt deceived, I think. I'd disappointed her and lost her trust. After the lawsuit and the state alcohol board enforcements, she felt I and others didn't stand strong enough with her against those responsible.

To aggravate the situation further, this was all happening at a time of palpable change in Wonder Valley. Roger, the retired Marine that passed his afternoons on the bar's patio, had just died of lung disease, for example. Jack McConaha, too, had taken a fall that had landed him in an old folks' home in town, while Rodney and Gerald, septuagenarian brothers who swept the bar in exchange for beer, had become ill and ceased coming in. At the same time, the valley was experiencing the real estate boom with speculators from out of the area buying up property and settling newcomers into the abandoned cabins, transforming the character of the valley. They drove up real estate prices, added traffic and dust to the roads, and erased the night sky with their lights. Some raced motorcycles across the desert, fired guns, others demanded the guns and off-road vehicles be banned. These newcomers didn't understand the social order here, the way things worked, many of them maintaining ties to LA, to down below, coming to Wonder Valley only on weekends and never becoming part of the community. Many of these newcomers were young, too, disaffected millennials whose views were inward, soul-searching, their tribe gathering in the ether, on Facebook and Instagram and Snapchat and Tinder, with little need or time for grizzled old desert rats, save as curiosities.

Of course, the lawsuit and the deaths and these newcomers weren't my doing, but I think Mary saw me somehow at the center of it all. For one thing, I as a newcomer, appeared on the scene just as it all began. I know she saw me as the ringleader of *those* people, too. In fact, she once openly accused me of encouraging their eccentric behavior. "Why are you putting them up to this?" she had demanded of me after hearing of someone doing something she didn't approve of. By then everyone at the bar knew me as Writer Bill and rumors I was writing some kind of big exposé about Wonder Valley surrounded me. Fearing what I would say, Mary reproached me for being deliberately provocative by glorifying the lives of the worst people out here—the worst in her opinion, like Larkin and Bud and Natalie. But while I found Larkin's life tragic, there wasn't much I could do to glorify it, even if I wanted to. The same with Bud and Natalie. They were just trying to zig and zag through the gauntlet of their unique situation as best they could. Suing Mary and The Palms may have been ill-advised considering the merit and implications of it, but I knew it wasn't a malicious act. They'd accrued hundreds of thousands of dollars in medical bills and worried they'd lose their home to it. Besides, they had assumed they were suing the bar's insurance company, not Mary herself. Without insurance, though, the suit was so much more personal, and Mary just couldn't understand why I and others didn't feel that insult as deeply as she did.

I think she also worried about what I would write about her and the bar. She saw me there every day and knew I saw everything that went on. Still reeling from the lawsuit and the state alcohol board enforcements, I think she feared I'd somehow expose her, feared she'd be considered complicit in the problems and even the rapid change in the valley. She capitalized, to some extent anyway, on what she saw as the degeneracy in Wonder Valley by taking meager money in exchange for cheap booze. With her beer prices as they were, it was cheaper to drink at The Palms than to drive to town and buy it. The guys she hired to work on her cabins, therefore, typically spent the money they earned from her in her bar, earning her back much of the wages she paid out. And while she was often contemptuous of them, thinking they should make better use of their money, she took it, nonetheless. She also bought scavenged materials and other things from them as well, items often found while Wonder Valley shopping or from some other even less savory source. I'm not saying she willfully or knowingly bought stolen merchandise, but The Palms was the first place anyone went when they had something to sell, and if it was something Mary wanted or needed, she often bought it, the money she paid out often going back to the bar in alcohol purchases or spent on other vices. Of the four most sought-after commodities in Wonder Valley—cigarettes, gasoline, Nattie Ice, and methamphetamine—The Palms was the valley's sole source for two of them. Back when George was selling gas out front from the back of his van and others allegedly dealing drugs inside, however, The Palms was one-stop shopping. I think Mary was genuinely troubled by this. And she certainly didn't want any suggestion of this made public.

The fact of the matter is, though, Mary didn't create or substantially encourage the bad out here anymore than I did. There were many alcoholics and drug addicts and mental patients living here before she came, and she and The Palms certainly weren't the ones attracting any more of them. Newcomers came or were pushed here for many reasons, The Palms the least of them. The newcomers brought their addictions with them, they were their own. So were their mental illnesses and criminality. We all make choices and our choices are ours. I was acutely aware, however, that each of us only had so much power, so much self-control or personal strength to bootstrap ourselves out of whatever hole we found ourselves in— whether we dug it ourselves or not. It was easier, though, to sweep these problems out of sight than to confront them. And having them exposed in print would make that confrontation inevitable.

None of this is to say The Palms was the valley's hotbed of moral degeneracy. It was common ground for all the various communities in Wonder Valley. Rarely, however, even at the bar, did these tribes interact. Like the Serengeti of Africa, herds of different species shared the land, but not each other's company. The retirees had

Sunday breakfast, the artists and musicians the bands of Saturday nights. The others, *those* people, had the afternoons. They were the drinkers, the ones who spent the money there. But Mary had bought The Palms as a place where James and Laura could play their instruments, have their band, The Sibleys, and was not to be simply a gathering place for desert low-lifes—Mary had told me this many times. Working as the bartender, though, had exposed her to the kind of place she owned, one where low-lifes, the afternoon regulars, embodied its public identity. I think she struggled with the moral and ethical implications this created for her. At any rate, it was wearing her out. She was fed up with it. Things had to change.

Thus, she devised a new strategy for running the bar: She would no longer trade beer for the paper towels and napkins Pizza Richard pinched from the pizza parlor. And you weren't going to find Richard's pizzas on the bar on Mondays anymore either. The Palms would be closed on Mondays now, and Tuesdays too. She also cut the bar's operating hours, from seven a day to just three. If there wasn't an event, the bar would only be open from three in the afternoon until six. That was time enough, Mary figured, for the regulars to come in, have a beer, maybe a burger, buy an 18-pack to go, and take their drama away with them. No longer would they be her problem. If you came to the bar now you were expected to behave. Don't bring your dog. Don't ask for credit. And don't even talk like you've got a weapon or drugs or some kind of mental illness.

The Palms would no longer be the epicenter of Wonder Valley's bullshit. She kicked Curtis out. Then George. George talked to people, he ran off business. He bothered the passers-though and weekenders with his stories about how his ex-wife ate a tuna fish sandwich and got pregnant, about his MBAs, his Master of Taxation, his law degree, his nasally laugh.

"He's driving me crazy!" Mary said to me as she made the decision to ban him. "He has to go because things around here are going to change." George just didn't fit into her new vision, Mary's new strategy for the bar. Besides, he had been on duty when Bud and Natalie were stabbed, and Mary just couldn't stand to look at him after that.

At first, after Mary kicked him out, George just ignored the edict. He returned with Biker Richard, but she ran him off again. He later called her, begged and pleaded. They came to an arrangement.

George explained the terms to me. "I can go to the bar if someone dies," he said. "I can attend wakes or memorials. Other than that, I can only go to the bar if I go with you."

That made no sense to me. "So, you can only come with me? Why me? Mary hates me!"

Mary, however, verified the deal. "He has to sit with you at the bar and leave when you leave," she said. "And he can't talk to passers-through unless they talk to him first. If he's going to come to the bar, you have to be responsible for him, you make sure he behaves, or he has to leave."

Why me of all people? I figured Mary just wanted George to annoy me as much as he annoyed her. If I was going to encourage the craziness out here, I needed to experience some of the craziness I encouraged.

But I liked George. I'd found that if I just asked more probing questions about whatever story he was droning on about, we could have an actual conversation. He had an interesting past, the grandson of a sea captain, a career in the Marines, did two tours in Vietnam. He was stationed at the base here outside of town where he married briefly and had a daughter before being reassigned elsewhere. He got his bachelor's degree in Hawaii while still in the Corps, then, upon retirement, moved to Ohio for his Doctor of Jurisprudence degree. He worked in admittance at the school and could take classes for free, so he did, completing that Master's in Taxation and a couple of MBAs. He returned to his then-teenage daughter in California when his ex-wife went to jail for fraud, but couldn't find work.

"Even the local banks wouldn't hire me," he said. "I was

overqualified." Knowing George like I did, though, I was sure there were other reasons. In fact, I couldn't imagine him working in a bank or anywhere else for that matter. But George had gotten by well enough on his military retirement augmented by the money he earned as a substitute math teacher.

I'll admit, a little George went a long way, but I tried to bring him to the bar once or twice a week. When he called and asked for a ride, he'd greet me with a "Is this Bill?" if I answered the phone or a forlorn "It's just George" if I didn't. I'd pick him up at his place, the now-oxidized MG convertible he bought after the war sitting on flat tires in the dirt of his yard next to the fast-looking boat Desert Dave gave him in repayment of a debt, the boat I now have a painting of. He lived in only one of the rooms of his homestead cabin because the others were jammed with stacks of books and the piles of magazines from the hundred-maybe subscriptions he didn't realize he didn't have to subscribe to to win the Publishers Clearinghouse Giveaway. Those books and magazines, as well as his university degrees and credentials, the bills and the junk mail that covered the floor and the table and lined the hallway in head-high stacks were all iced over with a thick layer of white pigeon shit from the birds that had invaded through the hole in the roof and roosted by the hundreds in his living room. He fed them—only outside—where he hoped to convince them to relocate.

At The Palms, he always sat right next to me, just as he was supposed to, humphing and grunting to himself, his wet, tired blue eyes peering out from under the weathered hat slouched on his head. Many passers-through and weekenders recognized him, having met him another time, another trip. He had always been part of the local color. Many greeted him with a Hey George! when they saw him. He didn't remember them, but he could talk to them since they spoke to him first, tell them about how his ex-wife was married nine times. If he got up and went over to them, though, Mary would flash me a look, one meant to remind me that he was my charge. I was to steer George back to his stool or out back for a smoke.

Frustration and embarrassment colored his face.

"But they started talking to *me*," he'd say as we shambled away together.

§§§

After finishing their breakfasts that first Sunday, the crowd slowly disappeared. The owners of the Glass Outhouse Gallery said their goodbyes, Jill, claiming something to do, slipped away. It was a changing of the guards, in a sense, the morning folks drifting away before the afternoon set arrived. I sat with the dregs of my coffee watching Mary on her stool behind the bar. It was just her and me now, and some old movie on the bar's TV, the sound off. Ignoring me, she had turned to the movie for company. A Bob Dylan song was on the music player. *I ain't a-saying you treated me unkind. You could have done better but I don't mind. You just kinda wasted my precious time.* I looked up at Mary and for a second, I imagined she was humming that tune. It became her lament. Suddenly, a pall of sadness shrouded me. I felt dismissed, written off. We didn't really know each other, Mary and me, but I think we could have been friends. I felt bad we never would. *Don't think twice, it's all right.* The song ended. I took a deep breath as silence consumed the bar.

On the television, black and white figures strode around melodramatically, silently making much ado about something lost in the silence. I stood and put a twenty on the counter. "Thanks," I said. Mary never took her eyes from the screen. I pushed the door open and I left.

Chapter 18

Wonder Valley had a particularly bad week the week Tonya died: Lou, an old timer and bar regular passed away. So had Devon Million, diabetes had taken his legs, but a bad heart took his life. And then there was the one they called Madriña. She'd studied shamanism in the jungles of Peru, boxes of research littered her lot. Red found her dead on her cabin floor. But while that spate of deaths was upsetting, Tonya's death was gut-wrenching. She hadn't died of old age like the others. She'd been murdered. She'd been found bound, her hands tied behind her back, hung by a dog leash from a tree in her yard. And everyone knew who had done it. Tonya had told them her ex was coming for her. In fact, people had seen him. He had been at The Palms looking for her the day it happened, the day she died. Her friends had called the police, told them everything they knew, but the police wouldn't do anything about it, wouldn't investigate, stopped returning calls. That's when her friends came to me. I was a reporter, they said. I could look into things.

Tonya's friends believed the police wouldn't investigate her murder because she was a felon, a former druggie. "They don't care about people like that, like her," Denise said.

It's true, sheriff's deputies out here did seem apathetic. Their response times were painfully slow, and while this was primarily due to the valley's isolation, it just added to the sense that the cops didn't care. And Wonder Valley's reputation as an end-of-the-line place also prejudiced police attitudes. Out here, everyone was suspect, their stories considered dubious. I knew with certainty that

Tonya's murder wouldn't get the attention it would have had it happened in a more affluent, urbanized area. I agreed to see what I could find out.

I figured I needed to talk to those closest to Tonya: Jill, Kassandra, Denise, the guys from the bar, see what they knew about this ex. I hadn't known Tonya very well myself, only from The Palms, and there, she mostly made small talk, bar talk, about the weather, music and movies. She'd linger in front of out-of-towners and passers-through if she thought they were tippers, leaning against the bar or wiping it down, her breasts heaving out of her leopard skin top or low-cut crop as she wiped, tendrils of brown hair cupping her chin on either side. She was always energetic and upbeat, though I thought her sad, knowing brown eyes revealed a kind of resignation, a weariness that conflicted with the smooth, youthfulness of the rest of her face.

For most of the guys at the bar, Tonya had been the only woman they encountered with any regularity, and many—Whitefeather, Scruffy Eddie, Pizza Richard—felt he had a special relationship with her. They felt like nobody knew her like he did. Talking to them, however, these guys seemed to know as little about her as I did. They didn't know about her past, for example—not really—nor about her exes or her boyfriends or fiancées, and still fewer knew she had a mother and a brother living in the area. I hadn't.

Tonya died in the trees behind the remote cabin she rented, a cabin on a desert island, a secluded knob of land surrounded by a wash, a sandy moat crossable only by four-wheel drive. It looked, from the distance, like a Gilligan's Island in a sea of sand. The story was that an eccentric old woman had owned the property, had dug the moat, kept emus and chickens and tracked the comings and goings of UFOs from there. The woman left the chicken coops and emu pens and a barn full of knickknacks and junk and odds and ends of furniture when she left, expecting to come back some day and retrieve them. She never did.

I went to check out the place—I had never been there when Tonya was alive. I wasn't sure what I was looking for. The compound was ringed by a dense thicket of trees, anything could go on there and no one would know, no one could see, no one would hear. The murder had had no witnesses, so I looked around for footprints and other clues. I stepped around Tonya's things strewn about everywhere, gone through and picked over—Wonder Valley shopping, an accepted practice to those figuring Tonya wasn't going to need any of this stuff anymore anyway. And she'd had a lot of stuff, too. They say you could ask Tonya for something and she always had it, that missing part, that just-the-right tool, that anything-you-needed because she had everything, rusty and old and broken maybe, moved with her from place to place, boyfriend to boyfriend, around the desert, but she had it, had one. At least one. It gave her comfort having it, knowing she had it to give you if you needed it. Scattered around the compound I found furniture enough for several households and clothes enough they filled a twenty-foot travel trailer—her closet, she'd called it. Behind the cabin was a swimming pool, empty and flaccid and deflated. I imagined Tonya floating in that pool in better times, drifting silently under the desert's vast sky surrounded by a lifetime's worth of accumulated possessions. Now, though, parts and tools and toys and doodads were flung about, things found worthless to those who had looted the place when they heard she was gone, things like clothes and photos, her panties, vibrators, a huge stuffed Big Foot and a teddy bear hanging from a noose that she told friends was her landlord hung in effigy. Other nooses littered the Gilligan's Island compound, too—Roger at the bar had showed her how to tie them. These were snapshots of her life, I thought, glimpses into her soul, hand-written poems, letters on pink paper in purple pen, a check receipt for a large sum of money, a letter alluding to the termination of a trust, runes, hieroglyphics, readable only to an expert, the police, an investigator, someone with training, someone other than me. I wasn't a reporter. I had a degree in creative writing, for Christ's sake. I didn't know what the hell I was doing. Yet her landlord was already hauling everything away, truck load after truck load, spreading it around various dumpsters across the valley, destroying whatever evidence was left. I took pictures with my phone. Under the tree where Tonya had hung from the dog leash, the marks from her dragging feet still marred the dirt. Seeing that, my knees went weak.

As I said, it was not like people out here hadn't tried to get an investigation opened. Denise had told the cops about the ex-fiancée; a man Tonya was terrified of. Because of her the guy went to prison, nine years. She had testified against him, or set him up, or somehow was responsible for his incarceration, and as he went to jail, he swore that when he got out, he'd get her, he'd kill her. Tonya had told this to Denise, as well as Jill and Kassandra. She told them all this herself, each independently, and their stories all corroborated. They each saw how serious she was when she told them, they could see it in her eyes, they could feel her fear. She was repeating this for them to remember, they knew, and they did remember, every detail, the ex's long lean build, his darting eyes, his gray ponytail, and when they found her hanging dead from that tree, her hands bound behind her back, they recalled it all, everything, unfortunately, except the ex-fiancée's name.

But Denise had seen him. The day of Tonya's murder he had returned to Wonder Valley. Denise had been out in front of the bar waiting for it to open when two men pulled up. One was chatty, he'd just gotten out of prison, he told her, after nine years. The other one, the one with the long, lean build and gray ponytail, the eyes darting from under his cap, was silent. He didn't say much inside the bar either, it was the other guy who asked about Tonya, spoke to the regulars. He was the one who got directions to Tonya's cabin. He was the one who drove when they left, heading in that direction.

§ § §

Tim Kralick was Tonya's boyfriend at the time of her death. He was a long-haul trucker who had also briefly been her boyfriend years before. Once upon a time, Tim had come to Wonder Valley to rescue some girl, but got stranded here himself for a while, he and his friend Fluffy having fallen into the local meth scene. He met Tonya at the bar, and they dated for a few weeks until Tonya dropped him for Fluffy, and Tim moved into the cabin cruiser at Larkin's with the girl he'd come to rescue. Then he moved away. But he and Tonya remained friends. As a trucker, he detoured through the area on occasion and they'd meet for drinks. They'd talk on the phone for hours, too, she in her bed, him on the road. Tim became her confidant, he told me. He had something special with her. No one knew her like he did.

Tim came back to Wonder Valley to rescue Tonya about six weeks before her death. "She'd called me in a panic," he said. "She said that if I didn't get her out of Wonder Valley, she'd lose her soul."

He picked her up with his big rig from the parking lot of The Palms. She left her nine dogs in the care of Scruffy Eddie who moved into her Gilligan's Island cabin to watch over her stuff. Tim told me that over the weeks they spent on the road together, Tonya slowly opened up to him, told him about herself, about her past. I had heard many stories about Tonya over the years, too, fables, tall tales, over-the-top epics. She had been on her own since she ran away to Hollywood, one story went, lived there on the streets, a teen turning tricks until some casting agent-cum-pedophile-john discovered her and got her a part on *General Hospital*——*General Hospital* or *One Life to Live*, no one could remember which. Tonya was eighteen by then. Or sixteen. Or maybe younger. Any kernel of truth in this story blossomed in Wonder Valley. Of course Tonya had been a TV star. It had to be true, someone as beautiful as her surely would have been discovered. Surely, she would have been pulled off the streets, a Cinderella finding her Prince Charming.

She had married young, the stories went, but couldn't have children. She'd been molested as a child. A janitor in her school pushed her into a closet and raped her, hurt her so badly she had to have surgery to repair the damage, though no one could repair it enough that she could ever have kids. Later, as a young adult she was raped again. Broken down, she hitched a ride with a man, leaving her sister with the car. He raped her before he brought her back. Right up to the day she died, it seems, Tonya had been a magnet for this particular class of depraved asshole.

Tonya's marriage was a tumultuous one, only lasting a few months or a few years. They separated. Or he committed suicide, one came before the other, no one could tell me which, or even if that's what really happened at all. It was after that, though, that Tonya came to Wonder Valley, to a single-wide trailer on thirty-five acres, a remnant of a 160-acre quarter-section homestead, the family vacation place she'd visited as a kid. Tonya hated the desert, she hated that property, but needing a place to go, she moved into that trailer next to the remains of the family's burned-down shack.

Tonya got by in Wonder Valley bartending. She replaced Sarah at The Palms after Mary let Sarah go. She met the man with the long lean build, the darting eyes, the gray ponytail around this time and moved to town with him. Or he moved to Wonder Valley with her. Then he killed someone. Or he beat someone up or he beat Tonya up or was cooking meth or trafficking drugs. Everyone had a different version, nothing actually corroborated. What was consistent, though, was that the man went to prison, hard time, nine years. He was put away because of her, they all remembered, and as his jailers hauled him off, he seethed that he was going to kill her.

Records show Tonya herself did time for drug possession and trafficking around that time too, and again the next year. In the meantime, her mother divorced Tonya's father and moved to the singlewide on the thirty-five acres, carting Tonya's failure-to-launch brother down from Central California with her. Getting out of jail, Tonya found another place to live and went back to work at the bar, again displacing Sarah who had covered her shifts. All told, Tonya worked at The Palms for a decade.

Losing her job after the stabbing and the lawsuit left Tonya without any income, destitute and desperate—not a situation a woman wants to find herself in out here. More than that, it seemed to me, she lost her identity, her reason to get dressed-up every day, to put on makeup, to be the center of attention, the Queen of Wonder Valley.

She got a part-time job working for her landlord, paperwork mostly, but sometimes manual labor as well. She wasn't earning enough to keep up with her rent, though, and the landlord hounded her for it. She owed him, he told her—grass, gas or ass, nobody rides for free. She shined him on, but his hounding became veiled threats, then not so veiled. He knew she was vulnerable, more vulnerable than she'd ever been in her life. Just once, he said. She owed him, he said. He took her to a motel in town.

On the road, Tonya, sobbing, told Tim Kralick that the landlord later forced her into a three-way, a ménage-a-trois with his wife. She told him the landlord was continually coming to her compound, crossing the sandy moat and entering the saltcedar trees that hid everything from view. Tonya tried to tell him no, but he threatened her with eviction, she'd lose her stuff, she'd lose her dogs.

"Her dogs were her life," Tim said, "they were her family. Her dog Bam Bam was like her child." Tonya panicked. She hid from the man. She moved a mattress to the roof of the cabin and slept where he couldn't find her. At least once, she told Tim, the landlord pushed her down and raped her.

"She said she didn't even fight back. She just laid there, staring at the ceiling." It was after that, she called Tim. "I had to get her out of Wonder Valley by the sixteenth of August. She said that was the landlord's birthday and the wife had promised her to him as a gift. She said she couldn't let that happen. She said that if she didn't get out of Wonder Valley, she would lose her soul."

Tim told me all this as we walked the wash leading to Tonya's place a few days after her death. In his truck, he said, they drove Pacific to Atlantic, Florida to Maine, and as they did, the stress and madness of Wonder Valley fell away from her.

"And she was clean," he said, "No drugs or drinking. Her complexion had improved, she smiled and laughed and teased and joked just like old times." She cried, though, when she told him about her life, about her past, about what her landlord was making her do. You'll never need to go back there again, Tim promised her.

But Tonya did need to go back. She still had her stuff here, and her dogs. She left them at her Gilligan's Island compound with Scruffy Eddie, but soon after she left, the landlord kicked him off the property. And then the messages started. *When are you coming home?* But Tonya was back east, up north, all over with Tim, going where the loads took them. The longer she stayed away, however, the more insistent the text became. *When are you coming back?* Worry began to eat at her. *They're going to take your dogs to the pound!* She had to return to Wonder Valley, she told Tim, one last time, just to take care of her dogs, her stuff, make arrangements. She would take only what she needed, absolutely needed, and ditch the rest. Then she'd tell that landlord to go fuck himself and abandon Wonder Valley forever, start over, maybe drive truck for a while, then find a place they could live and make a new life. Tim was deeply in love with her and, he said, she loved him too. He found a load that took them back west.

§ § §

I can't stop dwelling on what would have happened if Tonya had never come back. Her dogs would have gone to the pound, of course. And her stuff, her lifetime's accumulation of things, the furniture enough for several households, clothes enough to fill a twenty-foot travel trailer, the parts and tools and toys and doodads would have been pawed through, picked over and pocketed or tossed out into the dirt then thrown into a dumpster. But that's what happened anyway, and Tonya would still be alive.

When Tonya finally returned to Wonder Valley, she found eight of her nine dogs gone. Someone left the chrome leash they used to drag her dogs away draped over her gate. At Dingy and Fluffy's she found three of her missing dogs crammed into a single dog crate waiting to be taken away. They looked like they'd been in that crate for days. Crying, Tonya released them. She'd never leave them again, she promised.

"But you need to take care of your affairs so we can go," Tim reminded her. They argued. Frustrated, he left her outside her compound to park his truck for the night at a friend's a few miles down the road.

The landlord had changed the lock on the gate, so Tonya had to jump the fence. Inside the compound, the cabin was trashed. With Scruffy Eddie gone, her things had been ransacked, anything of value taken, the rest thrown out into the dirt of the yard. She spent the night there alone.

News of Tonya's return spread quickly. The next day Denise brought her a pint of tequila, Tonya's first drink in weeks. She smoked some meth with her, too. When Tim returned, they bickered again.

"You should be making arrangements for your dogs and grabbing what you need so we can get the hell out of here," he said.

"But I need more time!"

Christ, Tim thought. He was frustrated but tried to be practical. Maybe what they needed was some time apart. They'd been together six weeks, side by side day and night and now maybe they just needed some space. He left for a run into town. "I'll be back," he told her, "I'll talk to you later."

Over the course of the day and overnight, he got no calls from Tonya, so he left her alone. By the next afternoon, however, he realized his phone had been dead. Shit, he thought, he had forgotten to pay his bill. Reactivating it, he found he'd missed several calls and texts from her, messages that were at first lonely, but grew angrier, vitriolic, as Tonya, drinking, grew drunker.

He didn't listen to all the messages. Right away he called her. No answer. He quickly drove to her compound and jumped the fence. The cabin door was open and the lights were on, her makeup bag was there and her things where she'd left them, but Tonya was nowhere to be found. It was the dogs that put him on edge, though.

"They wouldn't let me approach," he said. "They were skittish yet seemed to need something." He gave them some water and left with a feeling that something was wrong.

Kassandra had received a phone message from Tonya, too. She'd been out all day, though, and didn't get the message until she got back that night. In the phone message, Tonya sounded desperate. She pleaded, "Please call me back! Please, please call me back!" But when Kassandra called, Tonya didn't answer. Right away she went up to the compound, but found the gate locked.

The next night, after Tim had gone there, Jason found her. A good friend of hers, he went to look for her, entering the compound by the back way, across the moat to the east, the opposite side from the landlord. There he found the dogs agitated, skittish, as if they were trying to alert him to something. He followed them into the trees that ringed the compound, shining his flashlight around. The compound was dark, the cabin lights off. He knelt to calm the dogs— they knew him, he'd been there many times before. As he knelt, he caught a glimpse of someone over his shoulder. Then something grazed against him. He jumped with a start. Above him she floated, her feet dragging the ground. He shined his light up at her eyes, black and bulging, her face bruised and spidered with broken veins. She looked like she'd been beaten. Her hands, too, were bound behind her back. He bolted, running across the wash to Dingy and Fluffy's where he banged on the door, Call the police! Tonya, he said, was dead. Murdered. The news flared through the valley like wildfire.

In Wonder Valley, everyone was in shock—I was in shock. There had been that spate of deaths here that week, but Tonya's was different: she wasn't old, she was young, in her early forties, and popular, like Wonder Valley royalty. And she'd been murdered. It was like a kick in the crotch. I hadn't known her very well, but we were friends, I think. I felt like I had something special with her, the knowing looks she gave me, the barbs and inside jokes we shared. Maybe she was just being a good bartender, but it seemed to me like something more. I felt I owed it to her to find out what had happened, I owed it to her friends.

Tim had told the police about the warnings and fears Tonya had expressed about her ex, how people had seen him at the bar the day she died. He also told them about the landlord, how he was forcing himself on her and was now destroying evidence by hauling all her stuff away before any investigation could be completed. The police listened patiently to him, then did nothing.

Denise told me she saw the ex and his friend follow her out of the bar as she left. They turned out behind her and followed her up the dirt road, too. And she knew they weren't from out here.

"They followed me too close," she said. "Everyone knows to fall back a bit, let the dust from the car in front clear, but these guys didn't. They ate my dust the whole way."

Later, about dusk, she saw the same guys parked at the top of the wash, saw them walking around as if trying to get their bearings, then she saw them head down the wash towards Tonya's. She said she later tracked them right to Tonya's compound.

The wash leading to the compound begins at Biker Richard's as a dirt road, on level ground, but soon cuts off across the desert as it gradually gouges deeper, becoming like a wound, a gaping scar, its walls head-high as it passes behind Tonya's landlord's place. Reaching Tonya's compound, it broadens and branches and forms the compound's moat. It had rained the day before Tim and I walked it, a thunderstorm having dumped a torrent on the valley, its flood flashing through the ravine, scouring it clean. Denise insisted she saw footprints, they led right to the compound, but when I walked it with Tim, we found only an unblemished canvas of smooth sand.

Tim said he was beginning to doubt the ex-fiancée-murderer theory anyway. "It's just too much of a coincidence that the ex had shown up just as Tonya returned to the valley and was going to leave again right away." The landlord, on the other hand, was the real person of interest. He lived right next door and Tim had evidence that placed him on the property the night of Tonya's death.

"Kassandra said the gate was locked from the inside when she went looking for Tonya the night she died," Tim said. "The lock was on the outside of the gate, though, when I showed up the next day." This suggests, Tim reasoned, that someone with a key to the gate—the landlord—was there, inside the compound on the night of Tonya's death, and had left through the gate by the time Tim arrived.

Tim confronted the landlord with this evidence. The landlord, however, insisted he hadn't even known Tonya was back, not until the police showed up.

"Bullshit!" Tim shouted. "Scruffy knew!" He lived in a travel trailer next to the landlord's property. "Scruffy said he could see the lights on in her cabin! Your employees had seen her, too. And she'd been *here* looking for her dogs! Yet you, her closest neighbor and the one demanding her return, *the one person with the key to the gate*, say you had no idea she was home? You're a liar!" Tim moved toward the landlord. Bystanders tried to restrain him. "Tonya told me everything! I know why she was afraid of you!"

The landlord threatened to call the police. Friends dragged Tim away before they arrived.

A few weeks later I got the coroner's report, their investigation into Tonya's death. It said officers had found Tonya hanging by a dog leash from a tree, the dog leash left across her gate after her dogs had been hauled to the pound. The report said nothing about her hands being bound. They found no evidence of struggle either—the marks on her body, her black and bulging eyes, bruised and spidered face consistent with death by hanging. Self-inflicted. Suicide, they concluded, not murder. There was no mention of sexual assault nor any indication of sexual activity in the hours leading up to her death. They found alcohol in her system, though, and methamphetamine. She had been depressed about her financial situation, the report concluded, "She was unable to pay her rent and was being threatened with eviction by her landlord." On her phone was a text she sent to

Jason, the friend who had found her, a suicide note of sorts. It said, *When you have time, send someone to get me out of this tree.*

§ § §

Few believed me when I told them Tonya hadn't been murdered, that she had killed herself.

"I had just seen her," Denise said. "She was happy! Things were finally looking up for her!"

"She was too much of a survivor," Kassandra added. "She'd been through so much."

"Besides, she would have used pills, or a noose, like the ones she tied all the time, like the ones laying all over her compound, not a dog leash—she wouldn't even use a leash on her dogs!"

"And what about the ex-fiancée asking about her at the bar, lurking in the wash the day of her death? And the landlord?" The cops were wrong, they all felt, I was wrong, nobody even investigated.

"Nobody cares about us out here," Denise repeated. "To you and everyone else, Tonya is just another dead felon."

But the cops had done their job, I insisted. They had investigated. They had collected evidence from the scene, interviewed Tim and Jason and the landlord. The coroner had done his job too. There was no sign of struggle, her hands had not been bound, the forensics were classic: suicide. Tonya had committed suicide.

I had to rationalize this even to myself. She had had such a great experience on the road with Tim, the time of her life. Why would she kill herself when she was only back for a few days before going off again to start a new life? I suspected that, coming back to Wonder Valley, she had been confronted with the realization of what she would need to give up to leave—the dogs, all her stuff—and she had to have been very conflicted. Then, drunk and unable to reach Tim or Kassandra or Jason, I bet she was already feeling abandoned and alone when her landlord came to confront her, made his demands or whatever, threatened her maybe, if he had gone to her at all—that was just my speculation, only he knows. At any rate, he didn't kill her. No one did. She killed herself. But no one wanted to believe me. Anger and frustration turned to hostility.

"That's bullshit!" Scruffy Eddie said to me at The Palms. "This is just a cover-up!"

"Why are you doing this?" another demanded of me. "Why is it any of your fucking business anyway?" I felt a groundswell of resentment and animosity surge up around me. I had the coroner's report, I could prove my assertions, but nobody wanted to see it. I was an outsider, I was reminded, a newcomer, a dumbshit from down below who didn't know a thing about Wonder Valley.

Clearly murder was what they all wanted to believe. It seemed consistent with her life, one where she fought and struggled, a survivor. My suicide narrative, though, contradicted this. By changing the way she died, I changed the way she lived. I was making her defenseless and susceptible, not such a survivor, but fragile. My version meant they hadn't known her like they thought they had. It meant they had been wrong about her. The murder version of the story served to exonerate everyone from her death, too, while suicide made us all complicit. The fact of the matter is that Tonya's tribe had abandoned her in the weeks before her death. She had become needy since she lost her job at The Palms, she'd become a burden before Tim came and took her away. She never had gas, couldn't keep her truck running, needed money and food and trips to town, giving everyone reasons to distance themselves from her until she had no one. Suicide would force everyone to confront that, confront their part in it. What if Mary hadn't fired her? What if someone had intervened when she told them about the landlord? We all knew about the landlord; I even knew about the landlord months before she died. What if someone had recognized the nooses she always tied or the morbid suicide jokes she often made for what they were, or if those closest to her had been more caring or more conscientious or more protective and supportive? Murder made Tonya courageous, a fighter to the end. Suicide made her vulnerable and everyone else pathetic and weak.

Jill had told me that one of Tonya's escape contingencies had always been to go visit her sister, a successful career woman living out of state—she couldn't understand why she hadn't called her. I looked her up.

"I used to send Tonya makeup and stuff, and money, sometimes," she told me over the phone. "Tonya was an unusually beautiful and charismatic child," she said. They had been raised upper middle class, the sisters with their brother, and had traveled all over the world with their father's import business. Tonya, her sister said, hadn't run away to Hollywood as the story went, but followed her there. "She slept on my couch and picked up work as an extra in *General Hospital*. You can see her in the background of restaurant scenes and stuff." She told me about Tonya's rapes, and about her failed marriage. "After that broke up, she needed a place to go, so she went to our property in Wonder Valley."

Tonya ended up in Wonder Valley like so many did, but stayed, the big fish in this small pond until that dried up and all hope withered, and she became mired here, living a life increasingly isolated in this land of isolation, everyone fighting their own fight with their own problems. Community, it seems, only goes so far.

I went back to my cabin and laid out in the dirt away from Brian's lights. The night sky out here is truly vast and limitless. Looking up, you see infinity. The sky appears torn from the earth, torn along the jagged edge of the mountains, the sand and shacks and me with them dissolving into a featureless black void below it. I felt shrouded in the dust of the Milky Way, the ancient pulse of countless stars. Under the weight of the heavens, you're reduced to just your breath rasping in your chest, your heart lub-dubbing in your ears. Life, the entirety of your existence, collapses to a mere spark, the briefest blush of daylight in this endless night.

That night, under that immense sky, my hold on the world felt tenuous. I felt upside down, hanging off the planet, hanging above the abyss, the stars pulling me to them. Gravity, the law of gravity was just another law in this lawless place, and that night I felt I could trip, could slip, could just lose my grip and fall, fall from the planet, fall into the void of space.

To most out here, Tonya's suicide was incomprehensible. It made no sense. But not to me. I had been there. Back when I was in my early twenties, back when I'd been trying to go to college and work and party, back when I fell into that deep depression, I once took an overdose of pills. I hadn't thought of it as suicide, I had just wanted to go into the abyss, to fall into the void and down into oblivion, to be swaddled like a newborn in nothingness. Instead, I spent three days alone, convulsing and vomiting in a nightmare delirium, believing I'd botched my death, having slipped into a parallel reality where I'd been rendered a vegetable, unable to speak but fully aware, made to live to eternity in a most noxious kind of hell. I came out of it knowing that things could be much worse for me. That's when I called my mother and she sent me a ticket home.

§ § §

A few weeks after Tonya's death, the chatty man seen at the bar with the "ex" knocked on Pizza Richard's door. His name was Eddie Galloway. He said he'd known Clyde Eddie years ago and was there to visit him, not knowing he'd rented the place to Richard. He'd just heard about Tonya's death, he said, and needed someone to talk to. I made room for him on the couch and Richard offered him a beer.

"I had just been to The Palms looking for her," he said. "We'd dated years ago. I helped her move out of her cabin after her mother got it. Only reason we broke up is I went to jail."

"Who was the guy with you?" I asked him—the long, lean man with the gray ponytail, the one everyone thought was the ex, the guy everyone suspected of killing her.

"Oh, he was just a buddy of mine. I'd told him about Wonder Valley. He'd never been here before. I was going to introduce him to Tonya."

Eddie opened the beer Richard handed him, then set it on the table without taking a sip. "Tonya was really special to me," he said. "I loved her." He leaned onto his knees and let his head drop, then gushed a sigh. "We'd had a lot of fun together," he said. "We understood each other." He looked up at me. "I guess no one really knew her like I did."

Chapter 19

Tonya's suicide reiterated that I was just a tourist here in this valley of death. I was walking a tightrope above this brink knowing I couldn't fall, knowing I had a safety net, that ticket home. I could live here in limbo, at the crossroads, and not be made to choose a route. I was starting to sense, though, that Ann had begun to plan for a life without me. She was reestablishing relationships with old friends, friends she'd lost touch with since we'd been married. She talked of selling our home or moving her widower father in. Feeling neglected and abandoned and finally fed up and frustrated with me, she became convinced that I no longer wanted to be married. Her attitude was changing subtly, but the realization of it hit me abruptly, coming to me like a visit from the ghost of Christmas Future, a vision of Ann cutting my tether to the outside world, leaving me to languish here. I had told Ann—and myself—that I was here to do research, eventually publish a book or something, an ethnography about Wonder Valley, but this wasn't research. Getting blackout drunk with misfits and miscreants on the margin of society wasn't research. I was simply dredging up the sordid details in the lives of others to avoid addressing those in my own. I'd gained thirty pounds in Wonder Valley, too, beer weight, and had built an impressive frat boy tolerance to alcohol. The signs of my downward spiral were obvious. Ann saw them. She knew my reasons for staying here were just excuses for not doing something else, anything else. Anymore, the justifications I invented for remaining here smacked of self-delusion even to me, or worse, lies.

But then, something changed everything. I turned fifty. It wasn't just my age or that birthday, but the events that surrounded it and because of it. It began with a surprise birthday barbeque. People who loved and cared about me came out to Wonder Valley. Old friends filled my bleached-white cabin. Ann spent the week here, too. At the barbeque my friends met and mingled with those from Wonder Valley: George and Larkin, Curtis, Paule, Pizza Richard and Jill. Bud and Natalie. Dingy and Fluffy. Clyde Eddie grilled the chicken.

Greg, a cinematographer friend I'd met at twenty while on my South Pacific odyssey, flew up from Australia. At my birthday barbecue I caught him, drunk, lifting Natalie's skirt and looking under it. She was bent over while he squinted and studied something under there, something he was apparently having trouble focusing on. He steadied himself against the wall and smiled a big smile, his nose bright red. I came around and looked, too.

"She has a koala on her ass!" He pronounced it 'koaler.' He again lifted her skirt to reveal a cuddly koala tattooed on her brown flesh. Of all my friends, Wonder Valley especially fascinated Greg—only in America could a place like this exist, he said. He spent the entirety of his visit here with a camera to his eye, filming. And in front of his camera, Wonder Valley shined. Paule was gregarious and funny. He took Greg on a scorpion hunt, demonstrated how his hair, dyed to match his clothes, fluoresced under black light. Slim, a former calf roper and rodeo clown, took Greg on a harrowing ride through the desert while he filmed. He attended Taco Tuesday at Pizza Richard's, toured Larkin's place, hung out at The Palms. After he left, he edited his footage into a short video set to a country song and posted it as a birthday gift to me on YouTube. Everyone in Wonder Valley loved it. We should do a TV show, they crowed, a reality show! It sounded like something from a Little Rascals episode.

I loved the video too—it captured the Wonder Valley I'd come to know so perfectly. We watched it over and over, laughing at ourselves and our antics. Meanwhile, views on YouTube slowly ticked upward into the thousands as people shared it outside of the valley. Then, one day, I got an email. A phone conversation followed it. An agent offered representation which led to an invitation to sit in on a conference call, then meetings in studio boardrooms listening to Hollywood executives and content experts zero in on a concept for a show. *Wonder Valley*, they'd call it, a reality TV show set in Wonder Valley, a show centered on the Wonder Valley Greg had captured in my video. And I was crucial to the project, they said. In fact, they said, they couldn't do it without me.

I was staggered, thrilled that these Hollywood guys *got it*, that they were as excited about Wonder Valley as I was. I couldn't wait to share the news. As I got to think about it, though, doubts began to fester. Was a reality show the best way to highlight the valley? I began to fear the effect a show like that would have on the place like this. I didn't want to make anyone out here look bad, I didn't want it to lampoon them or turn them into caricatures to be derided and mocked or displayed as specimens for shock value alone.

On the other hand, I knew there was ripe content for a reality show out here—things certainly as funny as anything those duck guys were doing. Just recently, for example, Whitefeather was out walking in the desert when a little pet pig approached him. People from out of the area had been dumping unwanted pets here for years to the extent it had created a dangerous feral dog problem. I figured someone must have unloaded this little pot-bellied pig. It was tame and friendly, craved human contact, but wouldn't let Whitefeather touch it. He worried coyotes would devour it if he didn't intervene, so he called Slim. Slim had won calf roping competitions over the years and figured he could make quick work of catching the animal. He and Desert Dave chased that pig up and down the rocks behind Whitefeather's cabin for hours, the pig always only an arm's reach away. Finally, Slim got a rope around a leg and hauled it squealing to Whitefeather's. Soon it got free again, however, and the chase started anew. In the end, Clyde Eddie arrived with a rifle and brought the poor pig down. It ended up in a barbeque pit at his place. Coyotes only got the gnawed-on bones.

As bad as I felt for that poor pig, I found it all uproariously funny. And it showed how the rules out here were different, how people out here come up with the most interesting and inventive—and often comical—ways to get by. But, thinking about it further, I wasn't so sure I wanted this kind of thing on television. An unapprised TV viewer might find this behavior disturbing, might see it as gruesome and even pathetic when witnessed without the context of the lives of the guys living it. Things like this so often had a tragic element to them and I doubted I could count on Hollywood to show the whys behind the ways everyone lived. These were the machinations necessary for survival, adaptations to limited opportunities, strategies rational only within the framework of Wonder Valley. And, funny as they might be, a show lampooning these hardships and struggles reeked to me of ridicule. It wasn't an easy life out here, and I, for one, didn't want anyone so disparaged.

When I eventually told the guys about the prospect of a show and explained my worries, however, they laughed them off. To them, this interest from Hollywood, this spotlight on them was electrifying. It commodified them, gave them value, and with that, purpose and meaning, meaning outside the forgotten confines of this desert. The thing I had to remember was that as isolated as this place was, virtually everyone here had known a life in the mainstream, had a past outside of Wonder Valley. But they all ended up here for one reason or another, victims of circumstance or bad decisions, mental illness or substance abuse and now had no way to escape. And they were very aware of their situations too—some like Slim and Larkin had fallen here off particularly high pedestals. For them, a TV show featuring themselves would go a long way to legitimize their existence here. That people would want to watch them might also affirm, to an extent, their life choices, return to them some of the esteem they'd lost. I realized all this even as I worried that with this show I was somehow the vector of assured disaster, patient zero of the plague. I felt it my duty to somehow protect the people of Wonder Valley, to keep the jackals of Hollywood from feasting on their souls—as if I had any idea how to do that, as if anyone needed me to look out for them. Even Curtis, despite his drunken, lobotomized guise, patched together enough moments of sophistication that he had lived out here more or less successfully for nearly thirty-five years. He, like the others, was a survivor.

The thing is, they all seemed to understand instinctively that they would be playing a character on TV, one separate and distinct from who they were off camera. They knew their lives would be considered disasters, but they'd be TV disasters, Hollywood disasters, if nothing else. They would be Wild Men from Borneo, Nanooks of the North, contrived and fake, playing a part. And they'd get paid. Hell, I'd get paid.

This TV show would go a long way to legitimize the time I'd spent here, too. It could go far to negate my failures, my years of stumbles, of foibles, of tripping-up and falling down, of hitting the floor sometimes really, really hard, to the point I'd become afraid to risk anything, afraid to fall again. It had become debilitating, leaving me with the defeatist attitude I struggled with, that crippling sense of the futility of life. It had left me trapped in a place mentally I couldn't escape from.

That Hollywood people wanting to develop this world I'd discovered into a TV show redeemed me. This was my Wonder Valley. *I* was PT Barnum and these guys out here were *my* Men from Borneo, *my* Nanooks of the North. This was my Jacques Cousteau moment, I convinced myself. It was validation of the life I'd lived, of my travels and experiences. I decided I was all-in to do a show.

It would be a hybrid show, the content experts and producers decided, part reality, part fiction. That was the new thing, they said—reality TV was dead. *Wonder Valley* would be a make-believe story of a pair of beautiful girls who inherit a run-down bar in the desert. The producers had a couple of known and established reality stars in mind for the job, and they, according to the storyline, would enlist the help of a cast of Wonder Valley misfits to get the bar up and running.

These girls, young and beautiful, were a necessary part of the concept, the Hollywood guys assured me. The whole thing had to be lighthearted. No one wanted to watch a bunch of middle-aged, marginally homeless white men, drunks, drug addicts and mental cases, struggle through life with no hope of redemption. Bernadette and Daisy, the girls they'd chosen, would give the whole project a positive spin. The plan was to shoot a pilot and shop it around to the networks. It would be my job, they told me, to select the local cast and scout locations. It was up to me, for example, to find a bar. That part was easy, I thought. Wonder Valley had only The Palms. And I would choose the cast from its most frequent customers.

§ § §

I arranged for crew to meet in the parking lot of The Palms on the morning we were to begin shooting. Bernadette was sitting in her car when I arrived. I watched her jerk alert as Desert Dave and Slim clattered up behind me, Dave on his ATV, Slim crumpled into a tiny trailer pulled behind it. She checked her doors and nonchalantly scrolled her phone while surreptitiously surveilling the men through aviator sunglasses. Under the mesquite tree on the side of the bar, Slim unpacked his lanky frame from the trailer, set his beer on the ground, and rolled himself a cigarette. Dave lifted a bottle of PowerAde to his mouth. The PowerAde was cola-brown, fortified as it was with a quantity of whiskey, and frozen to a slush. The two were filthy, too, their clothes the color of the sand and dust and mountains beyond, the streaks of black grease on them adding to their desert camouflage. I tapped on Bernadette's window and she jumped with a start. Recognizing me she got out of her car and gave me a hug.

It was eight o'clock Sunday morning. Daisy arrived with Patrick, the producer who would run the shoot, a few minutes later. Camera and sound guys showed up shortly after that. We all shook hands. Everyone seemed relaxed and calm: Slim and Desert Dave waited patiently in the shade, Bernadette and Daisy were nothing but professional, Patrick and the crew exuded confidence. I, on the other hand, was a wreck.

In addition to managing the local cast and procuring locations, I'd been given the responsibility to feed the crew, something, of course, I'd known about for weeks. I just figured we'd eat at The Palms after we shot the scenes there. I don't know why it never occurred to me that shooting in The Palms would be a problem. I knew of countless people who had photographed and filmed there over the years—my friend Greg had even shot much of our little video there. Others had too, anyone from random passers-through looking for some desert color to photographers shooting spreads for fashion magazines. George and Curtis and others had worked as extras in feature films and music videos there. Mary always seemed more than accommodating, cooperating and even assisting with all those projects. But the day before we were to begin shooting, when I finally I brought up filming some scenes to Mary, she turned cold. I had mentioned, obliquely, in the past, doing a reality show and I knew where she stood—she worried a reality TV show focusing on *those* people would ruin the valley's reputation—but I had arrived with an argument prepared to persuade her. As I started my spiel, though, she spun around away from me, her autonomic avoidance tactic, folding her arms across herself. Facing away from me she stood shaking her head. "I'll be quick," I said, trying to get in as many words as I could as fast as possible, "Just a screen test, really, just to see how it goes, no commitments or anything…"

"NO!" she replied, still shaking her head, "You are not making a mockery of this place!" With that she fled from behind the bar to the kitchen. She left me there mouthing my spiel to myself. Shit, I thought. We had no bar. And I would have to find an alternative for lunch.

I recalled that Clyde Eddie had once been a cook on a ranch or something. I drove to his place first thing in the morning and told him what I needed.

"Sure thing, Boss," he said. "No problem. I won't let you down." I left him with a couple hundred bucks and instructions to have the food ready by noon, then headed to The Palms in time to meet the crew and lay out the plans for the day. I had to deliver the news about the bar and somehow find an alternative but just as I was to pull Patrick aside, Pizza Richard called. He was set to appear in the first scene.

"Hey, hey, ahh," he said, fumbling for words, "you know, I don't usually get up this early, and I don't really want to be on TV anyway, so, umm, I think I'm going to give today a pass." While I was on the phone with him, Natalie texted that she had changed her mind too and probably wasn't going to show either. The weather was also troubling—the wind had blown a gale the day before, and, while it was predicted to let up, a stiff breeze still rustled the creosotes.

There was nothing I could do about the weather, but I grabbed Patrick, the producer, "We need to change the shooting schedule," I said, feigning confidence. "Something's come up. Pizza Richard will join us later." Quietly, I prayed he'd show. I then called Natalie and begged her to meet us as soon as possible. I still needed to tell Patrick about the bar.

I was on the phone with Natalie when Mary's car appeared on the low rise between her home and The Palms. She sat watching us. Shit. By the time it became clear we couldn't film at The Palms, it was too late to change it as the rallying point that morning. I had been sure, however, we'd be long gone by the time they'd arrive to open the bar for breakfast. It was now twenty 'til nine, though, and Mary was on her way. But she never came. In fact, a moment later her car was gone, disappeared over the backside of the hill.

"We should move," I told Patrick and the others. "We should get going," I said to everyone around me. I spun in place trying to get their attention. Bernadette moved toward her car, but no one else seemed to hear me.

Moments later, Mary's car came careening over the ridge leaving a contrail of dust, James's truck following closely. Together they came roaring towards us, skidding into the parking lot, springing from their cars like a tactical assault team, their hair in matted bed head helmets. Instead of weapons they carried signs at arm's length, signs depicting a camera with a slash across it.

"NO FILMING!" Mary screamed, as they backed toward the front door, Laura covering their rear, James on the flank. They retreated inside and barred the door closed.

A moment later, it cracked open.

"You guys go somewhere else," Mary shouted, slamming the door again. Then she reopened it. "And you," she said glaring at me with contempt, "forget about ever coming back!"

Mary's bold-faced contempt for me in front of everyone made me blush. But it didn't really surprise me. She was already cold to me, and with the talk of a reality show she became downright antipathetic. But seeing her there that morning, with her hair ratty, her clothes shabby, her car's bumper hanging, I think I finally understood her. As much as she hated running the bar day to day, she had a vision for The Palms, the vision she'd had since she bought the place. She wanted the bar to be a destination, like that bar in Pioneertown, a funky-cool desert dive that on holiday weekends attracted bands and their fans who drank bad beer and gloated about it on Instagram. Mary and her family would be at the center of that scene. They were its hosts first and foremost, The Sibleys the bar's house band. Already, on popular weekend nights, they played their kitschy pop songs to a packed house, garnering themselves a small following as well as a music video on YouTube and a CD out on an indie label. A song of theirs had recently been used in a TV show even. As newly-born public figures, they were being increasingly careful to preserve their brand and working ever harder to control the side of Wonder Valley visitors saw, monitoring who came into The Palms on those busy weekends, discouraging the locals and keeping the riff-raff who would normally be there, out. In fact, Mary had told me she would prefer to keep the bar closed except for these types of events.

The family's living conditions contradicted the public image they propagated, however. Like many people out here, they lived on a bare dirt lot surrounded by battered cars and old tires, broken flotsam and weather-beaten jetsam in a ramshackle shack full of hoarded junk. I could understand why they wouldn't want that on TV. What I hadn't understood, however, was that when I told Mary a reality show would be a weekly advertisement for her bar on national TV, it played right into her fears. I think she feared she'd lose control of their image, that people might see the little man behind the curtain. Mary, seeing me with a TV production crew there on her property, therefore, caused a panic in her. I was also defying her wishes, forcing a confrontation—something Mary was very averse to. That had never been my intention and I knew we needed to leave before she called the police. But no one moved. They just stared at me with puzzled expressions.

"Goddamn it!" I screamed, "WE NEED TO FUCKING GO!" I stomped my feet, my face a beef heart red. With arms spread wide, I wrangled everyone to their cars, urging them to move down the road to the location of the first scene.

To let Richard sleep, we'd start with Natalie. The scene would have Bernadette and Daisy, dressed in hot pants and halter tops, broken down on the side of the road. Natalie would then show up on her pink camouflaged ATV and lecture them about being prepared in the desert. She would be wearing an ankle-length sheath dress— not the most appropriate attire for the desert, either—and the result would be a funny interaction. I assured Patrick and the crew she'd be ready. She was on her way, I promised. Slim and Desert Dave would be in the scene after Natalie, followed, God willing, by Pizza Richard.

Thankfully, Natalie was waiting when we arrived, her ATV in the back of Bud's pickup. She nervously guzzled a beer in the cab as Bud unloaded the quad.

"Just relax," I told her. "You'll be fine. Remember, they're going to tell you what they want you to do, what they want you to say." Honestly, I had no better idea what was going to happen than she did, but she was visibly nervous, so I winged it with the advice. "Look, they're going to have you do your lines several times, so you'll have several opportunities to get it right. There is no way you can screw up." I gave her a pat on the shoulder.

In her scene, Natalie gunned her pink camo ATV down a dirt road to where Bernadette and Daisy had "broken down." She approached the girls and delivered the lines as instructed.

"It's pretty obvious y'all ain't from around here," she said. By the second take she seemed relaxed and comfortable.

In the next scene, Desert Dave and Slim were to "repair" the girls' car in Dave's dirt yard.

"You're fucked," Slim said to the girls on camera. "You let the turn signal fluid run low."

"No, it's the muffler bearing!" disputed Dave from under the hood. "I'll bet my left nut on it!" They squabbled good-naturedly back and forth until Dave directed the girls to his "waiting room," a truck's old bench seat lying in the dirt. The director had Dave take a shot of whiskey before delivering his lines. It took three takes—and three shots—until he was satisfied with the performance.

The plan after that was to shoot in the bar. I suggested we go back to The Palms, try to beg our way in. "Maybe you can negotiate something," I said to Patrick, "We just need to make sure Mary's fears are accommodated." Any misgivings she had about us shooting there were extensions of the misgivings she had about me, I knew. Patrick would have none of it, however.

"Find another bar," he said.

"There is one other place," I said. The Way Out, that old shuttered saloon out on the highway, way out past anything. Its asphalt was cracked, its sign lost to wind years before, but inside it still had the trappings of a bar—stools, a pool table, beer signs. "We could shoot there," I said, "Maybe find someone to let us in." I led the way.

Out at The Way Out, however, not a soul stirred. We shot some footage of the girls looking through the old bar's windows and then sitting on the stoop bantering back and forth acting giddy about opening it for business. To my relief, Pizza Richard had arrived while we were shooting at Dave's. He had inherited an old white Cadillac to replace his rattletrap truck, and now, at The Way Out, he sat in its back seat draining beer after beer as Daisy, with a homemade sign, tried to stop passing cars as if enticing them to the new business. No one stopped and the scene went on and on so that by the time Patrick was ready for Pizza Richard, he was dead drunk.

In his scene, he was to be in the backseat of his Caddie and say to Bernadette, "This was your Uncle Larry's bar, and now it's yours." But Richard had gotten up early despite his objections and had a couple of beers and a joint first thing to calm his nerves. He then had a few more beers while he waited, followed by those he drank in the Caddie before his cue, so that by the time he was in the back of the car with the girls he was uncomprehending.

"Who's Uncle Larry?" he asked, bewildered, looking at the girls for help. "I don't have an Uncle Larry. I don't even know a Larry!"

Patrick was patient. "No, Richard," he said, "This is just your line. You say, 'This was your Uncle Larry's bar, and now it's yours.'"

Richard looked around at everyone until a flash of realization crossed his face. "Oh, yeah, yeah," he said, "OK, so ah, 'This is my Uncle Larry's bar, and now it's mine!'"

Everyone laughed, but I felt my neck and face redden.

"No, Richard," Patrick said again, "Pretend you know an Uncle Larry and he had just given this bar to Bernadette."

"This is your bar?" Richard said to Bernadette, incredulous. Christ, I thought.

Finally, with some on-camera coaching and ad-lib from Bernadette and Daisy, we got a passable scene. Cut. Good enough. That's a wrap.

Now lunch.

We caravanned to Clyde Eddie's compound, arriving well after noon. What I saw clenched me in the grip of panic. A hodgepodge of chairs cluttered the dirt surrounding a mishmash of rickety tables as well as weathered plywood sheets and old doors on sawhorses. Bud and Natalie and Slim and Desert Dave and Curtis as well as an entire cabal of Wonder Valley locals stood around a jumble of aluminum foil-covered bowls and trays drinking beer. Empty beer cans littered the dirt of the yard. It looked like a hillbilly wedding. Or a wake.

Clyde Eddie bounded at me when he saw us arrive. "Goddammit!" he bellowed, "Everything's ruined! I had everything ready by noon, just like you said, and you didn't show up, I never heard anything from you!" I told him I tried to call, several times, over and over. He checked his missed messages and took a deep breath, "Looka here, Boss," he said, "I've been a little busy, don't you think?"

He had made pulled chicken tacos, rice and beans, homemade salsa, salad. An impressive spread despite the rudimentary conditions and the short notice. I thanked him for doing such a good job.

"Hey, uh, looka here," he said, "this is the chance I've been waiting for. I told you I wouldn't let you down." He then told me he'd gone a bit over budget. What with all the beer and the uninvited guests, I owed him another $200.

In spite of my nerves, I forced myself to eat. The crew seemed content—all except the cameraman, who, seeing the mess out in the dirt at Clyde Eddie's, took off toward town for food, not to return for hours. While we waited the Wonder Valley locals finished off a couple thirty-packs of Nattie Ice and a case of Corona. Natalie found a half-gallon jug of vodka and passed it around. As she drank, she grew confrontational, belligerent.

"Fuck these bitches," she said of Bernadette and Daisy, "all these guys drooling over them, coming here looking all hot in their short shorts while you made me dress like a soccer mom! Fuck them, fuck all these motherfuckers! And fuck Curtis!"

Natalie had been having an affair with Curtis, she revealed to everyone, but Curtis had dumped her right there for Carolyn, Carolyn being suddenly single since Biker Richard died the week before.

"I'm getting married!" Curtis said to Natalie as he spun around for her to take him all in. Natalie fumed and pounded vodka, growing increasingly morose. Bud, mortified at the news announced so publicly, consoled himself with beer after beer. Next to him Pizza Richard slumped in a chair, his head bobbing. When the cameraman returned, the crew shot interviews with potential cast members while everyone else drank and drank.

The shooting plan called for a cast photo at the "Welcome to Wonder Valley" sign in the golden light of the afternoon. The homemade sign was alongside the paved road as you entered the valley from the west; it had been there as long as anyone could remember. Knowing we were losing light, I ushered everyone to vehicles and led the way, down the dirt road from Clyde Eddie's and out onto the pavement, a snaking motorcade of cars and trucks, motorcycles and ATVs.

Arriving where I knew the sign to be, however, it was gone. I pulled over and turned around, the snake of cars and trucks fragmenting and dividing and recombining in U-turns and three-pointers behind me. I knew where the sign *was*, at least where it should have been. I stopped where it just the other day *had* been. My heart was racing. I felt the blood in my face. I needed to confer with Patrick but before I could, Bud grabbed me.

"You got to do something about Natalie and Curtis!" he demanded. Behind him, the two argued loudly in the cab of his truck. I dragged Curtis out of it and put him in mine. Others were now out of their cars, too, stumbling around in the road, laughing and running like children on a field trip. All the while Paule ran color commentary in his loud New Jersey slang. I wanted to scream. Goddamn it! The day was a disaster! I was shaking, my vision blurred. I worried I was having a stroke. Hyperventilating, I turned my back and stumbled out into the desert, out away from everyone and everything. I needed to find a bush I could curl up under and die.

After I staggered just ten feet, however, I found it, the sign, lying in the dirt. The hurricane-force wind the day before had taken it. After what was probably thirty years standing, the gale had snapped it off at the ground. I muscled it up and called the others over. Bernadette and Daisy held the sign erect while the crew, like paparazzi, snapped photos. Slowly others joined in, too, Slim and Desert Dave, Curtis, Bud, Clyde Eddie. Everyone crowded in, even me. Everyone except Natalie. She stood on the sidelines screaming obscenities, crying and raging.

"Fuck you! Fuck all of you!" Everyone tried to ignore her, but then she jumped into Bud's truck, threw it into gear, and charged us with it, burying it in sand to the hubs, thank god, before she could kill anyone. I begged Bud to take her home, but he wanted to stay, he said. He wanted to be on TV.

We shot the final scene later that evening. Curtis was now with me, and because of that, he was the only one still around. Everyone else was gone, passed out. I took Curtis home after the crew got into their cars and left. I was clammy with cold sweat, as though I'd just run a marathon.

I went back to Clyde Eddie's for a beer. He was just cleaning up. "This is all there is," he said, thrusting the plastic jug of vodka at me. "Just one swallow." I downed it and went home. I flopped down into a lounge chair in my dirt yard and looked up at the heavens. I felt I was going to cry. A shooting star raced across the sky, but I ignored it. I had made a lot of wishes on stars out here over the years, too many, and I thought one was finally coming true. This was to be my Jacques Cousteau opportunity, the culmination of my life nomadic, the validation and justification of my being here, of the choices I'd made. But we were just a bunch of middle-aged misfits and miscreants, drunks, drug addicts and mental cases struggling through life with no hope of redemption. I wasn't PT Barnum and these weren't my Wild Men from Borneo. There was a reason we were all out here, myself included. We were out here because we couldn't function in the real world. We were failures, losers, forever relegated to this land of the lost.

§ § §

The wind came up again the next day blowing fifty miles an hour, reducing visibility to mere feet. It had been so beautiful the day of the shoot, a gorgeous spring day, a perfect desert day, but today the wind trapped me inside. I didn't want to see anyone anyway. I'd left my windows down in my truck, though, and when I finally made a dash to roll them up, I found it with drifts of dust on the dash, the seats. It blew like smoke from the vents when I started it up.

I went back inside. In there, my phone rang. It was Patrick. I sat down, bracing myself for what was coming. I had an argument prepared, an excuse wrapped in an apology finishing with a pitch for a do-over. I hadn't set expectations, I planned to say. Next time I'd be sure to curb the drinking or find a different cast. I didn't have much confidence in my abilities to persuade him. The day had been such an overwhelming disaster.

"Yesterday," Patrick said. I stood up, anxiety and adrenaline triggering a fight or flight response. "Yesterday," he said again, "was the most rewarding day of filming in my career."

I pressed the phone to my ear uncertain what I was hearing. "What?"

"Best day of my career," he repeated.

"You're fucking with me."

"No, man, it was great, just great. Everyone was so genuine. They handled themselves perfectly."

"What about Natalie's raging?" I asked, "And Pizza Richard's drunken fumbling?"

He quieted me. "Everyone is nervous the first time on camera," he said, "usually worse than these guys were. They'll calm down and do fine once we start shooting a show for real."

He had been on the phone all morning, he said, talking with

network people and studio execs. "This show is going to be big," he repeated. "I think we've got a hit!" I started to shake. "We've got a hit," he said again. And again, I thought I might cry. I couldn't wait to tell everyone. I was Jacques Cousteau and Wonder Valley was *my* Galapagos!

Chapter 20

In the weeks after we filmed, Patrick's team edited the footage into a pilot. Despite the challenges, the drunken bickering and catty fighting, the finished product was a campy, lighthearted thing that looked like a TV show to me, no worse than anything you actually saw on television. Patrick was going to use the pilot as a sales tool to shop the project around Hollywood while we, in Wonder Valley, just waited. Time crept by like a stink bug up a sand dune. With each update, Patrick promised news. "Soon," he'd say, "Next Friday." Next Friday became like a wish on a star, nothing more than a euphemism for his optimism. Weeks turned to months and still we waited. But I remained hopeful.

In the meantime, circumstances forced me to give up my cabin. Virtually evicted, I found myself without a place in Wonder Valley for the first time in more than three years. The irony of it all was that I had to give the place up not because of that asshole Craig or even kooky Brian or anything to do with the Naborly Road feud. I had to give it up because of Paule.

An excruciating heat wave baked the valley early that summer. Temperatures surpassed 130 degrees in the shade, just a few degrees off the world record. Inside Paule's cabin it topped 150 degrees. As he said he would, he'd bought an air conditioner, ran if off a generator, but the AC struggled to churn out anywhere near enough coolness just as Paule struggled to keep the generator in gas. Worrying for him as temperatures spiked, Ann and I took him some ice and frozen water bottles and the key to my water tank so he had access to water, then we got the hell out of there.

I was still down the hill a week later when Paule called me.

"You need to call the water man, Chief," he said. "You're almost out of water!" I just had a load of water delivered before leaving, 2,000 gallons for ninety dollars, and my first thought was that someone— Brian or Craig or otherwise—had shot a hole in the tank. I rushed back to Wonder Valley, arriving after dark. In the morning, I found the source of the problem immediately: Paule had stretched a thousand feet of hose across the desert from my water tank to his new swimming pool! I could see him over there, sitting in the pool wearing an American flag Speedo under a shade tarp reading a book.

"You're about to run out of water, son," he said, as I walked up. "I just thought I should tell you."

That 2,000-gallons of water typically lasted me three months. This time, it lasted just two weeks.

"It's the fucking wind, man," Paule explained. "You can't keep the sand out of the pool!" Macie, too, the pit bull he'd adopted, tracked dirt into it as well, forcing him to drain and refill it regularly. "For hygiene purposes and such and such." I called the water delivery man for another load and went home to wait. Paule showed up a few minutes later wearing a hard hat, steel-toed work boots and that Speedo. He plopped down on my couch under the air conditioner.

"This is what I need, man," he said, looking around. "A place like this." He got up and walked around my cabin like it was an open house. I repeated the advice I'd given him months before: dump his place and buy something livable, something with a bathroom, hot and cold running water, a heater and AC. He had been trying to comply with the code enforcement requirements at his little yellow cabin, but with no money he was fighting a losing battle.

"The code man says he just wants to see progress," Paule said. "He doesn't want to make anyone homeless, so to speak." Despite Paule's optimism, though, it was clear they would condemn the cabin if drastic and immediate improvements weren't made. I tried my best to make that clear to him.

Finally, it seemed to have sunk in, because the next day he called the real estate agent who sold him his place and told her he would soon be evicted. He reminded her she knew when she sold him the cabin that it had no running water, no septic, yet she'd sold it to him as a residence.

"But it isn't a residence, not legally, so to speak. It was her job to know that, yadda yadda, such and such." Paule told her he was considering a lawsuit and a complaint to the state department of real estate, and shortly thereafter the agent arranged a settlement with the seller.

"She said as long as I list the property for sale, I don't have to make any more payments. So, with that extra money, I can afford to buy your place. I called Fangmeyer, he said $300 a month. In five years it will be paid off." He was buying my cabin out from under me.

We stood outside as he delivered this news. "Congratulations," I said, shaking his hand. Couldn't very well fault him for taking my advice, but it saddened me to be losing the place. I'd grown attached to it, so to speak. I wasn't finished with Wonder Valley, either, wasn't ready to leave yet. I had the promise of a TV show, for one thing.

More than the promise of a TV show, however, I liked it here. I had friends here now, Bud and Natalie, for example, and Pizza Richard. Clyde Eddie, Slim and Desert Dave. With the TV show we had a common goal, too, a common purpose. It made me happy to be part of that.

And I did feel a part of something here. I find it ironic that in a place where independence and self-reliance were so highly regarded, such a close-knit community had blossomed, something approaching a collective society. But with no employment opportunities, no stores or shopping or piped-in water, with unreliable fire and emergency services, the people of Wonder Valley were forced to band together to provide these things for themselves, forced by necessity to share time and resources. The communities and tribes out here were formed out of need. Individualism only goes so far.

But so does collectivism. It certainly wasn't a utopia out here. The prized sense of independence often led to all these differing tribal factions with countering philosophies squabbling with each other and even wielding the police and code enforcement to impose worldviews. Beyond that, I'd witnessed cruelly and neglect I hadn't before imagined, seen people at their worst, exhibiting a primitive, groupthink, herd mentality that shunned and even preyed upon the most vulnerable, those most needing support, most needing help. Single women were particularly susceptible to this type of abuse.

By and large, however, a live-and-let-live attitude prevailed, giving Wonder Valley its strange mix of small-town America and the wild, wild West. It was rough and uneven, certainly, and unforgiving to a dangerous end, but it was unique and genuine, dare I say authentic. Wonder Valley's natural beauty had grown on me, too, the mountains, the sunsets, the stars. Even the detritus of the old cabins had its allure. Standing in my yard with Paule I looked out at the charred hulk of Craig's municipal bus, my living room view for a few years now, and over at Brian's saltcedar compound, Wonder Valley State Penitentiary. No doubt Brian was hiding there now video recording us. I didn't care. I certainly wouldn't miss those lights of his.

My old cabin looked much the same as when I moved into it, still bleached white as dried bones, Fangmeyer's faded fake flowers gasping a pale dying breath of color in the yard. I loved those flowers. I had propped them up in the spirals of rusty bed springs I'd found in the desert, the fossil remains of an old mattress swept fleshless by sun and wind. I found a couple of headboards, too, old iron bedsteads rusted a deep umber with yellowed stencils of flowers faded faint as ancient inscriptions. I added them to the bedsprings. I called it my flowerbed. I thought it was funny. They were to be Paule's now.

Fangmeyer's old Chevy was to be Paule's now too. It still sat next to the cabin in the barren gravel yard, chalky-white and oxidized by the sun, its hood slightly ajar giving it the dead stare of a corpse, the eyelids closed in a last act of compassion. No matter what Paule told me about it, about how he was going to fix it up, how it just needed a new this or a reworked that, I knew all the future held for it was for the desert to devour it, for it to slowly decompose as the sun took the tires and scrappers everything else until the lifeless carcass was picked clean. People had already been asking me about it: Was it mine? Did it run? Do you think that radiator would fit a '93 Lumina? I laid a hand on its hood and called Ann to deliver the news that I was losing my place in the desert.

§ § §

Ann came out to help me pack my things. "I'm going to miss Wonder Valley," she said, looking around. "I'm going to miss having a place to come out to." I knew she loved the desert. She had introduced me to it, brought me out here all those years ago. She'd been coming out to Wonder Valley ever more frequently of late and spending long weekends and sometimes even entire weeks here. I was happy to have her with me. I appreciated her indulgence in what I was coming to recognize was nothing more than my protracted mid-life crisis.

"I agreed to this," she reminded me. "You told me before we got married that I couldn't expect you to always have a job, that you didn't want lead a normal life. I knew what I was getting into." I had forgotten that I had ever said that. She reminded me I had insisted we take time out to travel and that we not forget our obligations were to one another, not jobs or careers or material things. But I had forgotten. I had forgotten my own advice. I guess in my early twenties, I knew myself better than I know myself now. I'd been spending all my energy trying to recover what I felt I'd lost, as if by living my life and having these experiences I'd actually lost something, rather than gained insight and maturity, things I had clearly so valued in my youth.

From her phone, as I carried boxes to the car, Ann scrolled real estate listings in the area. "There is a place nearby," she said when I sat down to rest. "It's on Valle Vista, do you know where that is?" Valle Vista was a typical Wonder Valley road that stopped and started and dot dot dashed its way west to east. Without knowing the cross street, the property she found could be as far as twenty miles away from us.

"The map shows it just a mile or so from here," she said. "Want to go check it out?"

I recognized the place as soon as we drove up. I had driven around it while on patrol with Jack McConaha years before. "There's some kind of battle in court over it," he had said as we drove between it and the neighbor. As it turned out, the place had been in foreclosure.

The backdoor was open and Ann and I walked in. It was a sprawling "builtmore," the original homesteader's cabin nested inside layers of added rooms like a Russian doll, leaving windows that looked into other rooms or were boarded up, the glass left in place. It had been rented, then abandoned in the years since the previous owner, Joe Leonard, died. He had bequeathed it to a friend who had mortgaged it in the real estate boom, then defaulted.

Joe Leonard had been a giant of a man by all accounts, though the home he left behind sent mixed messages. The bathroom sink, for example, was sitting on a pedestal that raised it to close to five feet high. It was in the entryway foyer, too, outside the bathroom altogether, the bathroom only accessible through a twenty-inch wide portal sealed with an accordion curtain. A man of any stature or girth would have had to stoop and squeeze to pass through it. The showerhead in that bathroom, by contrast, snaked up to such a height water strained to reach it. In the kitchen, too, cabinets hovered unreachable, yet the breakfast bar squatted at knee height.

Because the place was bank-owned, it was clean, litter and rubbish-free, move-in ready. It was also the cheapest place in all of

California with five acres and a well.

"Should we buy it?" Ann asked. I couldn't believe what I was hearing. "You're going to need a place out here." I'd never before considered buying a place. "But it's so cheap!" she said. So cheap we could afford it. Ann's father had downsized his home, returning to us the money we had given him during the real estate boom. I quickly dialed the number listed on the for-sale sign.

§ § §

The day we took possession, the next-door neighbor, a woman in her eighties, rolled over in her golf cart, an old beagle riding shotgun. She had lived here for over thirty-five years, she said.

"I've seen that Clyde or Eddie or whatever he calls himself over here," she warned. Clyde Eddie's place was about a half mile away. Until recently, he'd been living on the other side of the valley while taking care of an elderly man, but after that man died, he moved home to his own cabin, displacing Pizza Richard to a cabin Mary owned walking distance to The Palms. "Watch out for him," she said. "There's been a rash of break-ins in the neighborhood since he got out of prison. We've been keeping an eye on him."

I laughed. "Clyde Eddie has never been to prison," I assured her. "He hasn't been breaking into cabins, either." I had gotten to know him pretty well since we shot the pilot. We had become friends.

"Well, since he's been back, we've noticed things going missing from the neighborhood."

I laughed again. Who was "we?" Her and her beagle? There was no one else around. And what neighborhood? It reminded me of that "armed neighborhood" sign I'd encountered working for the Census. This was no more a neighborhood than that was—of the fifty or so cabins in a mile radius of mine, only about a dozen were occupied.

"We have rules in this neighborhood," she continued, staring up at me from her golf cart, making sure I was listening. "First," she said, counting on her fingers, "no motorcycles. We don't like motorcycles around here." I didn't have a motorcycle, I told her. "Second, no guns. And third," she said, "no lights. We like the dark out here at night." Thank God. After living so long next to Brian I relished the thought of seeing the night sky once again. I told her we'd get along just fine.

Inside the cabin, Ann and I set about planning what we would do. It was indeed move-in ready—if you could live with the threadbare, dog-mauled carpet in the living room, or the plush mauve stuff in the bedroom or the blood-red, shit-stained stuff in the porch. It would need some TLC and redecorating, at least. I figured doing the work would give me something to do while we waited for word of the TV show.

Everyone who came over to see the place had an opinion about it. Clyde Eddie and others thought we were crazy ripping that carpet out. Slim even took the mauve stuff home and installed it in his cabin. He hauled it off as payment for scraping the popcorn from the vaulted ceilings in ours. With Desert Dave's help he chipped-up the eighties-vintage gray tile from the kitchen floor too—or started the work, Curtis and finally Clyde Eddie finished the job.

The nesting doll walls created dark, unwelcoming interior spaces, though I figured the compartmentalization would make the place easier to heat and cool. Ann and I debated what to do, unsure what walls we should or even could remove. To answer that question, Slim bashed a hole in one of them to inspect its insides. The rest of the nesting doll walls came down in much the same way, opening up the heart of the house into a large great room. The kitchen we separated from that with a new resized breakfast bar.

The work proceeded swiftly; I had no trouble finding people to do it—in fact, the place was like a party house all summer. As long as I had beer, work progressed, and mornings were often surprisingly productive. Clyde Eddie, Slim and Desert Dave would show up early, Curtis sometime later, though he'd be mostly in the way. Mark Bennett moved in and slept on a couch Slim brought over, using my truck for runs to town for materials. He stayed at my place because he had no electricity at his, a dispute over a $2 discrepancy in his bill and a stubborn standoff with the power company got his power cut off. Throughout the workday Bud and Natalie and maybe Dingy and Fluffy might stop by to drink beer and check on the progress, Larkin, occasionally, too. Paule and Jill Davis. Pizza Richard came by sometimes in the evenings. It was fun having everyone around.

We were all energized by the work. There was no real employment out here save the odd handyman job for a retiree or newcomer, so idleness along with the isolation took a toll on everyone. I think my big construction project gave everyone purpose where otherwise they had little to occupy themselves. Even the drinking, Wonder Valley's main pastime, lessened as we all became busy with the remodel. There was little specialization in Wonder Valley, so while some had more and different skills than others, to a degree, everyone had some idea how to do everything, though most were certain they knew how to do it better than anyone else. Arguments, therefore, were common. These disputes seemed to reinforce the hierarchy—or destroyed it as often—diffusing the tension through concessions, acknowledgements, compromises, the conflict, whatever it was, resolved by everyone as a group. Get too argumentative or combative and you faced the group's wrath, while the camaraderie of working together drew everyone closer. The satisfaction of finally having something to do worked wonders on everyone's morale and self-esteem, as well— even mine.

With Mark and everyone else practically living there, though, the house was a litter of beer cans and food wrappers, chunks of lumber and bent nails, the floor bespattered with drywall mud and sawdust—that is, when Ann wasn't around. When she was, the place sparkled, everyone cleaning and mopping and picking up the beer cans and cigarette butts and finding another place to pass out at night. She and I slept on an inflatable mattress on the floor of a bedroom, one we sealed-off as best we could from the construction dust and noise. We cooked and ate on sawhorse tables. As the major construction wound down, Ann picked the paint colors for the walls, colors with names like "Cactus Needle" and "Arroyo Sunset" and "Desert Dune."

I worried that our spending so much time and money on this remodel and our concern for its aesthetics would highlight the economic gulf between us and the guys volunteering their time. After all, most of them struggled to keep water flowing such was the state of their patched-together living conditions. Aesthetics were not typically a consideration. Still, that didn't stop them from having opinions.

"Looks like baby shit," Clyde Eddie said when I showed him the colors Ann had chosen for the interior walls.

"It's what she wants," I replied.

"Looka here," he said, "I got some paint at my place. I'll paint it." What Eddie had at his place was the mixed-together remains of several scavenged cans, something that approximated a lilac color. He had painted his own cabin with it. It was utilitarian, nothing more than basic protection from the elements, and I knew Ann didn't want that. I also knew that if I didn't act quickly, he would paint the place while I was away, so high was his opinion of his own stylistic sensibilities. Ann and I painted the interior surreptitiously over the next weekend. Same with the floors. Instead of carpet or tile, we wanted to stain the concrete, something no one out here had ever heard of doing before. After failing to communicate our idea, Ann and I stained the floors ourselves, working over another weekend she snuck in, the shades drawn and the lights dimmed so that no one discovered us there. I worried less about criticism than people trotting across the freshly stained and sealed floors. Consequently, Ann's are the only prints indelibly etched into them.

"I thought it was going to look like shit!" Eddie said seeing the paint and the floors for the first time. "But, man, it looks tits!" It really did look good. And Ann loved it. I was happy we had this to share.

I loved working side by side with her, too. Back when I was

buying and flipping houses, she often gave up her weekends to help me out—we did all the work ourselves in those houses. I had picked up my construction skills in a Building Trades class I took in high school, a class I had to take because, moving to California, my new school wouldn't recognize all the courses I had completed at my old school. They required I retake classes and stay after school in the evenings to earn filler credits—hence the Building Trades class. I got a lot out of that class, skills I used frequently, but for years I stewed about having to take it at all. Moving to California had shattered my college plans, the make-up classes keeping me out of the college prep courses I needed to transfer to a university. I felt that if my parents had pushed back harder against my new school's administrators for the arbitrary way they counted my credits, I could have avoided those make-up classes and the additional hours after school, but they hadn't. My parents were native Californians, certain the California school system I was transferring to was superior to the Mississippi one I left. I was lost at that new school, though, a huge one in Southern California's suburban sprawl where I had to integrate myself into a graduating class larger than the entire student body of my Mississippi small-town school system. I barely made it through to graduation. This was when I first felt my father's cold disappointment. In his eyes, I just didn't measure up. I resented him for this, too, and for not standing up for me, but, really, it was more complicated than that.

As it turned out, a career path in science—what I had aspired to in high school—was out of the question for me. More than simply the classes I'd missed, I just didn't have the aptitude. I struggled with basic math, for one thing, and I suffered with moderate to severe dyslexia, something I didn't fully understand until I went back to college in my forties. I knew, however, that I found it hard to read, hard to write, hard to focus on one thing for any length of time, which drew accusations of laziness from my father, accusations that I just wasn't trying. He was right, I had stopped trying. I had checked out, something I'm wont to do when life gets hard. The memory of this was fresh in my early twenties, I suppose, that's why I told Ann to moderate her expectations with me. Jesus Christ, she's been a saint.

Spelling continues to be a challenge. I rely on my fingers for math. And I still wake from nightmares about my time in that new school, nightmares in which I relive having to cover for incomplete homework and assignments and a learning disorder I didn't realize I had, as well as my father's disappointments which turned to disgust as I detached from school and family.

These days, Ann does all the complex mathematical calculations. She is the scientist. I'm the big picture guy, I tell her. Right-brained. Creative. And remodeling our new cabin fit right into that.

As I said, I liked doing the work, liked the finishing work particularly, as well as the plumbing and especially the electrical. I was the one who wired the lights and receptacles in the house before the drywall was installed, for instance; no one else wanted to touch it, afraid they'd burn the place down. I replaced the decaying swamp cooler with a mini-split air conditioner, wiring it in myself. I used a 220-volt circuit that had previously served a baseboard heater, pulling the wire through the wall to the outside where the AC's compressor would sit. Doing so, I found a spaghetti mass of other wires in the wall: spliced together odds and ends of cable and sundry extension cords leading seemingly nowhere. I cut and yanked that spaghetti mass out, wired in the AC, and sealed up the wall. The air conditioner worked as advertised, churning out delicious coolness. When I tested the switch to the circuit I would attach the ceiling fans to, however, it was dead. Same with the outside lights, the switches to them were on the same wall as the fans and AC. Shit. If I'd yanked needed wires when I pulled that spaghetti mass out, I'd have to tear out twenty feet of wall to fix it. I didn't know what to do.

I hesitated to call a specialist. So far, Ann and the guys and I had done all the renovation work ourselves and I didn't want to have to call anyone else in. Besides, finding someone to come all the way out from town would be hard. Desperate, though, I finally found an electrician.

Dana was a jolly guy who humphed and mumbled to himself as he worked, testing connections and flipping switches, making a great show of it.

"I don't see anything wrong," he said after a few minutes. "These circuits are fine."

"But I put a tester on the ceiling fan wires and when I flipped the switch, nothing happened," I replied.

"That's because these switches don't control the fan circuit." He called me over. "They control the outside lights. These over here control the fans." He flipped them on and off. "Flip the right switch for what you want to turn on and everything works fine! That will be $100." He laughed. I flushed. I felt like an idiot. As a favor, he offered to look at the wiring job I'd done for the AC and a couple of other things while he was there. Everything checked out. I hung the ceiling fans and of course they worked when I flipped the correct switches. I never told anyone about this.

The inside done, we furnished it with stuff Bud brought over from Jack McConaha's after Jack had fallen ill and could no longer live at home. Clyde Eddie contributed dressers and nightstands from his own Sanford and Son junkyard of stuff, too. Slim donated a bed and the couch and others carted in pots and pans and things found while shopping in the desert. Ann waxed some of the old battered furniture and chalk painted others, their rustic chic playing well with the desert palette on the walls, the muted greens and reds and browns and creams. We coordinated the furniture with photographs and desert artifacts and posters and art. Jill Davis gave us a painting she'd done of the human femur she'd found, the femur she'd shown me the first time we'd met. In the great room, we installed a nine-foot pool table Clyde Eddie had come up with. We had to take it apart to get it inside, however, Ann certain it would never go back together again. That pool table became the focal point for the Taco Tuesdays I began hosting, picking up on the tradition

Pizza Richard had started. Mary had banned me from The Palms, but that didn't matter. I didn't need that bar. We could all hang out at my place now.

I hired Clyde Eddie to paint the exterior, the last thing left to do, trading him the truck my father-in-law had given me to do the census work. Whenever I was away from Wonder Valley, which was more and more often now, Clyde Eddie and others borrowed it, so it was gone most of the time anyway. I'd have to hunt it down when I got back. The only time the truck sat idle, it seemed, was when it was out of gas. Mark Bennett had used it while he lived at our place and had damaged the radiator and the front-end trying not to get stuck in soft sand. He hadn't realized that Slim had disconnected the four-wheel drive because it started making a grinding noise while he had it. The rear window had mysteriously shattered while Slim had the truck, too, though he blamed that on Clyde Eddie. And no matter how I tried, it seemed, I just couldn't keep it in tires.

Eventually, Clyde Eddie relocated the truck at his place to make sure it was available when he needed it, it being the only registered vehicle out of the sundry dozen or so other cars and trucks and motorcycles and ATVs and trailers and motorhomes and bicycles and motorboats and canoes he had on his property, so, in reality, trading the truck to him for work meant I at least got something for a vehicle he had already taken possession of anyway.

The deal was, I would supply the paint and he would paint it, but Clyde Eddie didn't like the colors Ann had chosen. He particularly didn't like the color chosen for the front door—to the point he refused to paint it, certain that Ann, like him, would hate it. So I painted it, but while I was gone, he repainted it the color he preferred, forcing me to paint it again before Ann could see it. In the end, though, he admitted it looked pretty good.

"How do you like living in a museum?" Eddie asked Ann when the house was completed. That comment struck me with a pang of guilt. It was a beautiful home; one I was particularly proud of since all of us had worked so hard together to make it a reality. I knew they considered our house to be theirs too, in a way—at least to the extent that they had volunteered their time and skills and donated the furniture and other materials they had accumulated or found lying around. Because of this, I wanted them to be able to enjoy the place, so I handed out keys. Also, based on my experience with my truck, I knew they'd just break in to use the place if I didn't.

Chapter 21

Hindsight. I'd first heard that word in a pun my father made on a road trip in our family's yellow Plymouth station wagon, a pun I didn't at first understand but has now forever shaped the word as I have come to understanding it. On road trips, I loved riding in the "back in the back," that yellow Plymouth's pop-up, rear-facing rumble seat. I loved watching the world drift by in reverse, seeing where we'd been instead of where we were going. "Hindsight" my dad called it. I've come to think of that experience as an adequate representation of our journey through life. We know for sure only where we've been, never where we're going. You may know where the road goes, but you can never know for certain that you'll be on it.

I had met Nikos Lukaris at a New Year's Eve party, an open house get-together Ann and I had at our new place, a party for friends who gathered there before leaving us to head to The Palms for the countdown to midnight. Nikos arrived with a neighbor.

"I've heard a lot about you," he said, pressing a mitt at me, his face a dimpled smile. A braided goatee hung from his chin, his head shaved into a Krishna's topknot. I had heard stories about Nikos, too, wild and exotic stories, like how he'd once thrown a knife at a striking rattlesnake, killing it as he rode by on a motorcycle, or how he'd reengineered a snowmobile to ride in the sand and drove it to The Palms. I had seen him flying his lime-green ultralight airplane over the valley—as it turned out, he was the one that asshole Craig had seen flying over my bleached-bone cabin the day I rented it. I offered Nikos a beer.

"That would be beautiful! Yes! Yes!" he replied. He bit the cap off the bottle with his teeth. We stood together and talked about Wonder Valley, comparing notes about the places we'd been and the people we knew. He'd been here with his girlfriend, Rosie, for a few years, he said, and I wondered how I'd never met him, such was the affinity we shared. He was exuberant, energetic, enthusiastic about the desert and nature. He suggested we go motorcycle riding together sometime—he had one I could borrow, he said.

He left before midnight to meet Rosie at the bar, but we saw each other frequently after that. Nikos and Rosie came to Taco Tuesdays at my place and I sometimes went to barbeques at theirs. He and Rosie became dear to Ann as well.

Their place was a sprawling "builtmore" like ours, a long series of rooms interconnected one to another, furnished for comfort and entertaining with a collection of mementos from their frequent travels around the country. In their yard, Nikos had amassed an assortment of vehicles that matched his varied interests: Skiffs and jet skis and speedboats and rowboats he had saved from abandonment in the desert. The boats sat in the sand separate from the dirt bikes and ATVs, the quads and three-wheelers and trucks and street racers all in various stages of assembly that were his desert toys. In the drive he parked his seventies conversion van, Pursuit of Happiness, a big blue, four-wheel-drive shaggin' wagon in which he and Rosie made their summer evacuations to escape the desert heat.

He didn't really like the desert, he said. He missed lakes and trees. He preferred the Pacific Northwest and the mountains of Idaho and Montana, or the Adirondack Mountains of upstate New York where he'd grown up. His family had owned a zoo there, his father a former Navy SEAL-turned biology teacher, alligator wrestler, and professional clown, his mother a record-holding long-distance swimmer and Adirondacks celebrity. The family spent summers in that zoo, but over-wintered in Florida, the place Nikos considered home. The Florida Keys, specifically, were where he wanted to be. He was a pilot and scuba diver, a skier and outdoorsman. Not long after I met him, he traded his lime-green ultralight for a houseboat in the Keys, and it looked like he and Rosie would finally get down there to live.

Nikos made the best of his time in the desert, however. He had a passion for hot springs and motorcycles and had explored Wonder Valley as thoroughly as anybody I knew, riding the old mining roads in the mountains and the dunes in the center. He had learned to identify local medicinal plants and had become quite the desert tracker. He often quizzed Ann about rocks and desert formations and had a keen interest in the natural history of the valley. He had gathered around himself a disparate group of guys who would meet at his place with their motorcycles and ATVs for exploratory forays out into the desert. I hadn't gone riding with him, though, not until Nick Harmon showed up in the valley. He and Nikos quickly became friends.

Nick was a young writer from Verdigre, Nebraska, a town of only 600, where his family owned the gas station. His brother was the taxidermist there. By the time I met him, however, he was living in Texas with his wife, the recent and unexpected heiress to a casino magnate's fortune.

Coming from a small, isolated town and marrying into that kind of money, Nick found himself only a mouse-click from anything he wanted in the world. He and his wife could go anywhere they wanted to go, do anything they wanted to do, often in her family's executive jet. This money also freed Nick to write full-time. But that wealth of money proved to be a demotivating force, too, and as Nick and his wife soon ran out of things to want, places to go, Nick stopped writing. To overcome this, he went to back to college, where we met, as a way to reinvigorate his passion, the deadlines of school forcing him to get up and get to work. After graduating, though, the lethargy of money returned and he again lost steam, his motivation petered and his writing slowed. With this ennui, his relationship with his wife atrophied, too. She went elsewhere for love and stimulation, a clandestine affair that eventually broke their marriage apart. Cut-off and now broke, Nick wandered the West for a while, then called me and asked about my Wonder Valley place. I invited him to come out.

Nick had visited Wonder Valley once before with his wife. Together, we went to Taco Tuesday at Pizza Richard's rock guesthouse. There, he met Bud and Natalie, Whitefeather and Desert Dave, Dingy and Fluffy. Bartender Tonya was there, too, her last Taco Tuesday. In fact, it was the last time I saw her alive.

After his marriage broke up, Nick returned to Wonder Valley in a car stuffed with his worldly possessions, with photographs and books and sport coats and cardigans and an assortment of footwear, the accoutrements of his former lifestyle, none of which were appropriate for the desert. The trunk of the car held his tent and sleeping bag and cooler and camping gear that had been his home on the road.

At my place, he took up residence in the guest room, his books and photographs lining the walls. He would write, he said, that was his plan, finally finish the novel he had in the works, then take off to Mexico maybe, or Marfa, Texas, or some island somewhere where he could live out of the mainstream, find his own way, rebuild his life.

In Wonder Valley, Nick and Nikos couldn't have been more different, Nikos's exuberance the antipode to the reticence of Nick. Many afternoons found the two at The Palms together, gossiping with Pizza Richard and Clyde Eddie or planning adventures into the desert. The bar became their clubhouse. They'd often come back to my place to play pool after it closed at six.

Under Nikos's influence, Nick bought a motorcycle from Clyde Eddie, an eighties-era Yamaha, an ugly thing with faded orange paint, a cracked white fender, and a green naugahyde seat. "It doesn't matter what it looks like!" Nikos exclaimed. It had carburetor problems, though, and a broken throttle cable and stripped rear sprocket, but the bike had been Nikos's before, and with his help, Nick got it back on the road quickly.

On that motorcycle, Nick joined Nikos and his disparate group, riding out to the old mining roads in the gold fields or to the dunes in the center of the valley, or to The Swirls, as Nikos called the amphitheater-like erosional caves up past the Sheephole. On occasion, I'd borrow a bike and join them. For me, Nick and Nikos became the antidote to the loneliness, isolation, and social disconnection I often felt out here. They became bridges that connected Ann and my life at the coast with my new one here in Wonder Valley. After my TV show project abruptly failed, they were just what I needed.

§ § §

I had waited forever for word of that show. Updates had always come sporadically from Patrick, his upbeat "Next Friday" brushoffs what I'd come to expect. But then one day he called and was all business. A network had made a bid for the show, he said. Details dribbled in, specifics to be negotiated. "We should have contracts in place by next Friday," he assured me.

Those deadlines, however, continued to be as arbitrary and meaningless as ever. Negotiations inched forward at a snail's pace. Another six months passed, another twenty-four next Fridays. I called him monthly. I would be named co-creator and executive producer of the show, he said in one call. I'd get per-episode payments—not much the first season—he said in another. None of this registered as real progress, however. "These things take time," he said, "Next Friday we should know more." More waiting, more next Fridays. Then, one next Friday, he called me, "We start production in two weeks," he said. "The studio is sending out a producer and director the day after tomorrow. Show them around."

It took a moment for that to sink in. I'd been waiting a year and a half, and now, suddenly, it was happening. And I had just two days to prepare. I gathered everyone together to discuss what to do when the network people arrived. I really didn't know what to expect. I told them all just to be themselves—it had worked when we shot the pilot.

Curtis met the network people at the front door. "I'm a dead man walking," he said, flinging his arms wide. He bent forward for the producer to trace the scar across the top of his head. Desert Dave drove golf balls from the dirt of my yard, Slim threw a lasso at a bucket. Paule had dyed his hair electric blue, his beard shaped into two devil horns.

"Damn glad to meet you," he said to the director, pumping his hand. "I'm a Katrina survivor. Got PTSD, paranoia schizophrenic. I hear voices, yadda, yadda, such and such."

After the introductions, I loaded the director and producer into my truck, the new SUV I'd bought with Ann. For four hours, I drove them around the valley, filling them with stories about the derelict cabins, about their history, the people who had lived there, making stuff up on the fly about chemtrails and chupacabras and spirits and specters, camping up the kookiness of a place that already seemed so otherworldly to them. The director snapped pictures from the passenger-side window.

"There really is no third wall here," he said, agog. Wonder Valley was not a Hollywood set, I reminded them. It was the real deal.

"We'll be in touch," they said after the tour was complete. After they left, we celebrated with a barbecue at my house.

Then, two days later, I got an email. After seeing Wonder Valley for myself, the producer wrote, *I can 100% understand why you see so much potential and story in it. It's a fascinating place full of fascinating people.* But she didn't think the cast I had chosen was up to the rigors of a shooting schedule. She had expected, as she put it, *a cast that was alert, on time, and able to follow directions,* sober people without criminal records who could at least pass background checks. Based on that, she said, *we feel that this is not a show we can pursue further.* And that was that. Without further discussion, they'd backed out.

But weren't Bernadette and Daisy supposed to balance the locals out? I thought they were to give the whole project a positive spin. It seemed the network had other plans for them. They didn't need me after all. I thought about all the things I could have done differently. I could have recruited Nikos and Rosie for the show, for example, unique and energetic people who nevertheless led relatively stable lives. I should have revealed less about the kind of place Wonder Valley was, made it seem less kooky, less dangerous. Patrick was furious with me when he got the news. He blamed me for mishandling the Wonder Valley tour. He stopped taking my calls. Wonder Valley, the TV show, was dead.

A great pall of disappointment fell over me. Without the anticipation of that show and the camaraderie of remodeling the house, boredom took over. My relationship with everyone in the valley withered as well, and I spent less and less time out here. Until Nick arrived.

Most mornings, he and I would talk about books and movies over coffee. Clyde Eddie often came over to play pool, too, or Nikos might swing by and we'd all go riding.

Ann worried about me riding motorcycles, ever since I crashed and hurt myself a couple years before. Fluffy had had a quad with a souped-up race engine and bald, mismatched tires. I rolled it over on myself within seconds of boarding it, separating my shoulder. It never quite healed properly. Ann feared that on a motorcycle I'd maim myself worse.

"But I'll be riding with Nikos," I told her. "With him, we're safe, riding in formation, a group of us, sticking to the dirt roads where it was perfectly legal to ride." She reluctantly acquiesced.

I wasn't an experienced motorcycle rider, but I found I loved our forays. On our last excursion together, Nikos led Nick and Clyde Eddie and me to the place he called The Swirls, that series of erosional caves carved into the boulders. I crashed my motorcycle in deep sand as we headed out across the wash, and again in sand as we approached the Sheephole. Seeing me lifting the bike once again, Nikos rode back to me.

"Let me take some air out of those tires," he said. "I don't know why they're so hard. Soft tires take the sand better." Down on one knee he pressed a rock to the tires' valves; the air inside them hissed free. "And remember," he said, "you're basically riding two gyroscopes, the spinning wheels want to stand upright. If you start to go over, gas it. It will stand right up." The softer tires did take the sand better, and with that and the riding lesson, I made it the rest of the way to the Swirls without mishap.

At the Swirls, Nikos popped open some beers with his teeth and handed them around. He pinched off a spray of creosote bush, too, and stuffed it into the flask of vodka Clyde Eddie brought, transforming a swallow of that liquor into a shot of desert rain. With our beers, we climbed up onto the rocks for a view of the area, a natural amphitheater with a large open-mouth cave at its center. One cave Nikos had dubbed Ball-Cooler Caverns. It had a small vertical hole eroded between it and the cave below. Climbing up there, Nikos demonstrated how you stand above the hole for a refreshing caress when the breeze, caught by the cave below, blew up your shorts.

As evening approached, we sped off to watch the sunset from the dunes. To get there in time, Nikos led us right down the paved road. Riding on the pavement scared me, cars roaring past at seventy miles an hour shook the bike as they went. I worried less about those oncoming cars, though, than the ones speeding up behind me. I was afraid I wouldn't be able to get out of their way quickly enough, that if forced to bail off the road onto the sandy shoulder at that speed it wouldn't end well. Ann was in my head. "If you get hurt, I'll kill you," she'd said. It came as a relief when, ahead of me, Nikos slowed and turned off the pavement onto the dirt road to the salt mine.

From the Salt Mine road, Nikos jumped the berm and lit off down a small wash. Nick and I followed, Clyde Eddie behind. Nick's dust curled past me. As the wash widened, I twisted the accelerator, picking up speed until we burst out of the wash onto the expanse of the dry lakebed. The sun was just dropping into its sweet spot, the mountains to the west fracturing its rays into beams that set the Sheephole Mountains ablaze.

The lakebed playa beneath us was cumulus pillows of salt, mud crack clouds concealing the mucky mire below. I up-shifted and flew across those clouds, the bike rapped-out to redline. Before me, haloed by solar aureoles, Nikos soared across the very surface of the sun, a beer in one hand, shorts and sandals, Apollo on his chariot, a golden comet's tail of dust his contrail. Nick, behind him, stood on his foot pegs, a centurion to the sun god, his comet tail jet wash orange and black against the golden light, while Clyde Eddie, following, was a meteor, his blue bike a cold stone barreling at me, a roiling explosion of dust blasting him forward. I tucked down and flew, another heavenly body hurling across the sky.

The minutes of that ride are indelible to me. For all I've done in this life, the forty-foot seas, the moonbow, that orangutan, screaming across that lakebed, the sun's surface, the mountains ablaze around me, may have been the most exhilarating five minutes of my life. We were jets above those pillows of clouds, no sense we touched the earth at all.

Ahead, Nikos cut into a wash that led up into the dunes to the west. I continued straight, however, mesmerized, lost in the magic of the moment, hitting the lakes rim at fifty, its incline gentle, the wind having gathered sand into a ramp against it. With a sudden whump I found myself aloft, flying through the rays of the sun, literally separated from the surface of the earth and all but parted from the motorcycle, too, its handlebar's two grips being my sole points of contact as I soared with the bike through the air, the soles of my feet skyward, 'Oh shit,' my first thought, 'Ann's really going to kill me,' reminded in that instant that this was how Nikos's friend Warbird earned his nickname on this very lakebed after hitting a rock that sent him airborne like an eagle, wings spread across the glorious sunset, his impact with earth dislocating his clavicle and maybe breaking some ribs, but thankfully not his neck, which I was now in danger of doing, and this before Nikos ever gave me a nickname like he had Warbird and Nick who was Jim because he looked like a young William Shatner or Clydesdale for Clyde Eddie because that name fit him better than anything anyone had come up with for him yet.

Fortunately for me, gravity corrected the motorcycle's flight. I was riding two gyroscopes, after all. The bike crash-landed front wheel first, my testicles rejoining the seat with one, two, three bounces, while I willed my hand, which I desperately needed for control of the motorcycle, to back off on the fucking throttle, and my foot to find the goddamn brake. Adrenaline juiced through me. On the top of a nearby dune, Nikos watched while Nick, silhouetted against the sun, spun an exuberant Hills Are Alive, Julie Andrews, Sound of Music spin.

I joined them on top of that dune. "How's the balls?" Nikos asked. I fretted the nickname I might have just earned. He bit open a beer and handed it to me. Around us, the desert was a caldron, the dunes bubbles of molten gold, the lakebed leaden.

"Beautiful, yes, yes!" Nikos shouted, as the Sheephole Mountains smoldered fiery red, which slowly faded to magenta, then purple, then, just after the sun set, indigo black as a bruise.

We rode home to Nikos's after dark, Nick and I easing our way along the dirt path fronting the paved road, Clyde Eddie heading off across the dunes. He got lost. Nikos turned back to look for him while Nick and I opened a beer and waited.

That was the last time I rode with Nikos. He got a job installing wi-fi for a desert off-road event shortly after that and was working 16-hour days. He stopped by with Warbird at sunset on a rare day off and suggested we go riding the next day. Ann, however, had made plans for us and dinner with my parents that night.

"You want a flashlight or anything for the ride home," Nick asked Nikos as he and Warbird were about to depart. Neither bike had a headlight.

"We don't need a light!" Nikos exclaimed. "Look at that beautiful moon!" The sun was down but the moon was full, casting hard shadows in its fluorescent glow. Nikos and Warbird sped off with only that to guide them.

The next day, Nick rode up to the Swirls with them. That afternoon he texted me a picture, Nikos, the Greek god, six-three, standing on the rocks like a fist thrust at the sky. Man, how I wanted to be there. On the way to my parents' house, Ann and I stopped at The Palms for a beer, hoping to catch them when they returned. Nikos and Nick had negotiated my reinstatement into The Palms only about a month before, and I was excited to have a beer with them there, but we had to leave for dinner before they arrived.

Up at The Swirls, Nick and Warbird and Nikos watched the sunset from the rocks above the amphitheater. After that they headed to the bar, Nick and Nikos ripping down the paved road in the twilight at seventy miles an hour, Nick's headlight guiding them. We had just missed them. They rolled into The Palms parking lot right before six. But Warbird had gotten lost. He was Nikos's friend from the Adirondacks and had been to Wonder Valley a few times before but didn't really know his way around. Besides, the moon had not yet risen and it was dark. With no headlight of his own, he found the lights from the on-coming cars disorienting. He pulled to the dirt shoulder, unsure where he was. He thought he might have passed the bar by mistake.

"You couldn't have passed it," Nikos told him over the phone. "Hold on, I'll come find you." He set out while Nick ordered beers at the bar and waited.

We had just sat down to dinner at my parents' when Nick called.

"Man, Nikos went back for Warbird and he never came back. And I just saw some ambulances go by."

"Keep me posted," I said.

Ten minutes later I tried to call him. He didn't answer. I called Clyde Eddie.

"I heard there's a body on the road covered with a sheet," Eddie said.

Then Nick called.

"He's dead," was all he said.

§§§

Nikos, wearing no helmet or shoes or riding gear of any kind, had wrapped himself in a shred of blue tarpaulin he found to ward off the evening chill. Nick took a photo of him before he took off toward the deadman's bend in search of Warbird. It was the last photo of Nikos alive.

As he raced up the paved road, I'm sure Nikos would have been concerned about cars, especially those coming up behind him. He had no mirrors and wouldn't have been able to hear them over the roar of his bike, so he would have had to keep his speed up, fifty or sixty miles an hour to stay ahead of them. With no headlight of his own to counter them, the lights of oncoming cars would have been blinding for a moment as each one passed, just as they had Warbird, and with the moon not yet up, he would have been invisible to them. He had certainly been invisible to that F350 Super Duty, the monster-sized truck that veered out into his lane to pass a slower vehicle, the one that met Nikos head-on, blinding him in that moment, no way to swerve out of the way, to bail over to the shoulder, to evade, the impact totaling the Super Duty and instantly shattering Nikos's bike into a thousand pieces, Nikos along with it.

§§§

I imagine riding in the trundle seat of my childhood station wagon. Hindsight. In hindsight, Nikos should have taken Nick's bike, the one with the headlight. He should have stuck to the dirt, off the paved road, out of harm's way. He should have just talked Warbird in, explained over the phone how to find the bar. But in hindsight, you only know the wrong turns after you've made them, the zigs when you should have zagged.

Physics says all possibilities exist at once, that anything that can happen, does happen in an infinite array of parallel realities. What we feel and see and remember is but one iteration of what is, of what was, of what will be. Physics says all possible realities transpire, we just don't get to experience them. I lived the one, for example, where I lost my job, the TV show failed, and Nikos smacked his motorcycle head-on into a truck. Physics says other realities exist too, and in the days after Nikos's death, I found the idea of these parallel realities comforting, that for every mistake I made, in another reality, everything came out OK. I avoided missteps, or I just caught a lucky break. And in those realities, Nikos was still alive.

I drove out to the site where Nikos had died. Motorcycle shrapnel littered the roadside, blue confetti, the nylon chaff of that tarp he wore, twirled in the saltcedar trees, the trees themselves bespattered with gristle and sinew and shards of Nikos's own body. As I sat under the tree where he perished, an F350 veered into the left lane to pass a slow-moving vehicle. It thundered by at seventy, in the wrong lane, within feet of me, the trees flagging an unheeded warning at its rear. I thought again about those parallel realities.

A few days after the crash the tow truck driver who had picked up the remains of Nikos's bike returned to Wonder Valley, as if needing to come to terms with what he had seen. It was the worst crash he had ever witnessed, he told me. Immediately I thought of Nikos's favorite song, "Bat Out of Hell" by Meatloaf. It was so prescient in hindsight. That Meatloaf song is said to describe the worst motorcycle crash imaginable: *I'm gonna make my escape*, it says, but *I never see the sudden curve until it's way too late.*

Then I'm down in the bottom of a pit in the blazing sun

Torn and twisted at the foot of a burning bike,

I think somebody somewhere must be tolling a bell

And the last thing I see is my heart,

Still beating, still beating

Breaking out of my body, and flying away

Like a bat out of hell

Oh, like a bat out of hell

Death's scythe swings so wildly, randomly in Wonder Valley,

reaping arbitrarily, cutting down the weak with the strong. Ricka McGuire, whose death sent me on this journey. And Roger and Madriña and Lou and Devon Million. Biker Richard and George Stadler. Tonya. They had all touched me personally. Never before had I been this close to death. They all took part of me with them, and left a bit of themselves in me, but Nikos, that immortal Greek god, more than anyone.

Every time I thought about Nikos, my thoughts turned selfish: Who would take me riding now? Who would show me those secret spots? Who would keep me curious, keep alight that fire of wonder without Nikos at the bellows? He had rekindled my interest in writing, but had I, on my own, enough fuel to sustain it? I felt abandoned by him, cast adrift.

"He's not finished with you yet," Warbird said to me in the days after the crash. Already Nikos was deified, not a man, but a god. Shards of his bone found at the crash site were being passed around like holy relics. His deification seemed right, though, because I felt him like a holy spirit, a ghost haunting me in the best possible way, his vital essence seeping in from some parallel reality.

Nikos's death instigated some needed self-reflection. I had always looked for explanations, reasons, but there are no reasons, not really. I often conjured excuses for myself, ways to shift at least some of the responsibility off of me. I had spent countless hours reflecting over why I'd lost my job, searching for a suitable explanation. I blamed school administrators for my high school experience, I blamed my parents, I blamed dyslexia. I hurled my anger and hatred onto my father. He was the reason I was uprooted in high school. It was he who had dragged me from small-town Mississippi. I had been happy there, had known everyone in my high school. I felt a part of the community. I had my college track planned. But moving to California, I became a nobody, a small fry in a vast sea. I never fully assimilated into that school but found a marginalized clique to embed myself in. By then, at that age, I was too pissed off and bitter—anger and self-pity, my go-to emotions. Had I lived another reality, things would have been different, but I would never have met Ann, never have crossed the equator or sailed forty-foot seas. I never would have found Wonder Valley, for better or for worse.

I know my father did the best he could with me. He was only human, fallible, but a good man. As a family, we never wanted for anything, certainly not his love. My dad loved me and worried for me and grew frustrated with himself when he saw me slipping away from him. That's why he felt himself a failure as a father, because he didn't know what to do, because, try as he might, he, as a father, didn't know best. I know that now, in hindsight.

In Wonder Valley, I was to have had my Jacques Cousteau redemption, that fucking contrived reality TV bullshit thing was to have been my validation for living the life I'd lived. It escaped me suddenly why I had wanted that show so much, why I had invested so much of myself into it. Again, I searched for reasons, deflected responsibility, assigned blame. I had remained in Wonder Valley because I had checked out, given up. But I know I'm responsible for the life I've lived. I chose the course I am on.

Ann and I return to Wonder Valley often now because we like it here. We have friends here, own a house here, are part of a tribe. As much as I'd like to be, I can't be out here all the time because I now work part-time for Ann writing reports and doing research.

It's funny, but after the network balked at the show, no one was surprised. Actually, everyone seemed relieved. When I made the rounds telling them there would be no show, they all just shrugged.

"I didn't really want to do it anyway," Natalie said.

"It sounded like a lot of work to me," Pizza Richard replied. "I'm supposed to be retired! Exactly."

"I guess Wonder Valley is too real for reality TV!" Paule chimed in.

That made me laugh, the truth in it. Fucking Wonder Valley. Too real for reality TV.

"Fuck 'em," Slim said, cracking open a beer.

"Yeah," I said, opening a beer of my own. "Just fuck 'em."

Epilogue

Quantum theory says it is impossible to know both the position of a body and its momentum at the same time—the more you know about where a body is, the less you know about where it's going. And vice versa. In quantum theory, the entirety of the quantum world is merely a series of probabilities, the very act of observing bodies within it seals the outcome. You can never really *know* anything.

As with quantum theory, observing Wonder Valley sealed it as what it is for me. The Wonder Valley I found was shaped as much as anything by what I came looking for, by my state of mind when I arrived. I came looking for an end-of-the-line place, the bottom of a vortex where those shaken loose from society rolled, spiraling downward. A place that once you were here, if you'd no one to throw you a rope, you might never climb out. My Wonder Valley terrified me, as staring from the rim into an abyss does. I felt compelled to shine a light down into it, and what it revealed was not a pit at all, but a unique and varied community, a microcosm of the American society at large, a desert Galapagos where I got to play its Darwin. For a time, I was Jacques Cousteau. If you drive out this way, however, you won't find the place I found, the place I came to know. Your act of looking will seal a different place for you, different by a quantum leap.

§ § §

After Nikos died, Nick left, but returned, then left again. Wonder Valley had its strings on him, and he yoyoed back and forth until he bought a cabin for back taxes. It's about ten miles away from my place—Wonder Valley close. I'm glad he stayed, though I hope eventually he'll leave. We see each other often.

273

Nick gave me his motorcycle after Nikos died, but then bought another of his own. I ride with him to The Palms on the days it's open. In a lot of ways, nothing at The Palms had changed in the years I'd been banned from it. They'd cut their hours further still, down to four days a week, but you can still get Slim Jims and cigarettes and used t-shirts for a buck. The balls still jam in the pool table and the jukebox still doesn't work—though at one point I heard James got it working, but it was stuck on a George Michael record, so he unplugged it again. There is now a time machine near the window—an English-style phone booth with a plasma globe on top—and a guillotine out back, half-size but fully functioning, a relic from a Sibleys music video shot at the bar. And you can still get Nattie Ice, of course, but the Pabst on draft is cold year-round now and not only for the out-of-towners and passers-through, though they now pay out-of-towner prices, not the buck-fifty we locals are charged.

Pizza Richard still holds court from the end of the bar, but other than he and Nick, I know few people there. The old-timers I knew have their stools now occupied by newcomers, artists and musicians and disaffected millennials who spend an hour or so there becoming reacquainted with one another between texts to the outside world. To them I'm not Writer Bill or Reporter Bill, I'm just Nick's friend, the guy who sometimes comes in with him. They've no idea I'd ever been anything else out here.

I don't see Slim and Desert Dave and Clyde Eddie as often as I used to. Nor Larkin. He stewed over the depiction of himself in the video we shot until he finally asked me not to come around anymore. To register the point, his dogs attacked me the last time I visited, one biting me viciously, tearing my jeans. Those same dogs mauled Curtis not long after, chewing his legs to the bone. He nearly bled to death trying to crawl home. A passerby found him unconscious in the dirt. Doctors thought he'd never walk again. Now when he sees me, he throws his arms wide, "Double dead man walking!" he says, spinning around for me to take him all in.

Jack McConaha had taken that fall and ended up in that retirement home. Like an animal in a cage, I knew it was someplace he could never survive. He died within months thereafter.

Mark Bennett got sick around the same time as Jack's death, a lung thing. Valley Fever people said. He recovered as summer cooled, but the next summer, he fell ill again. Under the blast of the swamp cooler on Pizza Richard's couch, he failed to recover. An ambulance took him to the hospital, where, two days later he died.

Mark had been a musician, semi-pro football player, a hell-raiser and a head-knocker. As a carpenter and a contractor, he'd built some fabulous homes. Just being in my Wonder Valley home reminds me of his abilities. It is as much a tribute to him as it is to anybody out here.

After Whitefeather had his falling out with the valley, I stopped hanging out with him. Someone bought the rock cabin for taxes, though, so Whitefeather moved his belongings to the yard, awaiting the inevitable eviction. It never came, and he still lives there with his dozens upon dozens of cats.

Not long after Tonya died, a fire gutted her old place, collapsing the roof and blackening the desert around it. Scrappers, they say, coiled wire on the floor and lit it to burn off the insulation, the fire spreading to the walls. The cabin's charred hulk still sits there, Tonya's stuff in the dirt next to it, and probably will for a long time to come. I think it's too fitting a memorial to her to be torn down.

George's place burned down, too, lit by a candle left alight by a squatter named Sparky after George moved under the care of his daughter. I never saw George again.

I do see Jan, the German artist, though. He returns to Wonder Valley regularly, spending six or eight weeks each year at the Cat Ranch, often with a cadre of other artists and performers. He'd cleaned out the cat shit and negotiated away the code violations, paid his fines, then built a wood-burning sauna and invited artists and writers to visit. They sit in the sauna and drink espresso and listen to techno music pulsing through a solar-powered car stereo. When I visit, it seems they are always naked, even in the chill of winter.

Ann and I are old-timers here now. We spend our days trying to enjoy the quiet of the desert, though someone recently bought the abandoned place next to us and often rattles us awake on weekends with the groan of their generator and the whine of their saws as they remodel. To escape it we might go for a walk, or Nick and I might ride out to the dunes or up to Sheephole Pass and the cut-off to the Swirls. The view from up at the Sheephole was our first view of Wonder Valley, Ann and I, all those decades ago. I know this hardscrabble desert now, the mountains and the valley, the salt pan of the dry lake, the grid of dirt tracks. I'm a part of it and it's a part of me.

From up at the Sheephole I'm reminded the road through here runs both ways. The same road that takes you down into Wonder Valley takes you out of it too. I love the feeling of the drive up that grade, the valley falling away behind you. It looks like you're headed into the sky, nowhere to go but up. It feels so hopeful. This road will take you sea to shining sea if you let it. It stretches between here and everywhere. You can turn around at any time, though, flip a bitch, head back down if you want, just as I had. You probably won't though, few people do. And that's probably for the best.

Acknowledgements

This book would not have been possible without the very generous financial support of friends, family, and even some who I don't know personally, but believed enough in this project to contribute to it. In particular, I owe a cold beer and a big hug to Ken and Teresa Sitz, Steven Wilhelm, Phil Adams and Karen Thrasher, Todd Plesco, Malcolm and Julie Read, Ruarri Serpa, Kathy Neville and Chris Norton, Kate Lee Short, Carol and Steve Cross, Yeu Hong and Carol Yeo, Karoline Collins, Suzanne Dellinger, Michelle Haug, Alan and Kay Dohanyos, and Josh Henry. Thank you so much for your confidence and support.

There aren't hugs big enough to thank Faye Satterly and Dorothy Rice, great writers both, who read and re-read this manuscript. Their opinions, advice, and much-needed jabs of bare-knuckle criticism helped make this book what it is. I owe a thank you but also an apology to my friend Gary Tufel, who volunteered his time to copyedit my scribbles. I monkeyed with the pristine manuscript after Gary copyedited it, so any errors you find in it are my fault alone.

I owe a debt to other readers as well: Cynthia Romanowski, Mike Morshed, Kurt Taylor, Jenn-Anne Gledhill, Shannon Purchase, and Stephanie Green Smith. They all braved Wonder Valley's heat and dust with me as well as reading and re-reading the various iterations of this book. Their friendship, help, advice, and support have proved invaluable. Thank you all. And not to forget Nick Harmon, who, among other things, has found himself a character in this book. Our often hours-long discussions about music and literature and all things Wonder Valley shaped my writing in so many ways. Also, he gave me a motorcycle. Thanks, Nick!

A special thanks to Tim Covi, my editor at the Denver Voice. Besides being a great editor, Tim was a fabulous booster, sparking the fire that started this project.

I've dedicated this book to my parents, Bill and Maureen Hillyard, but I would be remiss if I didn't acknowledge all they've done for me, from providing basic shelter and sustenance to their own insight and knowledge about the desert and its denizens. We had a rough and rocky fifty-five years together, mom and dad, but please know that I love you.

Lee Fenner, my father-in-law, passed away before he could see this project completed, but had always been my biggest fan and supporter, having read every word I've written and sharing it enthusiastically. Thanks to Greg Dunstan, an extraordinary cinematographer and one of my oldest friends. His Wonder Valley photos and video footage added so much to my experience there. Similarly, I dragged my nephew, Preston Drake-Hillyard, all over this desert and often into some sketchy situations to get photographs for my Wonder Valley stories. His photo graces this book's cover, a cover designed by Wonder Valley's own Ven Voisey. Thanks Ven and Preston for making this book a beautiful thing to hold.

I must admit that the idea of the separate communities in Wonder Valley was not entirely my own. It was sparked by a conversation I had with Dr. Jacob Sowers, whose dissertation, *A Phenomenology of Place Identity for Wonder Valley, California: Homesteaders, Dystopics, and Utopics*, is required reading for any hardcore Wonder Valley-phile.

I would also be remiss if I didn't acknowledge Mary Sibley's contribution to this book project. We had a rocky relationship, she and I, but I know she was genuinely concerned for both her bar and the community.

Thanks, too, to my friends Richard and Stephen, Dominic and Naomi, Lindsay, Kate, Kacy and Nicholas, Kelly, Steven, Rosie and Norman, Paule, Phil and Karen, Dan and Nancy, Kyle and Catherine, Jan, Marvin, Dennis and Lena, Jill, Anderson and Diego, and Kevin. I lift a Nattie Ice to each of you.

Pour one out for Bill "Slim" Silva and Gary Heacock, who will live on in the pages of this book. Rest in peace, boys. God knows you deserve it.

And to my fabulous wife, Ann. Here's to our next adventure together. Thanks for standing by me. I love you.

Finally, I'd like to thank all of those that allowed me into their lives and shared their stories, warts and all, with me. I've changed many of the names in this book—and I did this with some reservation. Everyone was so open and candid with me and they certainly have nothing to be ashamed of. On the contrary, considering all they have overcome, I think they can stand proud knowing they are strong survivors of one of the harshest social and natural environments I can imagine. I am proud to have met them and still call many of them friends. While they certainly deserve recognition and a place in the world, I also feel I owe them a modicum of privacy even at the risk of perpetuating their anonymity. Head to The Palms, dear reader, if you wish to meet them for yourself. They will surely enrich your life as they have mine.

CPSIA information can be obtained
at www.ICGtesting.com
Printed in the USA
LVHW091433201120
672144LV00005B/284